ROMANIA

An Illustrated History

ILLUSTRATED HISTORIES

Arizona

Celtic World

China

Cracow

Egypt

England

France

Greece

Ireland

Israel

Korea: From Ancient Times to 1945

Mexico

Paris

Poland

Poland in WWII

Russia

Sicily

Tikal

Vietnam

ROMANIA

AN ILLUSTRATED HISTORY

Nicolae Klepper

HIPPOCRENE BOOKS, INC.
New York

Also by Nicolae Klepper
Taste of Romania

Third printing, 2007.

ISBN-13: 978-0-7818-0935-1
ISBN-10: 0-7818-0935-5

For information, address:
HIPPOCRENE BOOKS, INC.
171 Madison Avenue
New York, NY 10016
www.hippocrenebooks.com

Library of Congress Cataloging-in-Publication Data

Klepper, Nicolae.
Romania / Nicolae Klepper.
p. cm.
Includes bibliographical references and index.
ISBN 0-7818-0935-5
1. Romania--History. I. Title.

DR217 .K
949.8--dc21

2002191943

Printed in the United States of America.

Contents

Illustrations

Charts

Maps

Illustrations

Foreword

Romania is one of the most enchanting countries of East Central Europe. It is a beautiful land, rich in diversity and culture; it is bordered by Bulgaria to the south, Yugoslavia and Hungary to the west, the Ukraine to the north and east, and the Romanian territory of Bessarabia—today known as the Republic of Moldavia (Moldova)—to the east. The country is crossed in the center by the Carpathian Mountains, which provide breathtakingly beautiful scenery and include some of Romania's most remarkable tourist attractions, including the Peleş Castle in Sinaia and the world-renowned painted monasteries of northern Moldavia. To the south, the country is bordered by the Danube River. Near the Iron Gates, at Drobeta-Turnu Severin, the ruins of the bridge built by the Roman Emperor Trajan can still be seen.

The vast plains in the southern part of the country, known as Wallachia, have great agricultural potential. The capital city of Bucharest is located in this region. Today a modern metropolis of over two million inhabitants, Bucharest, with its many architectural treasures, was once known as the Paris of the East. The coast of the Black Sea and the Danube Delta, with its scenic beauty, fascinating wildlife, and favorable summer climate are favorite vacation spots for tourists from throughout the world.

The eastern part of the country, known as Moldavia, is rich in tradition and full of beauty. The landscape is dotted with historical monuments, among them monasteries from the fifteenth and sixteenth centuries, such as Voroneţ and Suceviţa, which are famous for their exterior mural paintings that have resisted the elements throughout many centuries and today are world heritage monuments. One of the most beautiful cities in the country, Iaşi, is built on seven hills and is filled with historical and religious treasures; it is the traditional capital of this region and is often referred to as the cultural capital of Romania.

Finally, the western part of the country, Transylvania, is a land steeped in Romanian tradition. The cradle of Romanian civilization and the heart of the former Roman province of Dacia, it was here that the Romanian people were formed. A region of cultural interaction throughout the centuries, the atmosphere in Transylvania is further enriched by the cultural contributions of the Hungarian and German minority populations. Cities such as Sibiu and Sighişoara are museums in and of themselves. With its forests, plains, mountains, hills, sea coast, and favorable continental climate, Romania is a land of cultural and geographic diversity, a land of tradition and spectacular beauty that offers something for everyone.

Throughout their long history, the Romanian lands have had much diversity and interaction. For centuries they served as a border between Orthodoxy and Catholicism and between the various empires that have exerted their domination over this region of Europe. This has contributed to the complexity of Romanian history, just as it inhibited the development of a Romanian national state until the middle of the nineteenth century. Soviet domination after World War II further halted development. It is only since the overthrow of the Communist regime in December 1989 that the Romanian nation again has the opportunity to affirm itself freely as a member of the European community, and it is now potentially the wealthiest and most important state in southeastern Europe.

This short history of Romania by Nicolae Klepper is an excellent introduction for those wishing to learn about this land of diversity. Klepper first shows the strong ties of this area to the classical world of Greece and Rome. Continuing on to the Middle Ages, he discusses the development of the Romanian people and some of the most fascinating personalities of Romanian and world history, including Vlad

III, the historical Dracula, and Stephen the Great. Klepper follows the story into modern times, looking at the formation of the modern Romanian nation-state and covering the triumphs and tragedies of the twentieth century. This includes the completion of national unity, followed by subjugation under oppressive Communist rule at the end of World War II, and up to 1989 when Romania resumed its rightful place among the free nations of the world. Klepper has extensively studied the history of the country where he was born. His years of research have resulted in this book, which surveys the most important personalities and events and provides a useful guide that makes a very complex country and people accessible to all. This book will serve as a starting point for tourists, students, and all those who wish to investigate further the rich history of this enchanting land.

DR. KURT W. TREPTOW

BIOGRAPHICAL NOTE: Kurt W. Treptow, a noted specialist of Romania and southeastern Europe, received his Ph.D. in history from the University of Illinois. He is the author of numerous books and articles on the history of the region, including *A History of Romania* (1997) and *Vlad III Dracula: The Life and Times of the Historical Dracula* (2000). Dr. Treptow is presently director of the Center for Romanian Studies in Iași, Romania.

Acknowledgments

I would like first to extend my thanks and gratitude to the staff of my publishers, Hippocrene Books—to George Blagowidow for entrusting me with this very interesting and highly challenging project, and to the editors with whom I had the pleasure of working—Carol Chitnis-Gress on my first book, *Taste of Romania*—Kara Migliorelli, Paul Simpson, and Caroline Gates on this book.

Especially helpful has been Simion Alb, a person of whom Romania can be proud. In his capacity as director of the Romanian National Tourist Office in New York, he has assisted me every step of the way, not only while I lived in the United States and was researching *Taste of Romania*, but even after I moved to Scotland and was writing this book. Each time he promised some information, Mr. Alb followed through, sometimes against all odds.

In Iaşi, my special thanks go to Dr. Kurt W. Treptow, for his hospitality and gracious support. He housed me at his Center for Romanian Studies while he and his staff guided and assisted me with my research. Dr. Treptow not only took time from his extremely busy schedule to review my manuscript but also honored me by writing the foreword to this book. The Center for Romanian Studies has also granted permission to reprint any of the maps contained in *A History of Romania* (3rd ed., Iaşi, 1997). Also in Iaşi, my friendship and gratitude goes to Bogdan Ulmu, author, humorist, and playwright, for his hospitality and assistance.

In Edinburgh, I am grateful for architect Vasile Toch's contribution to the sections devoted to architecture in Romania during the twentieth century.

Many other people helped me along the way, offering advice, showing interest in the project and encouraging me; supplying me with illustrations among which there are some unique prints and photographs; or simply offering basic information. I am particularly indebted to the Romanian Embassy in London, the Romanian Tourist Promotion Office in London, Mircea C. Carp, Dan and Isabella Jane Cirimpei, Dr. Radu Ioanid, Dan Ionescu, Dr. Crişan Muşeteanu, Dr. Andrei Pippidi, Elisabeth Raţiu, and Dr. Peter Wagner. If I left anyone out it is for no other reason except oversight, for which I apologize.

Introduction

> Ten years on, Romania has earned our help. [Since the 1989 revolution] the West has done little but watch as post-communist Romania struggled, mired in appalling poverty and systemic corruption. This inaction was possible because, unlike some of its Balkan neighbors, Romania remained basically stable—no civil war or genocide to trigger international concern. . . . In the case of Romania, we must not wait. A society can hold on only so long in the grip of misery and isolation. We have the opportunity to offer money and support while there is still a democracy to protect and stability to preserve. . . . The outside world has extended few helping hands. Romania has not been invited to join NATO. . . . it has been given little assistance to make entry [in the European Union] possible. Foreign investment is almost nonexistent—Western CEOs send their money to Hungary, Slovenia, Poland, almost anywhere but Romania. . . . It is wrong to dwell on how Romanians have "failed" to meet NATO or EU criteria; gauged by the sheer amount of social, political and economic change accomplished, Romanians have done more not less than, say Czechs.
>
> Daniel N. Nelson,
> "Ten Years On, Romania Has Earned Our Help,"
> *The Washington Post*, Dec. 26, 1999, B2.

The history of a nation is in fact the history of its people. Romania, as a state, has only been in existence since 1859, but the history of its people goes back a long way, to the late Bronze Age (around 1400 B.C.) and the early Iron Age (1200–1000 B.C.). Before embarking on this journey through the centuries that led the Romanian people from their forefathers, the Geto-Dacians and the Romans, to present-day Romanians, some background information might be helpful.

Romania is situated at the northern extremity of the Balkan Peninsula, with its southern frontiers along the Danube, bordering Yugoslavia and Bulgaria. It has Hungary as its western neighbor, with Ukraine to the north, and its Eastern borders face Moldova (Republic of Moldavia) along the Prut River, then a bit of Ukraine again as that country wraps itself around Moldova and, finally, the Black Sea. Romania's population of twenty-two million lives in an area about the combined size of New York and Pennsylvania and slightly smaller than the United Kingdom. It is a country endowed with good agricultural land, high majestic mountains, great forests, an abundance of rivers, good ports, and wide sandy beaches. A land such as this, located on the crossroads between east and west, proved throughout history to be a target of migrating tribes and invading powers. It was also a reason for the local populations to fight the intruders and to hold on to their land.

Studying the map on page 38, you will note that Romania is composed of a number of provinces, including Moldavia, Transylvania, and Wallachia. Although Romanians still call themselves Moldavians or Transylvanians, administratively these provinces have ceased to exist. Today's Romania is divided into forty counties (judeţe) and the Bucharest municipality (see map on page 202).

Chapters 1 through 3 cover prehistory and early history.

Chapters 4 through 6 cover the history of the Romanian principalities before their unification. Rather than moving simultaneously through the events that were taking place in these principalities, I chose, at the risk of some repetition, to cover each principality separately over each chapter's time span. This may avoid some confusion as to what was taking place in which principality.

Chapters 7 through 13 and the Epilogue cover the history of Romania since unification, including cultural history in the nineteenth and twentieth centuries in Chapters 9 and 13.

The Epilogue—"Post-Communist Romania"—is an abbreviated chapter, since this period belongs more to the political sciences than to history.

Most chapters in this book, beginning with Chapter 3, include a section called "Perspective" that gives a "bird's-eye view" of what was happening concurrently in other parts of Europe that may have had some effect on Romania, without which it is difficult to fully appreciate its history.

The manner in which the Romanian people evolved through history, the creation of the Romanian principalities, the struggle against empire-building powers, and the eventual unification of the principalities to found the state of Romania is a fascinating story. It is also the heartening tale of a people who even in this day and age continue to rise above all adversities to achieve a better life and to create a stronger nation that is appreciated and respected by the rest of the world. I wish Romania and its people a future of peace, security, and prosperity.

Pronunciation Guide

<u>Romanian</u>	<u>English</u>
Ă ă (χə)	*a*go
Â â, Î î (œ)	less*on*
Ş ş (ʃ)	*sh*ip
Ţ ţ (ts)	ge*ts*
Ci (‘tʃi)	*che*w

PREHISTORIC AGES

Anthropological Ages	Approximate Years	Implements
Stone Age		
Old Stone Age (Paleolithic)		
Lower Paleolithic	(2,000,000–100,000 B.C.)	Flints and stones shaped to fit man's fist. Rough tools by flaking.
Middle Paleolithic	(60,000–28,000 B.C.)	Special tools: hammers, anvils, scrapers, arrowheads, spearheads, and knives. Tools from single flakes, sharper and shapelier.
Upper Paleolithic	(28,000–10,000 B.C.)	More advanced tools and use of bone tools.
Transition to New Stone Age (Mesolithic)	(8,000–6,000 B.C.)	Smaller and more delicate stone and bone tools, pottery, and the use of the bow.
New Stone Age (Neolithic)	(6,000–2,000 B.C.)	Stone and bone implements were improved by grinding and polishing. Copper metallurgy begins sometime in the 4th millennium.
Bronze Age	(2,000–1,150 B.C.)	Metals were first used regularly in the manufacture of tools and weapons. Pure copper and bronze use.
Iron Age		
Lower (Hallstatt)	(1,150–850 B.C.)	General use of iron in manufacturing, first shaped by hammering; then by iron smelting
Middle (La Tène)	(850–650 B.C.)	
Upper (Hallstatt)	(650–440 B.C.)	

CHAPTER 1

Romanian Lands in Antiquity

The Geto-Dacians, forefathers of the Romanians, were first mentioned in the fourth century B.C. by the Greek historian Herodotus and probably made their appearance in the Carpatho-Danubian region within the boundary of present-day Romania sometime during the seventh century B.C. Populations of different cultures, however, inhabited that region long before that, during the prehistoric (undocumented) phase of human development, before the advent of writing systems and before mankind conceived the idea of recording historical events by writing them down. Prehistoric development took place over a period of about two-and-one-half million years, and we rely on the study of geological, environmental, and climatic changes, as well as on archaeological exploration, to reconstruct man's physical and cultural development.

Archaeological discoveries also give us clues about migrations, wars, and disappearance or assimilation of different ancient civilizations; of traditions and changing patterns of life, as well as of artistic, economic, and religious behavior. The three major divisions of prehistory according to the evolution of human skill in working with specific materials are the Stone Age, the Bronze Age, and the Iron Age. These successive changes took place at different times in different parts of the world, and the chronological periods shown here are generally for southwestern Europe, including the Carpatho-Danubian area of present-day Romania.

STONE AGE

The Stone Age is divided into the Old Stone Age (Paleolithic) and the New Stone Age (Neolithic). It stretches from about two million B.C. to 2000 B.C. During the Stone Age, humans evolved from ape-like creatures to *Homo sapiens*, then slowly changed from being hunters and food gatherers to producing foods through farming and animal husbandry.

Evidence of continuous human activity in the Carpatho-Danubian region down to the Black Sea goes back to the Middle Paleolithic Age (60,000 B.C.), and the peak of Neolithic development on Romanian soil dates back to the Aenolithic Age (fourth–third millennium B.C.), which is the period of transition between the Stone Age and the Bronze Age. Archaeological discoveries presumed different cultures brought by increasing waves of migratory newcomers; these cultures have been given names according to the localities where they were first found. One of the best-known works of art created during the Neolithic Age is a pair of tiny statuettes, barely five inches in height, of glossy black terra cotta, belonging to the Hamangia culture (c. 5500 B.C.) and found at the cemetery of Dealul Sofia near Cernavodă. Referred to as "The Thinker," this statue and its female partner are masterpieces of expressiveness, realism, and simplicity of line. Other cultures such as the Cucuteni, Gumelniţa, and Horodişte emerged toward the end of the Aenolithic Age.

BRONZE AGE

The Bronze Age was marked by increased specialization, along with the invention of the wheel and the ox-drawn or horse-drawn plow. Archaeological discoveries from that period include fortified settlements with ditches or walls, indicating defensive measures against migratory people. Discoveries on Romanian soil dating to the Bronze Age include the beginning of vine growing and the use of ox-drawn or horse-drawn carts. Gold, bronze, and copper were used as means of

The Thinker and its female partner, *Hamangia* statuettes (6th mill. B.C.)
Courtesy of Regia Autonomă "Monitorul Oficial," Romanian Parliament

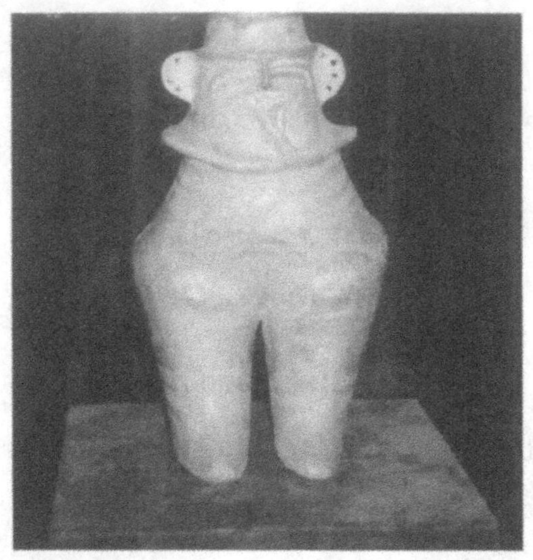

Anthromorphous vessel, Neolithic *Gumelnița* culture (4th–3rd mill. B.C.)
Courtesy of National Museum of History, Bucharest

Binocular-shaped vessels, Aenolithic *Cucuteni* culture (c. 4th mill. B.C.)
Courtesy of National Museum of History, Bucharest

exchange, and populations traded with neighbors, as well as with people in other parts of the world.

Indo-Europeans

The Bronze Age marks the beginning of migration of people from the Eurasian steppe, entering the area of the Old European civilization, creating and developing successive cultures which led to the establishment and propagation of an Indo-European population. Over the next 1,500 years, in three great waves of migration, Indo-Europeans spread from east to west and southward. After the second wave of migration and expansion of Indo-Europeans, which took place in the third millennium B.C., the Carpatho-Danubian area and the whole region south of the Haemus Mountains down to the Aegean Sea was inhabited by the Thracians.

Thracians

The Thracians consisted of a large number of tribes speaking different dialects of the same basic language. At a point in history, the homeland of these tribes covered a large portion of southwestern Europe, stretching from the north Aegean Sea to the northern foothills of the Carpathian Mountains, and from the Vardar River (in Macedonia), the Theiss (Tisa, Tisza) Valley, through most of Slovakia, eastward into northwestern Anatolia. The Thracians could have become one of the great powers of the classical period, were it not for their seeming inability to unite their tribes. Herodotus (c. 484–424 B.C.), the Greek historian, known as the father of history, wrote:

> The Thracians are the most powerful people in the world, except, of course, the Indians; and if they had one head, or were agreed among themselves, it is my belief that their match could not be found anywhere, and that they would very far surpass all other nations. But such union is impossible for them, and there are no means of ever bringing it about.[1]

The third great migration of people, beginning in the second millennium B.C., also caused dislocation of a number of Thracian tribes. Various factors—such as the new mix of people and cultures, influences of neighboring civilizations, and different geographic and political environments—resulted in an increasing disparity between the northern Thracians and the southern Thracians. Those who lived north of the Haemus Mountains, including the Geto-Dacians, continued to be subjected to invasions by nomadic tribes, slowing down their development. Their principal contact with more advanced civilizations was the trade and cultural exchange with Dorian and Ionian colonies on the Black Sea. Other tribes inhabiting the land that is now Romania were the Cimmerians and the Scythians.

IRON AGE

The Iron Age was the last of the prehistoric ages, beginning about 1150 B.C. and continuing into history. Knowledge of iron smelting passed during the third great migration through Greece and the Balkans, and spread from there through the rest of Europe. The people of the Iron Age developed the basic economic innovations of the Bronze Age and laid foundations for a feudal organization. Ox-drawn plows and wheeled vehicles acquired new importance and changed agricultural patterns. Villages were fortified, and warfare was conducted on horseback and horse-drawn chariots. Alphabetic writing based on the Phoenician script became widespread. Distinctive art styles in metal, pottery, and stone characterized many Iron Age cultures.

Early Geto-Dacians

The Roman geographer Pliny the Elder tells us that "Getae" was the Greek name and "Dacians" was the Latin name for the same Thracian tribe. It is also possible that they were separate tribes speaking the same Thracian dialect. The Greek geographer Strabo writes:

Bronze ritual chariot, Iron Age

Courtesy of National Museum of History, Bucharest

> [S]ome of the people are called Daci whereas others are called Getae—Getae those who incline towards the Pontus and the East, and Daci, those who incline in the opposite direction, towards Germany and the source of the Ister. The Daci, I think, were called Daï in the early times, whence the slave names "Geta" and "Daïs" which prevailed among the Attic people.[2]

Herodotus is the first historian who, in the fifth century B.C., mentions the Getae. He writes about Persian King Darius I who runs into the Getae during his campaign against the Scythians (512 B.C.) to prevent shipment of grain to Greece. Here is how he describes them:

> Before arriving at the Ister, the first people whom he subdued were the Getae who believe in their immortality. The Thracians of Salmydessus, and those who dwelt above the cities of Appolonia and Messembria—the Scyrmidae and Nipsaeans, as they are called—gave themselves up to Darius without a struggle; but the Getae obstinately defending themselves, were forthwith enslaved, notwithstanding that they are the noblest as well as the most just of the Thracian tribes.[3]

The earliest known Getic site is Zimnicea, on the northern bank of the Danube, about sixty miles southwest of where Bucharest now stands. The inhabitants lived in thatched- or reed-roofed log cabins, and objects found at this site indicate that these natives wore imported bronze and gold jewelry from Thrace and used imported Greek oil and wine. These luxury products were probably acquired through trade with Greek colonies that established themselves on the coast of the Black Sea and along the Danube Delta.

Greek City-States

In the mid-seventh century B.C., Dorian and Ionian merchants traveled north and set up a number of trading posts, which developed into the city-states of Tomis, Calattis, Histria, Dionysopolis, Tyras, and Axiopolis. From the local population they bought slaves, fish, furs, and grains, as well as gold and silver that were mined by the Dacians living in the western Carpathians. In return, the merchants sold imported luxury products, wine, and oil to the natives. Regular trading contact with these Greek colonies had a profound effect on the development of the Geto-Dacians, as they gradually entered the sphere of influence of the more advanced Hellenic civilization. Much later, this process facilitated their Romanization under the Romans.

Geto-Dacians From 650 B.C. to A.D. 106

Other influences on Geto-Dacian life came from the neighboring Scythians and from the Celts. Thucydides, the Greek historian, tells us that "the Getae beyond the Danube" were neighbors of the Scythians and had weapons like the Scythians, and all of them were expert archers and horsemen.

During the fourth century B.C., the Celts reached the Danube in the Pannonian Plain, and in the third century they advanced to the center of Transylvania and to the steppe of southeastern Moldavia. For a while, the Celts dominated Transylvania, but by the end of the second century B.C. their influence began to wane, and they either departed or were assimilated by the Dacians.

The Geto-Dacians' homeland was one of the most densely populated areas of the ancient world. It was a desirable place to live—rich in iron, gold, and silver and with fertile plains, hills that were well suited to raising sheep and cattle, mountains and forests in which to take refuge from invaders, and plenty of rivers for an abundant supply of fish. The Geto-Dacians generally were blond and of medium height. The men were bearded, and their hair was long; they wore long, loose-fitting trousers, over which they wore shirts tied with a belt. They also wore short, sleeveless cloaks and, in the winter, long sheepskin coats and hoods. The women wore short-sleeved blouses and skirts, over which they threw cloaks; their heads were covered with kerchiefs.

Bust of a Dacian nobleman (Pileatus)
Courtesy of National Museum of History, Bucharest

Bust of a Dacian commoner (Comatus)

Courtesy of National Museum of History, Bucharest

There existed a nobility, and the noblemen wore a fur hat to distinguish them from the commoners who went bare-headed. The Geto-Dacians were a hardworking, heroic, and religious people. Their religion was based on the teachings of Zalmoxis (Zamolxis), who was their god.

The story of Zalmoxis is interesting and is told by Herodotus and again, much later, by Strabo. According to both historians, Zalmoxis was a Dacian slave in the house of Pythagoras at Samos. While in his service, Zalmoxis learned a great deal about heavenly bodies from his master and from their travels to Egypt. In his Dacian homeland, the word spread that Zalmoxis could make predictions from celestial signs. Hearing about this, the king made him high priest on the basis of his ability to report the will of the gods. According to Strabo, "he was even addressed as God, and having taken possession of a certain cavernous place that was inaccessible to anyone else, he spent the rest of his life there, only rarely meeting with any people outside except the king and his own attendants."[4]

Herodotus tells this story:

> They think that they do not really die, but that when they depart this life they go to Zalmoxis. To this god every five years they send a messenger, who is chosen by lot out of the whole nation, and charged to bear him their several requests. Their mode of sending him is this. A number of them stand in order, each holding in his hand three darts: others take the man who is to be sent to Zalmoxis; and swinging him by his hands and feet, toss him into the air so that he falls upon the points of the weapons. If he is pierced and dies, they think that the god is propitious to them; but if not, they lay the fault on the messenger, who (they say) is a wicked man; so they choose another to send away. The messages are given while the man is still alive.[5]

During the Iron Age new and more sophisticated methods of manufacturing weapons and of conducting warfare made it increasingly more difficult for the Getae and the Dacians—living as they were in separate, individual tribal villages scattered across their homeland—to defend themselves against marauding tribes and invading armies. At some point they formed a united Geto-Dacian state with their capital located about thirteen miles southwest of Bucharest.

In 335 B.C. Alexander the Great, son of Philip II of Macedon, then a general, launched campaigns against Thrace to put down unrest in the region. We have two accounts about these expeditions—one by Strabo and the other by Arrian. Strabo writes:

> When Alexander, the son of Philip, on his expedition against the Thracians beyond the Haemus, invaded the country of the Triballians (a Thracian tribe) and saw that it extended as far as the Ister, and that the island of Peuce in the Ister, and that the parts on the far side were held by the Getae, he went as far as that (as far as the island), it is said, but could not disembark upon the island because of scarcity of boats. He did, however, cross over to the country of the Getae, took their city, and returned with all speed to his home-land, after receiving gifts from the tribes in question.[6]

Arrian writes:

> In the spring he went Thraceward. . . . After numerous battles and victories against the Thracians and the Triballians, Alexander reached the Ister, the greatest river of Europe. . . . There Alexander found at the mouth of the river warships come to join him from Byzantium through the Black Sea. These he manned with archers and men-at-arms and sailed against the island where the Triballians and Thracians had taken refuge, and endeavored to force a landing. The island was too steep for landing, however, and the armed tribesmen kept swooping down to the riverbanks, and the river currents were too swift. Thereupon Alexander withdrew his troops and decided instead

> to cross the Ister to attack the Getae who were settled on the farther side, both because he saw a large force of them gathered at the bank, to repel him, should he cross—there were about four thousand mounted men, and more than ten thousand on foot—and also because he had been seized with a desire to land on the farther side. . . . The Getae did not sustain even the first charge of the cavalry; for Alexander's bold stroke came as a great shock to them, in that he so easily crossed the Ister, greatest of rivers, in one night without so much as bridging the stream. The Getae retreated first to their city, and then fled to the mountains. Alexander captured the city, plundered it and razed it to the ground. Then, in daylight he took all his force safe and sound back to the camp, taking with them whatever plunder the Getae left behind.[7]

After the death of Alexander the Great (in 323 B.C.), the Macedonian Empire was divided among his generals, weakening their control over the Danube region. This allowed the Geto-Dacians to improve their organization and become an important power in the area.

Macedonia and Thrace south of the Haemus were ruled by Lysimach, king of Thrace. In 322 B.C., after several internal power struggles, rebellions and battles, Lysimach consolidated his control in his kingdom, and since he now faced the Getae, he decided, in the year 300 B.C., to attack them. The Geto-Dacians had made considerable progress in terms of organizational and military capability since the days of Alexander the Great. Now their troops, under King Dromichaites, defeated the Macedonians and took Lysimach prisoner. The Getic king appears to have been not only an astute statesman but also of a kind nature. He invited his captured enemy to a royal dinner and later on formed an alliance with the Macedonians, bound by his marriage with Lysimach's daughter.

For the remaining years of the third century and for the second century B.C. there is very little historical information about the Geto-Dacians.

History again focuses on the Geto-Dacians during the first century B.C. with the rise to power of Burebista, one of the greatest of Getic kings. Through strong leadership, he was able to unite all the Geto-Dacian tribes, as well as all other tribes in the region, for the first time into one kingdom, which now stretched from the Pannonian valley in the west to the Black Sea and southward into Thrace. Strabo writes:

> Boerobistas (Burebista, Byrebistas), a Getan, on setting himself in authority over the tribe, restored the people, who had been reduced to an evil plight by numerous wars, and raised them to such a height through training, sobriety, and obedience to his commands that within only a few years he had established a great empire and subordinated to the Getae most of the neighboring people. And he began to be formidable even to the Romans because he would cross the Ister with impunity, and plunder Thrace as far as Macedonia and the Illyrian country; and he not only lay waste the country of the Celti (Celts) who were intermingled with the Thracians and the Illyrians, but actually caused the complete disappearance of the Boii (also a Celtic tribe) and also of the Taurisci (also a Celtic tribe).[8]

Burebista even imposed his control over the Greek Black Sea city-states. To increase discipline in his people, he attempted to eliminate drunkenness, which was widespread in those days, by ordering the destruction of all the vineyards.

Burebista's kingdom soon became the strongest power north of the Roman Empire. In A.D. 45–44, Burebista joined Pompey in a plot to overthrow Caesar, who was planning an expedition against the Dacians. As it happened, Caesar was assassinated before he could go through with his plan. Shortly afterward, King Burebista himself was assassinated by some of his own chiefs. After his death, his kingdom broke up again and was not to be reunited until some one hundred years later, under King Decebal. Cassius Dio wrote about him:

> He was very skilled in drawing up battle plans and carrying them out, knowing when to attack the enemy and when to withdraw. Ingenious in laying ambushes, he was a brave warrior who knew how to turn to good account a victory and how to escape the dangers of defeat. That is why for a long time he had been a most dangerous enemy of the Romans.[9]

In 85, the Dacians crossed the Danube and defeated a Roman army led by Oppius Sabinius, who died on the battleground. In retaliation, Roman troops under Cornelius Fuscus entered Dacian territory and moved up toward the capital, Sarmizegetusa, but they were defeated once again. Under Emperor Domitian, in 89, a third campaign by the Romans successfully battled their way to the Dacian capital, whereupon Decebal sent a mission to Rome and concluded a very favorable peace agreement. Rome recognized Dacia as a state and Decebal as king of the Dacians. Under this agreement, Rome was also to pay the Dacians annual subsidies, as well as provide them with weapons, construction engineers, and other war equipment. Decebal introduced Roman discipline and fighting methods into his army and built fortifications using Roman designs and technique. Peace lasted for twelve years, but to the Roman senate the humiliation of paying tribute to the Dacians was too much to bear. Dacia was also becoming too much of a threat to the security of the empire.

During this time Roman Emperor Nerva, who had no children, was searching for a successor. He chose Marcus Ulpius Trajanus (Trajan). Born in Spain, Trajan was the first non-Italian to become head of the empire. He was born and bred to be a soldier. His father, a legionary soldier who worked his way up to the governorship of Asia, raised his son in the military tradition. On October 27, 97, Nerva adopted Trajan and named him his successor. The Senate confirmed the choice, and upon Nerva's death on January 25, 98, he was proclaimed Emperor Trajan (ruled 98–117).

As soon as Trajan took charge of the empire, he realized that it was in jeopardy. Instead of going to Rome, he went north to the Dacian

Dacian King Decebal
Courtesy of Romanian National Tourist Office

Roman Emperor Trajan, bronze head discovered at Sarmizegetusa
Private collection of Bogdan Ulmu

frontier to set in motion his plan to attack and conquer the kingdom of Dacia, which he felt was vital for the security of the empire.

Preparations for his attack took three years. He ordered new military roads to be built so that his army could move to the Danube rapidly. In the spring of 101, one of the largest armies that had ever been amassed crossed the Danube at Viminacium into Dacia. A force of fourteen to fifteen legions and non-Roman auxiliaries estimated at 100,000 to 150,000 men took part in the campaign. Although they were able to reach Tapae, just west of the capital, their troops were halted there, and a powerful counterattack by the Dacians sent the Roman troops in retreat. In a second offensive, in 102, the Romans again reached the walls of Sarmizegetusa, and this time Decebal negotiated a peace with Trajan.

The king was allowed to keep his crown but had to accept a Roman garrison and a civil adviser. Strabo writes:

> "Although the Getae and Daci once attained to very great power, so that they actually could send forth an expedition of 200,000 men, they now find themselves reduced to as few as 40,000, and they have come close to the point of yielding obedience to the Romans."[10]

To secure his communication with Dacia, Trajan called on the famous architect, Apollodorus from Damascus, who later designed Trajan's forum in Rome, to build a bridge across the Danube, a bridge that was considered a masterpiece of engineering. It crossed the Danube at Drobeta. In July 105, war broke out again as Decebal tried to rid himself of Roman control. This time a massive Roman offensive on two fronts finally defeated the Dacians, and in 106, Dacia officially became a province of the Roman Empire.

NOTES

1. Herodotus *Histories* V.3.
2. Strabo *The Geography* 7.III.12.
3. Herodotus *Histories* IV.93.
4. Strabo *The Geography* 7.III.5.
5. Herodotus *Histories* IV.94.
6. Strabo *The Geography* 7.III.8.
7. Arrian *Anabasis of Alexander* I, I. 1–5.
8. Strabo *The Geography* 7.III.11.
9. Cassius Dio *Roman History* 67.6.1.
10. Strabo *The Geography* 7.III.13.

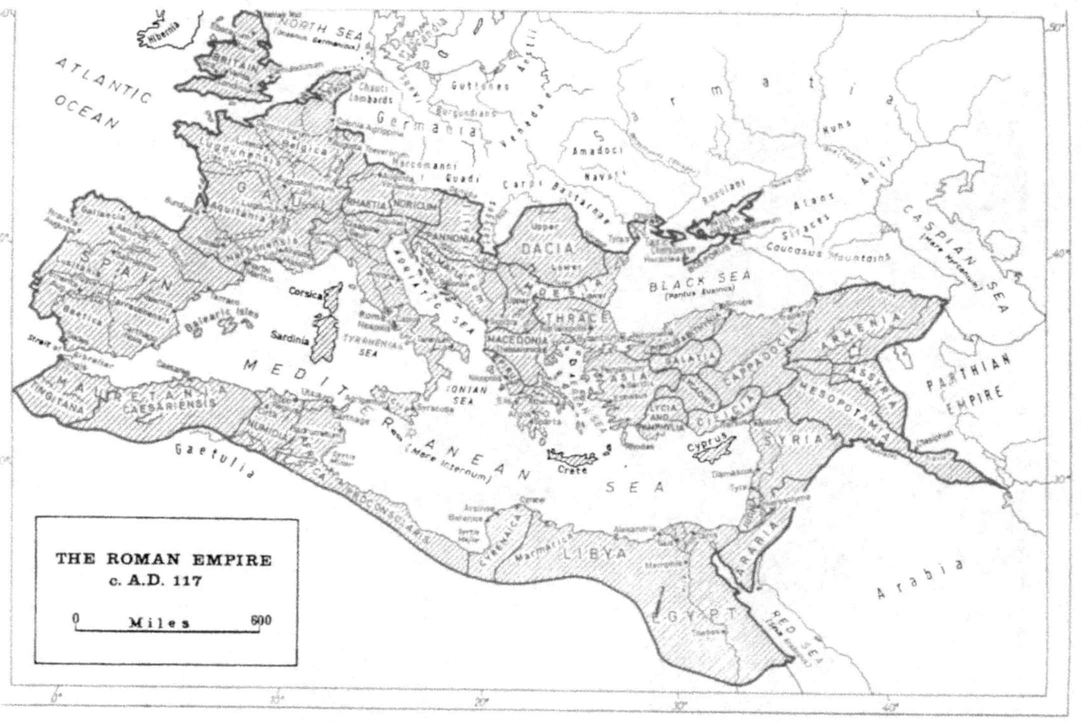

THE ROMAN EMPIRE
c. A.D. 117
0 Miles 600
ATLANTIC OCEAN
NORTH SEA
Hibernia
BRITAIN
Germania
Guttones
Chauci
Lombards
Burgundians
Marcomanni
Quadi
Amadoci
Carpi
Bastarnae
Roxolani
Huns
Alans
Caucasus Mountains
CASPIAN SEA
PARTHIAN EMPIRE
GAUL
Belgica
Lugdunensis
Aquitania
Narbonensis
RHAETIA
NORICUM
PANNONIA
DACIA
MOESIA
THRACE
MACEDONIA
SPAIN
Baetica
Corsica
Sardinia
Balearic Isles
ADRIATIC SEA
TYRRHENIAN SEA
IONIAN SEA
AEGEAN SEA
BLACK SEA
(Pontus Euxinus)
MEDITERRANEAN SEA
(Mare Internum)
ASIA
GALATIA
CAPPADOCIA
ARMENIA
ASSYRIA
MESOPOTAMIA
SYRIA
CILICIA
LYCIA AND
Cyprus
Crete
MAURETANIA TINGITANA
MAURETANIA CAESARIENSIS
NUMIDIA
AFRICA PROCONSULARIS
Gaetulia
CYRENAICA
Marmarica
LIBYA
EGYPT
ARABIA
Arabia
RED SEA

Dacia as a Roman Province

Reprinted with permission from the Center for Romanian Studies.

CHAPTER 2

Dacia as a Roman Province
(106 to 271)

ROMAN VICTORY

The Dacian conquest was completed after two major campaigns that lasted over two years, and Emperor Trajan returned to Rome in glory to celebrate his definitive subjugation of the Dacian kingdom. The festivities lasted four months. The Dacian wars and Trajan's victory were immortalized by the erection of a magnificent monument on the site of Trajan's forum in Rome. *Trajan's Column*, designed by Apollodor, the same famous architect from Damascus who designed the bridge crossing the Danube at Drobeta, stands 130 feet high. It is sculpted in stone and some 2,500 bas-relief figures spiral around the column, with each panel capturing a different war scene. Scenes of battles, of suffering and cruelty, and of heroism and victory are carved with remarkable accuracy. There are Dacians dressed in mantles and tunics, the nobles wearing the kind of caps one can still see Romanians wearing in today's villages. One scene depicts Dacians setting fire to their capital, Sarmizegetusa, before the arrival of the Roman conquerors, while others drink poison from a large vessel, some already lying on the ground in agony, preferring to die rather than be captured. Still other scenes show the Dacians surrendering to the Romans, Trajan as victor, and soldiers carrying the head of Decebal.

Trajan's Column, Trajan's forum, Rome
From author's collection

"Crossing the Danube landing at Dobrogea," a scene from *Trajan's Column*
Courtesy of Museum of History, Iași

Trajan's Column has withstood more than 1,700 years and is practically intact. Trajan's body lies buried underneath it, but his statue, which stood on the column's summit, was removed by one of the popes and replaced with a statue of St. Peter.

There was much to celebrate in the year 106. Not only was it strategically important for the empire to eliminate the threat of the Dacian kingdom and to use the province as a buffer against the mounting danger from invading barbarian armies, but also the wealth of gold and silver from Dacian mines helped prop up the depleting Roman coffers. Every Roman taxpayer received a gift of 650 dinars from their emperor on that occasion.

PROVINCE OF DACIA AND ITS SURROUNDINGS

The territory that became a Roman province in A.D. 106 was limited to that portion of the Geto-Dacian homeland which comprised Decebal's kingdom of Dacia. It consisted of eastern and southeastern Transylvania, the Banat, and Oltenia. During the next 130 years, various neighboring areas were to be incorporated into the province. Dacia's borders then ran along the Tisa River from where it flows into the Danube, up to where it merges with the Mureş River, then along the Mureş, north along the western side of the Apuseni Mountains, east along the Samus (Someş) River and along the Carpathians as far as Cumidava (Râşnov in the county of Braşov), then south across the mountains over the Bran Pass, ending at the northern bank of the Danube in western Muntenia.

To the south and east of Dacia's borders was the Roman province of Moesia, which in the year 86 had been divided by Emperor Domitian into Moesia Superior, with its capital Singidunum (Belgrade, Serbia) and Moesia Inferior, with its capital at Tomis (Constanţa, Romania). Moesia Inferior extended north of the Danube and covered parts of Wallachia, Moldavia, and Transylvania. During the reign of Emperor

Hadrian (ruled 117–138), some of its territories were incorporated into the new province of Dacia, so that Moesia Inferior no longer included any territory north of the Danube, with the exception of strategic bridgeheads. Moesia Inferior also included all of Dobrogea.

Yazyges, a Sarmatian tribe related to the Scythians, inhabited the Pannonian Plain (Hungary) along Dacia's western border. The northern part of Transylvania was inhabited by Free Dacians and Costobocs, another Dacian tribe, while northern Moldavia and the former Romanian province of Bessarabia were inhabited by two Sarmatian tribes (the Carps and the Roxolani), by Bastarns, and by Tyragetae (another Geto-Dacian tribe).

LIFE IN DACIA FELIX

The Romans wasted no time in turning the war-ravaged nation into an organized, fully functioning Roman province. The first requirement to accomplish this was to supplement what remained of the local population with specialists and workers in all fields—from military personnel to doctors and civil servants; from engineers and architects to veterans of Roman legions. An intensive colonization program was set up. Word spread about opportunities that the rich and beautiful land of Dacia offered, and people from Rome and all other parts of the empire rushed to take advantage of it. Romans called the new province *Dacia Felix* (Dacia the blessed). They settled there, built homes, married Dacians, and raised families; their offspring created a new Daco-Roman race.

The next priority was to set up military and administrative infrastructures. One of the main functions of the new province was to act as a buffer against attacks from incessant barbarian invasions and incursions that began in the second century A.D. and were to continue for the next ten centuries. Dacia was not an easy territory to defend since it stuck out into barbarian territory like the proverbial "sore thumb." Four major military roads traversed Dacia, three of them connecting all major cities and one, Trajan's Road, crossing the Carpathians from Transylvania into Wallachia. Some 100 fortified camps spread across the province, manned by an army and auxiliary staff that numbered 50,000.

For administrative purposes, Dacia was at first divided into two departments: Dacia Superior, with Apulum (Alba-Iulia) as its capital; and Dacia Inferior, with Drobeta (Turnu-Severin) as its capital. Later, Emperor Hadrian reorganized defenses and created a third department, Dacia Porolissensis, with Napoca (Cluj-Napoca) as its capital.

About twenty miles from Decebal's old capital, Sarmizegetusa, a new, elegant city complete with temples, amphitheaters, aqueducts, and baths was created and named Ulpia Trajanus. It became the provincial capital with a single appointed governor for the three Dacian departments. Dacia became the empire's most urbanized province, with at least eleven identified major cities, which were laid out in the same manner as any Roman city and with all their amenities, such as theaters, aqueducts, sewers, and baths. Eight cities were classified as *coloniae* (equivalent to "city"). These included Ulpia Trajanus, Apulum, Napoca, and Drobeta, as well as Dierna (near Orşova), Potaissa (Turda, fifty miles north of Apulum), Romula (Reşca), and Aquae (Călan). Three others were classified as *municipae* (equivalent to "town"). They were Porolissum (Moigrad), Tibiscum (Jupa, near Caransebeş), and Ampelum (Zlatna, in the Apuseni Mountains).

A period of peace, stability, and prosperity followed. Agriculture, stockbreeding, and commerce flourished. New mines were opened, and ore extraction intensified. Vineyards that had been destroyed during the reign of Burebista were replanted. Dacia began to supply grains not only to the military personnel stationed in the province but also to the rest of the Balkan area. Craftsmen were organized into guilds. While no great literary works from that period have been uncovered, many religious documents have been found, which indicate that different deities were worshiped.

ROMANIZATION OF THE DACIANS

Roman influence on the Dacians by no means started with the occupation of Dacia. It probably began with trade between Moesia and Dacia since the end of the last century B.C. Later on, during the reign of Emperor Titus (ruled 79–81), influence became stronger when many skilled Roman engineers, craftsmen, and workers were brought in by Decebal to settle in Dacia and build fortresses in the Roman fashion.

In cities, Romans far outnumbered the local populations, making it a necessity for Dacians who worked and lived there to speak Latin. The Latin they learned was not classical Latin but the common dialect spoken by the soldiers and civil servants. In the rest of the province, in rural areas, Roman settlers (*coloni*) and veterans of Roman legions were allowed to lease tracts of land, and there they built their villas and settled down. They used the local population to work the land. Here the Dacians far outnumbered the Romans, and they clung to their language and traditions. Nevertheless, since many of them worked for the Roman settlers, they learned to speak Latin, too. Furthermore, Roman legions also included many Dacian cohorts.[1] In fact one of the "milecastles"[2] along Hadrian's Wall in Great Britain (built in c. 121–127) was occupied by the First Aelian Cohort of Dacians. The locality was called Camboglanna (Crooked Glen), later known successively as Aeliana, Tetriciana, and Gordiana. Today it is called Birdoswald.

In 212, Emperor Caracalla granted Roman citizenship to all free inhabitants of the empire, Dacians included, and Latin was decreed the official language. Gradually, over the next three generations, the influence of Roman culture and way of life, change of religion, and intermarriage resulted in a new Daco-Roman population that spoke a common Latin, mixed with some Dacian words: a people who physically resembled Romans, but who kept some of the old Dacian customs and traditions. From this synthesis of two cultures, the Romanian culture gradually evolved.

WITHDRAWAL OF THE ROMANS FROM DACIA

Toward the end of the second century and the beginning of the third, the Roman Empire was heading toward a crisis that was to signal its eventual collapse. Rome was suffering from internal strife and intrigue, and the empire was too large to be effectively controlled. This encouraged barbarian tribes in the Danubian region to invade, ransack, and plunder Roman provinces, while in Rome corrupt officials were buying their way to the throne. The Romans lost the fortitude to rule, and in 193, people appealed to the provincial military legions to depose Emperor Didius Julianus. The Pannonian commander, Lucius Septimius Severus, brought his troops to Rome, had Julianus decapitated, and became emperor.

Septimius was born in Africa of Punic-speaking Phoenicians, and he became the first of a Semite dynasty of emperors, with orientation to the East. He was a military man who devoted his career to trying to bring order and stability to the empire. His son Caracalla succeeded him, but after only six years, he was murdered by his successor. A number of inept emperors followed, bringing the empire to the brink of chaos.

At the same time, the empire faced some of the worst defeats in Roman history in the battles against barbarian attacks. In 248, the Goths invaded Moesia. In 251, Emperor Gallus bribed the Goths to retreat, with their booty and prisoners, into Muntenia and Moldavia, thus creating an isolating gap between Dacia and Dobrogea. A further five Gothic attacks, however, took place between 248 and 268, one of which cost Roman Emperor Decius's life. Then, in 270, Lucius Domitius Aurelianus (Aurelian) became emperor. He was to become one of Rome's greatest: he regained Britain, Gaul, Spain, Egypt, Syria, and Mesopotamia; and for a while, he removed the barbarian threat to the Danubian provinces.

To enforce his defenses, Aurelian resolved to evacuate Dacia and consolidate his forces along the banks of the Danube. Beginning in

271, the Roman legions and the government officials began their retreat, and by about 275 the Daco-Roman population that remained behind was left to fend for itself. Dacia had been the last province to be added to the Roman Empire and was the first to be abandoned.

NOTES

1. One of ten divisions of a Roman legion.
2. Small stone forts built against Hadrian's Wall, with a gateway through the wall, a tower above, and another gate on the south wall. They provided accommodation for up to sixty-four men.

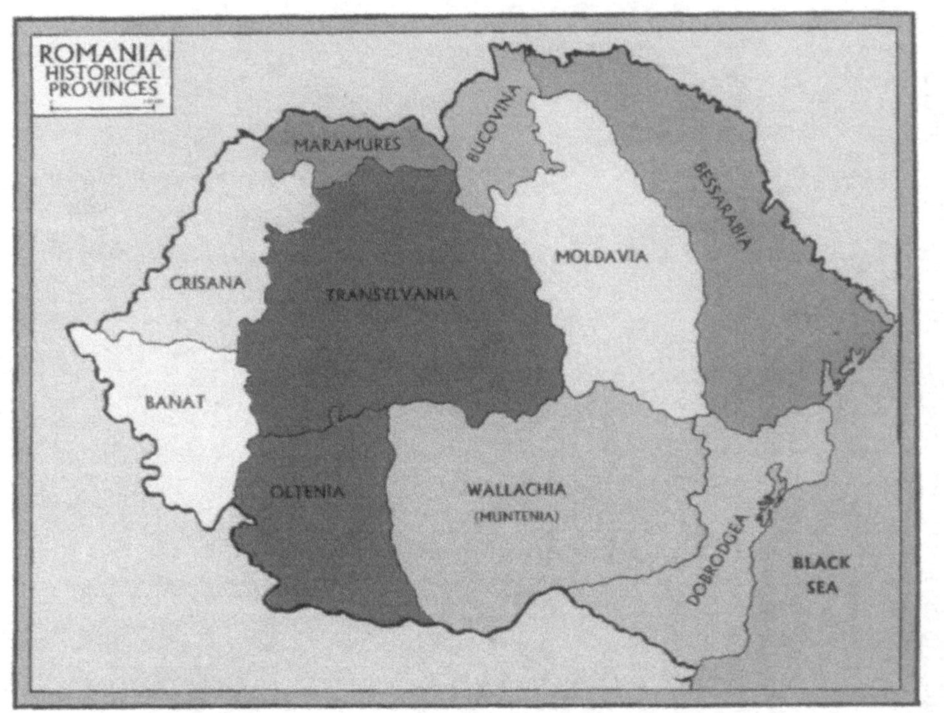

The Road to Statehood

Reprinted with permission from the Center for Romanian Studies.

CHAPTER 3

Into and Out of the Dark Ages
(Second–Fourteenth Centuries)

PERSPECTIVE

The Roman Empire had reached its greatest expansion by the year 180 A.D. Across the whole empire, people enjoyed peace, order, and prosperity. The arts, architecture, science, and medicine flourished. Towns had water supplies, baths for all classes, and modern roads, while the privileged class even enjoyed central heating. There was a postal service as well as police and fire departments. This period was known as the Golden Age of the empire. All of Rome's provinces, including Dacia, were partaking in these benefits equally. In 212 Emperor Caracalla had even extended Roman citizenship to all free inhabitants of the empire.

The Golden Age ended, however, by the third century. In Rome, corruption, rivalry, and conspiracy were on the increase. With the rise of Christianity, violent persecutions were continuing against the Christians, invasions by the Goths were weakening the empire, Emperor Valerian was captured by the Persians, and a virulent epidemic is said to have caused the death of over 5,000 Romans.

It was against this backdrop of events that Dacia was abandoned by Aurelian in 271 to 275. The Dark Ages are generally considered as the period following the disintegration of Rome in the fourth and fifth centuries and lasting until the eleventh century. In Dacia and the rest of the Romanized region north of the Danube, the Dark Ages could be said to begin when the Romans left. For almost 1,000 years, until the formation of the principality of Wallachia in 1317, the Carpatho-Danubian territory was to be crisscrossed by migrating populations from the north, the west, and the east, who ravaged everything in their path, and, in succession, ruled over parts of the region. As for the native population, historians have left us with very little written information. During this millennium, Europe was undergoing fundamental changes that would affect the evolution of the Romanians and the ultimate formation of Romanian states.

Emperor Diocletian (ruled 285–305) divided the empire into the East Roman Empire and the West Roman Empire in 286 and Emperor Constantine I (ruled 305–337) moved the capital to Byzantium, renaming it Constantinople in 330. The two administrative units soon split, and Rome rapidly lost its political importance. Italy was ravaged by invaders, and Rome was taken, first by the Goths, then by the Vandals in 455. Christianity, which was made the official religion of the empire in 313, grew in importance as the empire's power diminished.

Hispania was overrun by the Suevis and the Vandals, followed by the Visigoths, who established their kingdom in Spain in 419. Gaul was invaded by the Vandals and others who had crossed the Rhine in 406. Shortly thereafter, the Visigoths were settled by treaty in the province of Aquitania. Finally, Clovis I had conquered most of Gaul by the end of the sixth century and it became part of the kingdom of the Franks. In 476 the last of the emperors of the West, Romulus Augustulus, was deposed by Odoacer, the barbarian mercenary and king of the Heruli. The Ostrogoths, who overthrew Odoacer in 493, controlled Rome until the Byzantine Empire reconquered Italy in the Gothic War (535–555). However, the coronation of Charlemagne in 800 as emperor of the West ended Byzantine rule over Rome and brought about a period of power struggles between emperors and popes.

Charlemagne's Carolingian empire ended with the partition among Emperor Louis I's three sons in 843 and was concluded by the Treaty of Verdun in 843. Louis the German received the eastern portion (later to become Germany). Louis I's eldest son, Lothair, received the central portion (later to be called the Low Countries, as well as Lorraine, Alsace, Burgundy, Provence, and most of Italy). Lothair also inherited the imperial title, and upon Louis I's death, became Roman emperor as Lothair I. In 855, as Lothair became seriously ill, he divided his lands between his three sons.

Otto I (Otto the Great), a son of the German King Henry I, Duke of Saxony, was crowned king of Germany in 936. In 951 he was crowned king of Lombardy and in 961 he crossed the Alps to invigorate an ineffective papacy and was crowned king of Italy. The next year, Pope John XII proclaimed Otto emperor. Many historians consider his coronation as the beginning of a European empire that dominated the political life of the Middle Ages, and lasted until 1806. Later it came to be known as the Holy Roman Empire.

In the east, the Byzantine Emperor Justinian (ruled 526–565) was confident that he could restore the old boundaries of the Roman Empire and heal the doctrinal differences within the Christian Church. He achieved the re-conquest of Italy, North Africa, and part of Spain, and reestablished Byzantine influence in the eastern Black Sea trading area. During the eighth and ninth centuries, the East Roman Empire, known as the Byzantine Empire, reached the peak of its power. It had become completely Hellenized and its language was Greek. The Byzantine Empire flourished for nearly a thousand years.

After 1025, the empire had to face increasing attacks from migratory tribes from the north of the Danube and from the east. However, in the face of innumerable difficulties, including the sacking of Constantinople by the armies of the Fourth Crusade, the Byzantine Empire survived by the use of astute international diplomacy and military force for nearly three more centuries.

QUESTION OF IDENTITY

Once the Romans withdrew from Dacia, the inhabitants of the Carpatho-Danubian region north of the Danube were no longer of interest to historians. Neither was Emperor Aurelian eager to make the Romans aware that he was abandoning one of their provinces. He therefore immediately created a new "Dacia" south of the Danube, in part of Moesia. Semi-official Roman historians noted that the population of Dacia was moved south. With respect to the north, history, for the next six centuries, records for the most part only the struggle of the Roman Empire against barbarian invaders and the effect that the invasions may have had on the rest of Europe. Because of this lengthy period of historical stealth, two theories about the origin of Romanians developed, theories that were subsequently exploited for political reasons.

One theory holds that the whole population of Dacia was moved south of the Danube and that the deserted region was settled by nomadic migratory people of Germanic, Asian, and Slavic origin. Adherents to this theory argue that in any event most of the Dacian population was exterminated when the Romans occupied Dacia, and that 165 years of occupation was not sufficient to Romanize a whole population. According to this theory, the Romanians developed in the Balkans, south of the Danube, from Romanized tribes who, in the tenth century, were called Vlachs by Byzantine and Bulgarian writers. These Vlachs then crossed the Danube and settled in the region that is now Romania. In the thirteenth century some of them crossed the Alps to settle in Transylvania in response to the Hungarian king's policy of colonization by foreigners.

The opposing theory argues that with Aurelian's Roman legions went the magistrates, the wealthy, the urban population, and the merchants. The vast majority, the Daco-Roman peasants and shepherds, stayed behind, having no reason to leave and no place to go. Those who adhere to this theory conclude that there has been a continuous Daco-Roman presence in Transylvania and the rest of the Carpatho-Danubian region and that this population, together with Romanized people of Thracian/Dacian stock coming from the south, evolved into proto-Romanians and finally the Romanians of today. There is today ample evidence—archaeological, linguistic, and religious—to support this latter position.

MILLENNIUM OF INVASIONS

While Dacia was still a province of the Roman Empire, it faced attacks and incursions by Free Dacians, Sarmatians, Carps, and, as early as 211, the first of the Gothic invasions. As Dacia was heavily fortified and protected by Roman legions, migrating populations who were directing their attacks against the Roman provinces south of the Danube soon found it more expedient to circumvent Dacia. This resulted in a period of relative calm in the province, while incursions continued and intensified across the Danube into Moesia, Thracia, Dalmatia, and Pannonia.

It was during this period, in 271, that Emperor Aurelian made the decision to reinforce his defenses along the Danube by withdrawing the troops from Dacia, virtually leaving its Daco-Roman population to fend for itself. Some historians argue that this decision sent a message to all the migrating barbarian hordes that the power of the empire was weakening. In fact, the attacks, plunders, incursions, and invasions increased both in frequency and in intensity from that point on and were to continue for a whole millennium. Most of the migrating people either went across parts of the territory that is now Romania or settled there, or they paused there for some years before continuing their migration. Most of them left untold devastation in their path, and most took turns in dominating and ruling over the native population.

Between 275 and 567, Moldavian, Wallachian, and Transylvanian regions were overrun by Visigoths, Vandals, Victuals, Taifals, and Huns. The Huns were the first in a long series of Asian migratory hordes to enter Europe, and they had a great effect on European history. These invasions weakened the Roman Empire and eventually led to the disintegration of Rome.

Avars

The Avars, a nomadic people originating in central Asia, were driven from their homeland by Turkish tribes; they entered Dobrogea in 567 and settled down for some years. Some of the Avars went further west and settled in parts of Pannonia, Crişana, the Banat, and Transylvania. For more than two centuries, the Avars dominated eastern and central Europe. Several incursions into the Byzantine Empire opened the gates for a major invasion by the Slavs in 602, which was to change the history of the Balkan Peninsula. The Avars were defeated in 791 to 796 by the Frankish armies of Charlemagne, who drove them across the Tisa River, where they were totally annihilated by the Bulgars under the Khan Krum in 803.

Slavs and Petchenegs

The origin of the Slavs is believed to be in an area of the Pripet Marshes near Kiev (Ukraine). They were dominated in succession by the Scythians and the Sarmatians, and then by the Goths, the Huns, and the Avars. At the beginning of the sixth century, a succession of massive Slavic invasions into Europe took place and continued into the tenth century. The Slavs came from an area between the Dnieper and Vistula Rivers and reached the Danube in 517. More and more Slavic people arrived with each successive migrating wave. They settled with the Avars and proto-Romanians in the area between the Carpathian Mountains and the Danube. Then, in 602, the largest portion of this population crossed the Danube and resettled permanently in the area of Bulgaria, changing the ethnic structure of the Balkan Peninsula. Those Slavs who remained north of the Danube were gradually assimilated by the proto-Romanian population, and during the ninth and tenth centuries, they were Christianized by missionaries from south of the Danube. The process of assimilation was completed by the thirteenth century. During this process, many Slavic words entered into the Romanian language, completing the evolution from the Danubian Latin and Dacian/Thracian to Romanian.

From about 890 to 1122, the Petchenegs (Patzinaks), a Turkic tribe from beyond the Volga and the Urals, settled on Romanian lands and began incursions into the Byzantine Empire. These raids continued until 1122, when the Petchenegs were finally crushed in battle by Roman Emperor John II.

Bulgars

The Bulgars, a Turkic-speaking people originating along the banks of the Volga, appeared in 619 at the mouth of the Danube and dominated southern Bessarabia and the Banat. One branch of Bulgars, the Eastern Bulgars, moved into Dobrogea in 679/680 and settled in the territory of present-day Bulgaria. There they subjugated Slavic tribes who had established themselves in Thrace and Moesia since 602 and settled permanently in the territory of present-day Bulgaria. They merged with the Slavs by the ninth century.

The First Bulgarian Empire lasted until the second half of the tenth century when, after repeated battles, the Bulgarian territory was regained by the Byzantine Empire. The Second Bulgarian Empire (or Vlacho-Bulgarian Empire) was established as a result of the 1185 revolt of the Bulgarians and the Vlachs against the Byzantine Empire, led by two Vlach brothers, Peter and Asam. This turned into a Bulgarian state that lasted until 1396, when it was conquered by the Ottoman Empire.

Cumans

An old Turkish people related to the Petchenegs, the Cumans came from the Black Sea steppes. They entered Moldavia and Wallachia in 1057, swept the Petchenegs aside, and replaced them as masters over that region. Settling down, the Cumans were converted to Christianity and became sedentary. Their domination ended in 1241 with the invasion of the Tatars.

Tatars (Tartars)

The last of the migrating populations to inflict themselves on the Romanians were the Tatars. They did not stay long but left behind them a devastated Moldavia and Wallachia. The Tatars, a Turkic-speaking people, came from east central Asia or central Siberia. They were related to the Petchenegs and the Cumans. The Mongols under Genghis Khan merged with the Tatars in about 1167, and in 1237 they attacked the Cuman empire, reaching the Dnieper River. In 1241, under Batu Khan, they invaded Romanian, Hungarian, and German territory. Fortunately for the Romanians and the rest of Europe, Batu Khan was recalled in 1242 in order to participate in elections. He died during his campaigns, and the invasions of Europe were never again renewed.

The Tatars were the last of the migrating hordes to enter Europe. After the wave of invasions receded eastward, however, the Tatars continued to dominate nearly all of Russia, Ukraine, and Siberia, as well as the area that later became the principality of Moldavia. Their successors, known as the Golden Horde, adopted Islam as their religion in the fourteenth century. Internal division and the appearance of the Ottoman Turks contributed to its disintegration.

FROM DACO-ROMANS TO ROMANIANS

The present-day Romanians evolved from the Geto-Dacians, a people who, unlike others in the area, were not migrants but had lived in the region of present-day Romania for centuries in prehistory and who continued to live on the same soil, as they became Daco-Romans, proto-Romanians, and finally Romanians. They are essentially a Latin people, influenced over time by the West and by the East, and spiritually by their Eastern Orthodox religion.

The evolution from Dacians to Romanians began with contacts between Dacians and Romans even before Dacia became a Roman province in 106. Romanization of the Dacian population intensified during the 165 years of occupation and with the introduction of Roman law and Latin as the official language, as well as education, economic and social intercourse, and intermarriage. When the Romans withdrew from Dacia in 271, they left a population that was already fully Romanized: a Daco-Roman people, speaking the Danubian Latin dialect, carrying on with a Roman way of life, while preserving ancestral Dacian traditions. Contact with Romans, Moesians, and other Romanized people south of the Danube continued uninterrupted for the next three decades, sustaining the Roman influence.

At first, the Danubian Latin was continually reinforced, but as the seat of power of the Roman Empire shifted to the east, so did the sphere of influence shift from Rome to Constantinople. Nevertheless, normal contact between the Daco-Romans and the Roman world continued uninterrupted as long as the Byzantine Empire still controlled the Danube. In fact, between 295 and 378, the Romans even launched a number of expeditions north of the Danube against the Visigoths, establishing control over parts of the Wallachian plain. However, by 447, under pressure from the Huns, the Romans abandoned their bridgeheads along the Danube, thereby increasing the isolation of the Daco-Roman population. The sixth century brought with it the beginning of great Slavic invasions, which continued into the tenth century.

In 602, new waves of Slavic migrations across the Danube into Moesia forced the Byzantine Empire to withdraw altogether from the lower Danube region, completely isolating the Romanized population north of the river. Those who inhabited Moesia and the Aurelian Dacia were being assimilated first by the Slavs, then by the Bulgars. Others were pushed north by the Slavs. Only three enclaves of Romanized people remained in the Balkan Peninsula. They were the Vlachs, and spoke a dialect of the same language as the Daco-Romans north of the Danube. Only one of these branches survived into the nineteenth century.

In the meantime, north of the Danube the Daco-Romans and other Romanized populations slowly assimilated the Slavs who settled there. In the process, many Slavic words entered the spoken Danubian Latin, which was henceforth called Proto-Romanian. The process of fusion continued into the twelfth century. It is not known at what exact point in history the transition between Proto-Romanian and Romanian occurred. It was only after the end of the Tatar invasions and the inception of feudal states that historians first used the term *Romanian,* but it is generally considered that the process was completed by the ninth or tenth century.

Language

During the Roman colonization of Dacia in the first century A.D., Latin was made the official language of the province. The Latin spoken by the colonists, military, and civil servants was not the literary Latin of Cicero but a common dialect that became known as Danubian Latin. This was spoken throughout the provinces of Pannonia, Dacia, and Moesia. The local population spoke a Thracian dialect. By the time the Romans pulled out of Dacia, the Daco-Romans spoke Danubian Latin with added Dacian words that became part of the language. Approximately 160 words of Geto-Dacian origin remain in the Romanian language. Examples include *buză* (lip), *gușă* (goiter), *băiat* (boy), *copil* (child), *vatră* (hearth), *mânz* (colt), and *urdă* (soft cheese).

Some 60 percent of the words in the Romanian vocabulary are directly derived from Latin. These are generally words used in everyday conversation, basic concepts of life, human activities, politics, and basic religious concepts. The grammatical structure of the language is Latin as well. Examples of words derived from Latin include:

English	Latin	Romanian
wine	vinum	vin
green	verde	verde
gold	aurum	aur
supper	cena	cină
evening	sera	seară
church	basilica	biserică
God	Domine Deus	Dumnezeu
cross	crucem	cruce

The fusion of the Daco-Romans with Slav settlers that began in the seventh century, resulted in a significant change in the Daco-Roman language, which then became known as Proto-Romanian. Some 20 percent of Romanian is derived from Slavic. Examples include prince (*voievod*), nobleman (*boier*), old woman (*babă*), sheepskin jacket (*cojoc*), and illness (*boală*).

The rest of the Romanian vocabulary includes words derived from other migrating tribes such as the Petchenegs and Cumans and, finally, words of Greek, Hungarian, and Turkish origin.

Religion

Religion played a major role in the evolutionary process of the Romanians. Before the Roman occupation, the Geto-Dacians were the only people in the region to practice a monotheistic religion, that of Zalmoxis, and therefore were easily converted to Christianity by missionaries from Rome. After the Milan Decree in 313, when the Christian religion was made the official religion of the Roman Empire, its spread by Roman missionaries intensified throughout the Carpatho-Danubian region. Most of the Daco-Roman population converted, thus establishing a strong link to Rome and to the Latin world. As the sphere of influence shifted from Rome to Constantinople, the church began to look eastward. During the eighth and ninth centuries, the Byzantine Empire had become completely Hellenized and a schism between the Eastern and Latin Christian churches developed in the middle of the eleventh century. By then, the Romanian population was surrounded by Slavic and Bulgarian nations, with no direct contact with Constantinople. However, in Bulgaria, Serbia, and Russia, missionaries were spreading Eastern Christianity. The Bible and liturgy were translated into the Slavonic language, which also became the church language in Romania and remained its official language into the seventeenth century.

ROAD TO STATEHOOD

When the Roman legions withdrew from Dacia in 271, and with them most of the urban population, the deserted towns and cities with their magnificent buildings, roads, and water systems began to crumble. Nature took over, and what remained of man-made structures was looted and burned by migrant populations. The natives who remained in the Carpatho-Danubian region consisted mostly of peasants who lived in the rural areas and were an agricultural and sheepherding society.

The Daco-Romans, faced with repeated invasions and changes in tribal rulers over the region, were slow to follow the unification processes that were taking place in other areas of Europe. It was not until the seventh century, during a period of relative stability, that this process began to take shape. At the time, the local inhabitants were ruled by "wise elders" who were empowered by the villagers to make decisions in matters that affected the community. They were called juzi (from Lat. *Judex*), or cnezi. As a pre-feudal system began to emerge in the tenth century, these cnezi were given lands by overlords, such as Hungarian kings, in return for loyalty or military duty. These landowners were considered "nobles" (*boieri* in Romanian). To better protect their lands and villagers working on the land, some of these nobles formed unions with other landowners, creating political groupings known as cnezates, or voievodates for larger groups. They were led by elected dukes, known as cnezi or voievods.

Transylvania, Banat, Crişana, and Maramureş

Transylvania is the largest of the Romanian principalities; it was also the last to be integrated into modern Romania (1918). Its Latin name, *trans sillva* (the land beyond the forest), first appeared in the twelfth century. The Hungarian *Erdély* and the Romanian *Ardeal* both mean land of the forest. Transylvania was once the core of the kingdom of Dacia with its capital at Sarmizegetusa and later was part of the

Roman province of Dacia. After the withdrawal of the Romans in 271, the region became for centuries the prey of the various migrating populations. The Magyars, the people of Hungary, who originally came from a region of the Altay Mountains, were forced by other nomadic tribes to migrate westward about 896. Under their semilegendary leader, Árpád, the Magyars crossed the Carpathians and settled down in the plain of Pannonia.

At the end of the ninth century, the Hungarians began raids into Transylvania. According to a chronicle written by the notary of one of Hungary's kings,[1] the Hungarians came across three cnezates: that of Duke Menumorut, whose residence was in the fortress Byhor in Crişana; that of Duke Gelu, described as being "a certain Romanian," whose cnezate was in Transylvania; and that of Duke Glad, whose residence was in Keve, on the left bank of the Danube (in Serbian Banat). The Hungarians defeated the three dukedoms, and an agreement was reached whereby the dukedoms of Crişana and Banat remained separate entities under Hungarian suzerainty.

In 1001, under King Stephen I (Stephen the Saint) the Hungarians pushed further into Transylvania, and finally, in the twelfth and thirteenth centuries, Transylvania was conquered in its entirety. It was given the status of dukedom (voievodate) in 1176, and its first leader was Voievod Leustachius. The title of voievod continued to be used for all rulers through the late sixteenth century, when the title was changed to "prince." Since the days of Duke Gelu, Transylvania, although a part of the kingdom of Hungary, had a different tradition, with a predominantly Romanian population. It developed a different political organization from that of the other Hungarian provinces.

During the twelfth century, the Hungarians initiated a policy of colonization in Transylvania and Crişana. So-called Saxons—who were Germans from Westphalia, Hesse, Thuringia, and Bavaria—settled in areas that they called *Siebenbürgen*, after the original seven villages where they settled, which were to become major commercial and cultural centers. Hungarian-speaking Szeklers colonized part of Crişana and eastern Transylvania.

Wallachia

In 1247, with the conquest of Transylvania completed, King Bella IV had his eyes on the regions south and east of the Carpathians. He issued a charter to the Knights Hospitalers (members of the military and religious Order of the Hospital of St. John of Jerusalem, sometimes called the Knights of St. John, who had been organized during the twelfth century by crusaders to combat the Muslims) to protect the Hungarian kingdom from further attacks by the Tatars. This charter mentions that in return for their service, they would be given the whole land of Severin, as well as the cnezates of John (Ioan) and Farkaş, as far as the Olt River. It also stipulates that the cnezates of Voievods Litovoi and Seneslau were to be left "to the Romanians as they have owned them until now."

Toward the end of the thirteenth century the cnezate of Seneslau, east of the Olt River, grew in importance when a number of Romanian nobles from Transylvania extended their control over Romanian lands that were still independent. This stimulated the movement for unification, and in c. 1310 it was achieved by Voievod Basarab I the Great (Basarab I cel Mare; ruled c. 1310–1352). The principality of Wallachia extended from the Carpathians to the Danube and the Black Sea. It also included an area in the Danube Delta, now part of the Republic of Moldova, and Dobrogea. The formation of Wallachia was also facilitated by a political crisis in Hungary after the end of the Árpád dynasty in 1301. Voievod Basarab strengthened his position by entering into alliances with the Bulgarian and Serbian rulers. He then refused to pay any further vassalage tributes to the kingdom of Hungary.

In 1330, King Charles I of Hungary (Charles Robert of Anjou), leading a Hungarian army, launched an expedition into Wallachia to restore his authority over that area. A large contingent of Wallachian soldiers was waiting for the Hungarians at Posada, and as they were winding their way through a narrow valley, the Hungarians found themselves trapped. On November 12, 1330, after three days of fighting, with the Wallachian soldiers battering them with a barrage of arrows and stones thrown from cliffs on both sides of the path, Voievod Basarab defeated the Hungarian forces. He obtained international recognition for the independent principality of Wallachia and became Prince (Voievod) Basarab I of Wallachia, with the capital at Câmpulung (later Argeş). The remains of his palace can still be seen there. He is remembered as Basarab the Great because he terminated the Hungarian king's suzerainty over Wallachia and defeated repeated incursions by the Tatars. As an independent state under him, Wallachia experienced a period of stability and prosperity.

Moldavia

While Wallachia became an independent principality, the Tatars were still in control of the area east of the Carpathian Mountains (now Moldavia). This area suffered the most from the incessant invasions from the east, especially from the devastation left there by the Tatars. During the fourteenth century, Hungary and Poland were both competing for supremacy over the small dukedoms east of the Carpathians. In 1352, Hungarian King Louis I (the Great) launched an expedition across the mountains to create a fortified buffer state whose mission was to protect the Transylvanian borders against further Tatar incursions and to maintain Hungarian influence in the region. Documents mention Voievod Dragoş from Maramureş who took part in the expedition. He was made ruler of the fortified state and was a vassal of the king. Many historians consider Dragoş to be the first ruler of Moldavia. He was succeeded by his son, Sas, who ruled until 1358, followed by Sas's son, Balc.

In 1359 another Romanian voievod from Maramureş by the name of Bogdan crossed the mountain accompanied by about 200 other dukes who were in search of full political freedom. There they joined with local dukes in a revolt against Hungarian domination. Bogdan forced Balc to flee to Transylvania, and Moldavia became the second Romanian independent principality after Wallachia. Prince Bogdan I ruled from 1359 to 1365.

Dobrogea

Dobrogea also became a state in the fourteenth century. It covered an area roughly equal to that of present-day Bulgaria and Dobrogea. In 1346, Balic, its leader, fought in the Byzantine army and was awarded the title "despot." He was succeeded by Dobrotch. At first, Dobrogea was under the suzerainty of the Byzantine Empire, but later Dobrotch ruled as an autonomous leader. He extended his authority to the Danube. In 1388, a great Turkish expedition threatened to turn the whole area between the Danube and the sea into a Turkish pashalik, but with the assistance of Wallachia, that danger was removed and Dobrogea was united with Wallachia.

NOTE

1. *Gesta Hungarorum* (Hungarian Deeds). 12th c.

Prince Basarab I of Wallachia

The Romanian Principalities

Reprinted with permission from the Center for Romanian Studies.

CHAPTER 4

The Romanian Principalities—First 300 Years (Fourteenth–Sixteenth Centuries)

PERSPECTIVE

No sooner had Moldavia and Wallachia emerged as new autonomous principalities, and the great Tatar hordes retreated to their homelands, than a new menace rose from Asia Minor—the Ottoman Empire. The Turkish Seljuk empire, which reigned over large parts of Asia in the eleventh and twelfth centuries, began to fall apart toward the end of the thirteenth century. The dynasties of the Seljuk family collapsed after the death of their last sultan in c. 1300, but the Turkish empire founded by them continued to exist under the rising dynasty of the Osmali Turks. Their first historic ruler, Osman I (Uthman), began the conquest of neighboring regions and founded the Ottoman Empire (c.1300), giving it his name.

The Ottoman Empire began to expand through military campaigns, alliances, and outright purchases of territory, and by 1353 it reached European shores at the Dardanelles. By the end of the fourteenth century, southeastern Europe consisted of the Byzantine Empire, the Ottoman Empire, and sixteen other states. In 1453, after repeated attacks on the Byzantine Empire, Constantinople fell, and by the end of the fifteenth century, the Ottomans were in possession of most of what had been the Byzantine Empire. As the sixteenth century began, only six states remained in southeast Europe: the Ottoman Empire, which had doubled its territory and now spread across three continents, the Hungarian kingdom, Venice, Ragusa, Moldavia, and Wallachia.

The expanding Islamic empire of the Ottomans had now become a direct threat to Wallachia and Moldavia and also a risk for the whole of Europe's Christian population. Not only did the Romanian principalities play a major part in containing the Ottoman expansion toward central and western Europe, but also their own survival was sustained by support and intervention from other European powers.

In the meantime, the kingdom of Poland was created in 1025 by the unification of several feudal states, including Great Poland, Little Poland, Silesia, and part of Pomerania. The Hapsburg monarchy can be traced back to the eleventh century. During the twelfth and thirteenth centuries, the Hapsburgs were closely associated with the Hohenstaufen emperors; they supplied Austrian rulers from 1278 to 1804, emperors of the Holy Roman Empire from 1438 to 1806, kings of Spain from 1515 to 1700, kings of Hungary and Bohemia from 1556 to 1564, and Austrian emperors from 1804 to 1918.

The kingdom of Hungary ceased to exist as an independent state in 1541 when it was partitioned between the Ottoman and the Hapsburg Empires, while Transylvania emerged as an autonomous principality under the Ottoman government's (the Porte) suzerainty.

TRANSYLVANIA

During the thirteenth and fourteenth centuries, a number of Romanian districts continued to be recognized as cnezates (dukedoms), while the Hungarians established counties that were superimposed on the cnezates. The king of Hungary exerted his authority over Transylvania through its dukes and through his royal high officials. Until the mid-fourteenth century, Hungarian, Saxon, Szekler, and Romanian nobility participated in both political and military life. Gradually, however, the position of the Romanian nobility deteriorated due to ethnic and religious discrimination. Some of the nobles became Catholic and joined the Hungarian nobility, but most of them either crossed the Carpathian Mountains and moved to neighboring states or remained and gradually became peasants.

By the end of the fourteenth century, the Ottoman Empire's armies began expansionary campaigns against Hungary, including Transylvania, menacing not only Hungary but all of central Europe.

During this period, there emerged a great political and military leader. Famous for his battles against the Ottoman Turks, he helped not only Transylvania but also neighboring Moldavia and Wallachia in their efforts to resist the Turkish attacks. He was John Hunyadi (Romanian, Iancu de Hunedoara; Hungarian, János Hunyadi—1387?–1456). Born in Transylvania to a Romanian noble family, he entered the service of King Sigismund of Hungary in c. 1410. Hunyadi having distinguished himself as one of the most capable military leaders of his time, after the death of King Sigismund, the new king of Hungary, Albert I of Hapsburg, named him governor of Timişoara in 1438. In 1441 he was chosen voievod of Transylvania (ruled 1441–1446). In 1443 he organized an expedition in an attempt to liberate the Balkan Peninsula from Turkish domination, and reached as far as Sofia. In 1448, as governor of Hungary, he led forces from Transylvania, Wallachia, and Moldova, but was defeated by the Ottomans at Kosovo.

Hunyadi's last victory took place on July 4–22, 1456, in the battle of Belgrade, where he defeated a Turkish army attempting to capture the fortress, thereby delaying their advance toward central Europe for more than half a century. On that occasion, Pope Calixtus III (served 1455–1458) called him the most valiant among Christian champions. Hunyadi died of the plague shortly thereafter, on August 11, 1456. In the meantime, Transylvania continued to be ruled by Hungarian-appointed voievods for the rest of the fifteenth century.

In the early sixteenth century the feudal system in Transylvania was becoming increasingly oppressive. Serfdom was harsher, and exploitation of the free peasants by the Hungarian nobility reached

John Hunyadi (Iancu de Hunedoara)
Courtesy of Romanian National Tourist Office

such unbearable proportions that the Hungarian, Romanian, and Szekler peasants united in a massive and widespread uprising. The leader of the revolt, George Doja, a Szekler captain and member of the lesser nobility, led a peasant army on July 15, 1514, to confront the nobility. They were met by an army of nobles under the command of Stephen Báthory II, governor of Timişoara. The peasant army was defeated, and the uprising was ruthlessly crushed. Doja and other leaders of the revolt were captured, tortured, and publicly executed. It is said that Doja was stripped naked and tied to a red-hot seat. Cooked alive, chunks of his flesh were ripped off with tongs and fed to his supporters who were forced to eat it. Needless to say, the peasant armies were henceforth not easily persuaded to join in battles against Ottomans in defense of Christianity.

In 1521 the Belgrade fortress fell to the Ottomans, and in 1526 the Hungarian army was annihilated at the battle of Mohács, where Hungarian King Louis II met his death. A struggle for the crown of Hungary and Bohemia led to military clashes between the contenders: Ferdinand of Hapsburg, brother-in-law of Louis II, and the Ottoman candidate, John Zápolya, voievod of Transylvania (1511–1526), who was crowned King John I of Hungary (1526–1540). John's death in 1540 and the accession of John II (John Sigismund Zápolya) were pretexts for Sultan Suleiman I to send an expedition against Hungary in 1541, capturing Buda and annexing the southern and central regions of Hungary, which remained under Ottoman rule for the next 150 years as a Turkish district (pashalik). The district was brutally reduced to a wasteland during this period. Western and northern Hungary remained under the rule of the Hapsburgs, while Transylvania—including Banat, Crişana, and some districts of Hungary—was allowed to become an autonomous principality, ruled by noble families who were vassals of the Ottoman Porte. Transylvania developed into a flourishing state. For the next two centuries, Austrians and Turks vied for domination of this principality. In 1552, Banat and part of Crişana were annexed by the Ottoman Empire and turned into a Turkish district (pashalik) with Timişoara as its capital.

Stephen Báthory II was a loyal adherent of King John I of Hungary (John Zápolyi). He was elected voievod of Transylvania in 1529. In 1571, under Stephen's youngest son, Stephen Báthory III, Transylvania became the first European state to institute equality and mutual religious tolerance. Although five major religions were practiced in the principality—Catholic, Calvinist, Lutheran, Unitarian, and Romanian Orthodox—this tolerance was not extended to the Orthodox religion because Romanians were excluded from political and religious life. Stephen became king of Poland in 1575 and was succeeded as voievod of Transylvania by his brother, Christopher. Sigismund Báthory, Christopher's son, came to power in 1583. He was a loyal vassal of the Hapsburg king of Hungary (Emperor Rudolf II). In 1594, Sigismund crushed the pro-Turkish faction of nobles and was in return recognized by Rudolf as hereditary prince of Transylvania. In 1597, Sigismund abdicated in order to devote the rest of his life to religion, but he had a change of heart and returned to power in 1598 as a vassal of the Porte. In March 1599, Sigismund abdicated again, this time in favor of his cousin, Andrew Cardinal Báthory. Unlike his cousin, the new prince had close ties with Poland and he began to negotiate a treaty with the Ottomans as soon as he came to power.

WALLACHIA

The son and successor of Prince Basarab I, Nicholas Alexander (ruled 1352–1364) continued to build on Wallachia's good relations with neighboring powers, and he did this through marriage. He married one of his daughters to the Bulgarian czar, his second to a Serbian prince, and his third to a Hungarian duke. He was very supportive of the Orthodox Church and had many church buildings erected. He also founded, in 1359, the first Metropolitan Church of Wallachia at the Curtea de Argeş. His successor, Vladislav I Vlaicu (ruled 1364–1377), continued the tradition of support for the church by having a second Metropolitan Church built at Severin, as well as a number of monasteries. The first Wallachian coins were minted under his rule. They were of silver with Latin inscriptions.

Toward the end of the fourteenth century, the expansion of the Ottoman Empire reached the southern bank of the Danube, thus directly threatening the newly formed Romanian principalities of Wallachia and Moldavia. To preserve their independence, the two principalities were forced to fight repeated wars against the Turks, often with the support of Hungarian kings and Transylvanian princes.

Mircea the Old

It was during the reign of Mircea the Old (Mircea cel Bătrân: ruled 1386–1395 and 1397–1418) that Wallachia had its first confrontation with the Ottoman Empire at Ravine, on October 10, 1394. With support from Hungary, a combined Wallachian and Hungarian army forced the Turkish troops back across the Danube.

Mircea the Old is considered one of the great Romanian princes of his time. As a capable and brave military leader and an astute negotiator, he was able to maintain the principality's autonomy and to prevent the Ottoman troops from crossing north of the Danube. The local nobility, however, abandoned him and, in 1395, installed his rival, Vlad I, on the throne. Mircea was forced to flee to Transylvania, where he participated in the Crusade of Nicopolis against the Turks in September 1396. He regained his throne in 1397.

Three more attempts by Turkish forces to cross the Danube—in 1397, 1400, and 1408—were foiled by the Wallachians. However, in 1417 Sultan Mehmed I launched a powerful offensive, in the course of which most of Dobrogea fell, and Mircea the Old was forced to sign a treaty, agreeing to pay yearly tributes to the Porte in return for a guarantee against future attacks. Mircea died on January 31, 1418, after a thirty-year reign.

During the rest of the fifteenth century, confrontations with the Ottomans continued and were further complicated by internal Wallachian rivalries for the throne. These rivalries were the result of

Mircea the Old, ruler of Wallachia

Courtesy of Regia Autonomă "Monitorul Oficial," Romanian Parliament

the hereditary-elective principle derived from Slavic law: all legitimate or illegitimate male offspring of a ruling prince had equal right to the throne. It was up to each pretender to seek the support of local nobility, as well as one or another of the neighboring states that vied for sway over Wallachia, mainly the Hapsburg and Ottoman Empires and the kingdom of Hungary. The same problem prevailed in Moldavia as well. In Wallachia, ten princes succeeded each other sixteen times in thirty-four years. Before Mircea died, he tried to assure a smooth succession by appointing his eldest son, Michael I (ruled 1418–1420) as associate ruler as early as 1391. However, Michael was overthrown by Dan II, a son of Mircea's brother Dan I (ruled c. 1383–1386). For the next eleven years the throne alternated four times between Dan II and Radu Praznaglava, another of Mircea's sons.

Alexander Aldea

Alexander the Good (Alexandru cel Bun) of Moldavia (ruled 1400–1432), who took an interest in the political situation in Wallachia, helped Prince Aldea to succeed Dan II to the throne. In return, Prince Aldea took his benefactor's name, calling himself Alexander I Aldea (ruled 1431–1436), and became his strong ally against the Turks. With Alexander the Good's death, Aldea lost an ally, and he failed to receive the support he sought from other states. His only recourse was to negotiate with Sultan Murad II (ruled 1421–1451). He joined the sultan in an invasion of Transylvania in 1432, but tried to maintain good relations with Hungary at the same time. Alexander Aldea died in 1436 and was succeeded by Prince Vlad Dracul.

Vlad Dracul

Vlad Dracul (ruled 1436–1442 and 1443–1447) was one of those princes who switched allegiance between the Turks, the Hungarians, and the Hapsburgs. He was seeking Emperor Sigismund I's backing in his bid for the throne when, in Nuremberg, he was bestowed with the Order of the Dragon, a crusading order. In Romanian, at that time, the word for dragon was *dracul*, and when he became ruler of Wallachia in 1436, he was called Vlad Dracul (Vlad the Dragon). After an Ottoman attack in November of that year, he was forced to sign another vassalage agreement with Sultan Murad II, but in 1442 he supported Prince John Hunyadi of Transylvania in a battle against the Turks. As a result, he was called to Adrianople for a meeting with the sultan but was arrested instead, together with two of his sons, Vlad and Radu. When the sultan was told that Hunyadi had installed the sultan's candidate, Basarab II, as Prince of Wallachia, he released Vlad Dracul but kept his two sons as hostages to assure Vlad's loyalty. Vlad invaded Wallachia and recaptured his throne. In 1447 Hunyadi invaded Wallachia and installed Vladislav II on the throne. Vlad Dracul and his eldest son, Mircea, were assassinated by order of Hunyadi.

Vlad III Dracula

Upon Vlad Dracul's death, Sultan Murad II released Vlad's two sons. Vlad was the eldest and thereby pretender to the throne of Wallachia, so he went to Transylvania, where he waited for the opportune moment to present itself. In October 1448 he seized the opportunity when Vladislav II was fighting the Turks at Kosovo, but a month later Vladislav returned from battle and ousted Vlad, who fled to Transylvania and tried to gain John Hunyadi's support. In 1456, while Vladislav was again engaged in fighting the Turks, this time defending Belgrade, Vlad seized the throne as Vlad III Dracula (ruled 1448, 1456–1462, and 1476). (Draculă means "the son of Dracul.")

In 1461, when Vlad Dracula refused to pay any further tributes to the Porte and attacked Turkish forces along the Danube and in Bulgaria, Sultan Mehmed II (ruled 1451–1481) sent a large expedition into Wallachia and ousted Vlad, replacing him with his youngest brother, Radu. Vlad fled to Transylvania but was arrested there by Matthias Corvinus, king of Hungary and son-in-law of John Hunyadi.

Vlad III Dracula (Vlad the Impaler), ruler of Wallachia

Courtesy of Regia Autonomă "Monitorul Oficial," Romanian Parliament

The Forest of Stakes engraving, reproduced in *Dracole Wayda*, Ambr. Huber Edition, Nürnberg, 1499 (depicts Vlad the Impaler having his meal as Turkish prisoners die in agony)

Private collection of Bogdan Ulmu

He spent many years in prison, but in 1476 he again became Hungary's candidate for the throne of Wallachia. For the third and last time he seized the throne, ousting Prince Basarab Laiotă, this time with support from Hungary and Moldavia. His rule was to last only one month. In December 1476, Turkish forces entered Wallachia and reinstated Basarab Laiotă.

Vlad Dracula died on the battlefield. He came to be known as Vlad Țepeș (Vlad the Impaler) for the atrocities he committed against his prisoners, and, in 1897, he became the inspiration for Bram Stoker's book *Dracula*.

Tightening of Ottoman Control

After the death of Vlad III Dracula, for the rest of the fifteenth century and the sixteenth century, Wallachia's dependence on the Ottoman Empire increased, as in neighboring Moldavia. Their military forces were now expected to join in Ottoman campaigns under Turkish commanders. Ruling princes who were previously elected by the local nobility began to be appointed directly by the Turkish sultans and often were brought in from other regions. The appointments were changed frequently to limit the ruler's ability to gain authority, to conspire, or to plot against the Ottoman Empire. Also, the crown became negotiable, according to the largest tribute offered: twenty-seven princes succeeded themselves forty times during this period. Increasingly, the Ottomans demanded a supply of products and labor, in addition to yearly tributes. Expensive gifts to the sultan were also expected. To meet these obligations, taxes were raised, and when peasants were not able to pay, their land and cattle were sold off and they were forced into serfdom.

On the other hand, the two principalities, Wallachia and Moldavia, were able to maintain their autonomy at a time when the Balkans were occupied and turned into Turkish pashaliks. They thus could continue to develop their economies and cultures, as well as their own laws and social structures.

During the reign of Neagoe Basarab (ruled 1512–1521), unlike during the short reigns preceding and following him, Wallachia experienced some internal stability and cultural growth. In its foreign relations, Wallachia continued to honor its obligations toward Turkey's government while it accepted the suzerainty of Hungary. Contacts were also established with Poland, Venice, and the Vatican. After Neagoe Basarab's death, the Turks tried to appoint Wallachia's princes in an attempt to turn the principality into a Turkish pashalik. However, their plans met with strong opposition and many battles were fought to maintain Wallachia's autonomy. From 1521 to 1593, eighteen princes succeeded themselves twenty-nine times.

Michael the Brave

Prince Michael was a wealthy and influential nobleman who owned twenty villages by the age of thirty and became the wealthiest landowner in Wallachia. Michael obtained the approval of the Porte and the support of Edward Barton, English ambassador to Constantinople, as well as that of the Greek banker, Andronicus Cantacuzino, to become ruler of Wallachia as Michael the Brave (Mihai Viteazul; ruled 1593–1601).

In the meantime, an anti-Ottoman Holy League, led by the Hapsburgs, was being organized in Europe. It was made up of the Holy Roman Empire, Spain, Venice, the papal states, and some Italian states. Emperor Rudolf II invited the principalities of Wallachia and Moldavia to join. As soon as Michael ascended the throne, he turned against the Ottomans and joined the Holy League. Wallachia owed large sums of money to Turkish moneylenders, borrowed to pay the extortionate tributary obligations to the Porte. Michael's first anti-Ottoman act was to summon all his creditors to his palace under the pretext of dividing some of the money owed between them. They were directed to one of the buildings on the palace grounds, and when they were all inside he gave the order to his soldiers to set fire to the building. All the creditors, as well as the financial records, perished in

Michael the Brave

Courtesy of Romanian National Tourist Office

the fire. He then ordered the massacre of all Turks in Wallachia. Michael won his first victory in battle in 1594. One year later, on August 23, 1595, he defeated a large Turkish army at Călugăreni and became famous overnight throughout the Christian world. He became known as Michael the Brave. After several more major battles over the next three years, the Ottomans concluded a treaty with Michael in 1598 recognizing Wallachia's total independence.

During the same year in Transylvania, Prince Sigismund Báthory abdicated and ceded his rights to the throne to the Hapsburg Emperor Rudolf II. Prince Michael tried to negotiate with both the Ottomans and the Hapsburgs in an effort to secure his position. Not succeeding in this effort, he signed a treaty with the Hapsburgs who became his new suzerains. The treaty was signed in June 1598 at the Monastery of Dealu.

MOLDAVIA

In the years after the rule of Bogdan I (ruled c. 1359–1365), the process of unification of territories within Moldavia continued and was completed by 1392, during the reign of Prince Roman I Muşat (ruled 1391–1394). It then included the lands of Bucovina and Bessarabia. In a document dated March 30, 1392, Prince Roman I is described as ruler of the country of Moldavia, from the mountain to the sea.

Alexander the Good

Alexander the Good (Alexandru cel Bun; ruled 1400–1432), son of Roman I Muşat, came to the throne with support from Mircea the Old of Wallachia. He brought a long period of economic prosperity and international prestige to Moldavia. He also promoted the organization of the Orthodox Church.

Faced with expansionist threats from both the Ottoman Empire and Hungary, Alexander continued the policy of cooperation with Poland.

Moldavian armies often fought alongside those of Poland and Lithuania against the Teutonic knights, gaining distinction in the battles of Grünewald in 1440 and Marienburg in 1422. In 1420 Alexander succeeded in repulsing the first Ottoman attack on Moldavia.

After the death of Mircea the Old, Alexander took advantage of the internal struggles in Wallachia to seize, in 1421, the strategic fortress of Chilia along the Danube.

After Alexander the Good's death, Moldavia went through a period of internal struggles for the throne similar to the situation in Wallachia after Mircea the Old's death. Eight princes succeeded each other sixteen times until, in 1457, Stephen the Great ascended to the throne. The conquest of Constantinople by the Ottomans in 1453 was a severe blow to the Christian world. The Orthodox Church was threatened since Greece, Bulgaria, and Serbia were also under Turkish rule. The only Orthodox Christians who were still autonomous were those in the Romanian principalities.

Stephen the Great

Stephen became known as Stephen the Great (Ştefan cel Mare; ruled 1457–1504) because of his tireless and successful battles against the onslaught of Turks from the south, and that of his expansionist neighbors to the north and west, Poland and Hungary. He was the son of Prince Bogdan II (ruled 1449–1451), and grandson of Alexander the Good (ruled 1400–1432). In 1451, when his father was assassinated, Stephen fled from Moldavia. In the spring of 1457, with the assistance of his cousin Vlad III Draculă, he invaded Moldavia and seized the throne. At the time, the principality had gone through a quarter of a century of internal power struggle among the nobility and external pressure from Hungary and Poland, and Stephen's predecessor, Peter Aron, had just entered into a vassalage treaty with the Ottoman Porte.

At first Stephen tried to maintain good relations with both the Ottoman Empire and Poland, but this policy caused relations to deteriorate with Hungary and Wallachia, as both were allies against the

Stephen the Great (Ştefan cel Mare) (r. 1457–1504)
Courtesy of Romanian National Tourist Office

Stephen the Great, Piața Culturei, Iași
Photo by author

Turks. In 1462 the Ottomans, joined by a Moldavian army detachment led by Stephen the Great, attacked Wallachia and laid siege to the fortress of Chilia (again under Wallachian control). They were defeated, and Stephen was wounded in battle. Three years later he captured the fortress. When in 1466/1467 Stephen began to support a separatist movement in Transylvania, Hungarian forces invaded Moldavia and destroyed the towns of Bacău, Roman, and Neamţ. Stephen and his troops retreated, but during the night of December 14, 1467, he launched a surprise counterattack at Baia, defeating the Hungarians. The Hungarian king, Matthias Corvinus, was wounded while fleeing in retreat.

Stephen's first confrontation with the Ottoman Empire took place in 1474 as a result of his involvement in a number of anti-Ottoman activities, including the removal of Radu the Handsome from the Wallachian throne to be replaced with his own candidate, Basarab Laiotă. Prince Radu had been placed there under Ottoman military pressure. When Stephen refused to turn over the fortresses of Chilia and Cetatea Albă to the Ottomans, and stopped paying tribute to the Porte, Sultan Mehmed II launched a major invasion of Moldavia under the command of his general, Suleiman Pasha. Stephen, using his well-proven warfare technique, retreated until they reached Podul Înalt (near Vaslui). There, on January 10, 1475, his men counterattacked and were victorious, although they were outnumbered three to one. Following this victory, Stephen sent messages to the rulers of Europe and to the Vatican, warning them of the threat that the Ottoman Empire presented to the whole Christian world. In return, Pope Sixtus IV sent a message of praise and encouragement to Stephen, proclaiming him "Athlete of Christ," but no action was taken. Stephen the Great then strengthened his relations with Matthias Corvinus, who was king of Hungary, accepting his suzerainty in return for the support of the Holy Alliance against future Turkish attacks.

In May 1476 Sultan Mehmed II launched his most powerful offensive against Moldavia, and this time the Tatars, his allies, attacked simultaneously from the east. Stephen was forced to retreat to avoid the massacre of his troops, laying to waste everything behind him. The Ottomans advanced all the way to Suceava, where a violent battle took place at Războieni on July 26. The Moldovian army was crushed, but Stephen escaped. The sultan's troops then attacked the fortress of Neamţ, but the fortress had been so well designed and reinforced by Stephen that it withstood the siege. In the meantime, the outbreak of a plague and a shortage of food supplies forced the Turkish troops to retreat and abandon Moldavia.

That same year, allied Moldavian and Transylvanian forces entered Wallachia and placed Vlad III Dracula, Stephen's cousin, on the throne.

In 1484, after the death of Mehmed II, Sultan Bayezid II attacked once again, and this time he took control of the fortresses of Chilia and Cetatea Albă. Not being able to obtain the support he sought from Poland and the Holy Alliance, Stephen the Great was forced to accept the Porte's suzerainty once again.

Stephen the Great died on July 2, 1504, after a reign of more than forty-seven years, the longest reign of any Romanian leader with the exception of that of King Carol I (ruled 1866–1914). In defending Moldavia against external conquest, he fought thirty-six battles, thirty-four of which he won. He became known not just for his military skill but also for his diplomatic and political adroitness. During his reign he commissioned many monasteries and churches to be built, usually in gratitude for successful battles; some of these can still be visited. They are recognized worldwide as unique masterpieces of art and architecture.

Transylvania's transformation into a vassal state of the Porte in 1540 made Moldavia's struggle for total independence that much more difficult to attain. Moldavia continued the policy of Stephen the Great by encouraging other Christian countries to join forces in the struggle against the Ottoman Empire. Prince Peter (Petru) Rareş (ruled 1527–1538 and 1541–1546), an illegitimate son of Stephen the

Voroneţ Monastery, Gura Humorului, Moldavia
Oldest of painted churches built in 1488 by order of Stephen the Great
Photo by author

Great, signed a treaty with the king of Hungary, but some of the Moldavian nobles betrayed him and forced his abdication in favor of the first in a number of princes appointed by the Ottoman sultan. Thus Moldavia reverted to the status of a vassal state of the Porte. During his reign, Rareş ordered many churches and monasteries to be constructed or repaired. Among them is the Monastery of Moldoviţa, renowned for the beauty of its exterior murals.

After Peter's reign, the political situation in the Romanian principalities began to deteriorate. The Ottoman Empire's control became more oppressive, and princes were changed frequently, each with the approval of the Porte and open to financial negotiations. Another effort to liberate Moldavia from Turkish domination took place when Prince John (ruled 1572–1574), having bought his way to the throne, turned anti-Ottoman. In 1574 John refused to pay the yearly tribute which had just been doubled, whereupon a combined Turkish-Wallachian army invaded Moldavia. John, who came to be known as John the Brave and John the Terrible, met the invaders and defeated them. Two years later, Sultan Salim II, supported by Wallachian and Tatar troops, led a massive attack against him. Salim forced John into retreat and then, after a battle that lasted three days, John the Brave surrendered on June 13, 1574, at Cahul. When John chose not to abide by the terms of the surrender, however, he and his supporters were massacred and Moldavia once again was submitted to vassalage.

It was not until 1595 that Moldavia attempted once more to throw off the Turkish yoke. Transylvanian Prince Sigismund Báthory had launched an attack on Moldavia and installed his candidate, Stephen (Ştefan) Răzvan (ruled April–August 1595) on the throne. When Michael the Brave, ruler of Wallachia, was fighting the invading Ottoman troops with the aid of Transylvanian forces, Stephen decided to join in the struggle. However, Poland now invaded Moldavia, removed him, and replaced him with a Moldavian nobleman, Ieremia Movilă (1595–1600), who was pro-Polish and pro-Ottoman.

A SHORT-LIVED UNION

Wallachia's continuing struggle to remain independent was now threatened because both Transylvania and Moldavia, its neighboring principalities, were ruled by pro-Polish, pro-Ottoman rulers. Michael the Brave, prince of Wallachia, organized an expedition into Transylvania with support from the Hapsburgs, and removed Andrew Cardinal Báthory from his throne. In October 1599, Michael the Brave was acknowledged Prince of Transylvania by the Diet, which consisted of Hungarians, Szeklers, and Saxon nobility.

Having successfully rid Transylvania of the pro-Polish, pro-Ottoman regime, Michael now decided to undertake the same action in Moldavia. Consequently, he invaded that principality and ousted Ieremia Movilă, claiming that it was in the name of Emperor Rudolf II, who in fact was opposed to the plan. In July 1660, in the Moldavian capital Iaşi, Michael the Brave was proclaimed Prince of Wallachia, Transylvania, and Moldavia.

Thus Michael the Brave achieved what, much later, Romanians everywhere aspired to—the union of the three Romanian principalities. At the beginning of the seventeenth century, union was not yet a concept to which states aspired, and it collapsed almost as soon as it came into being. Michael made some crucial errors of judgment. To maintain good relations with the nobility of Transylvania, he imposed severe measures against the peasants who were in revolt against their masters. As it turned out, while he lost the support of the peasantry, he never won the favors of the nobility who considered him an outsider because he was a Wallachian. He also managed to alienate the Austrian emperor. A revolt led by the Hungarian nobility, aided by the imperial army, defeated Michael, and Sigismund Báthory was reinstated ruler of Transylvania. Michael presented himself at the imperial court in Vienna and persuaded the emperor to allow him to resume his reign over Transylvania. Shortly thereafter, in 1601, the nobles, aided by the Austrian General George Basta, surprised Michael while he was sleeping and stabbed him to death. In a letter dated September

Michael the Brave (r. 1593–1601), Piața Universității, Bucharest
Photo by author

12, 1601, Henry Lello, English ambassador to the Ottoman Porte, wrote to Sir Robert Cecil, Earl of Salisbury:

> Right Honorable. Fourteen dayes past myne advised your Honour how Maximillian together with Michaell had geven Sigismondus overthrowe and were entered into Transilvania. . . . Maximillian, who rested without upon the confines. . . . in his place sent Georgio Basty, betwene whom and Michaell happened a great difference whether should be cheife Governor, and as Michaell was asleepe in his pavillion Basty besett him round about and slewe him, the manner whereof and cause of the difference ys yet so uncertaine until further and more perfect advise that I thincke yt not fytt to trouble your Honour therewith until my next.[1]

After Michael the Brave's death, Wallachia and Moldavia reverted to Turkish suzerainty while Transylvania came under Austrian domination. Although the first union of the principalities was short-lived, its achievement continued to be an inspiration to generations of Romanians to come.

NOTE

1. Tappes, *Documents Concerning Romanian History*, no. 216.

CHAPTER 5

The Romanian Principalities
(1601 to 1821)

PERSPECTIVE

As the Middle Ages came to an end, the political and military landscape of southeastern Europe changed and became more complex. By 1640 the Ottoman Empire had attained its limits of expansion with some minor exceptions. In 1683 the Turkish armies laid siege to Vienna, but with support from Poland and Germany, the imperial armies repelled them. The balance of power began to turn. In 1686 Buda fell; Mohács was recaptured in 1687, and in 1699 the Turks were driven out of Hungary. The Ottoman Empire began to face increasing external pressure while internally, corruption and decadence were on the rise. Nevertheless it continued to be a major power for the next 300 years and exerted its supremacy on Wallachia and Moldavia well into the nineteenth century.

Toward the end of the seventeenth century, Russia entered the European power struggle. Czar Peter the Great tried unsuccessfully to form a European Christian alliance against the Ottoman Empire, but attempts to find an outlet on the Black Sea and to dominate the Balkan Peninsula led Russia to a series of confrontations and major wars with Turkey throughout the eighteenth and nineteenth centuries, ending in the Russo-Turkish war of 1877–1878. The eighteenth century also witnessed the growth of Prussia and the dismemberment of Poland, which after 800 years of existence was then among the largest European states. Between 1772 and 1775 it was partitioned between Austria, Prussia, and Russia, and it ceased to exist until 1918 when the World War I Allies reestablished its independence. As the eighteenth century came to a close, France began to exercise its influence on European events, beginning with Louis XVI's declaration of war on Austria in 1792 and continuing with the French Revolution and the Napoleonic Wars.

Throughout these wars and power struggles, Wallachia and Moldavia remained autonomous principalities.

TRANSYLVANIA

After the death of Michael the Brave in 1601, Transylvania was ruled by an imperial military commission until 1606, when Sultan Ahmed I (ruled 1603–1617), facing the threat of Persian expansion, decided to free his forces in the west. He signed the Treaty of Zsitva-Török with Austria on November 11, 1606, putting an end to a war that lasted more than thirteen years. The importance of this treaty was that it gave the first indication of the decline of the Ottoman Empire's power. Under the treaty, the sultan acknowledged the Hapsburg emperor as an equal, and Austria's yearly tribute to the Porte was cancelled. Prince Stephen Bocskai, who had fought on the side of the Turks against Austria, was rewarded with the title of king of Middle Hungary. He was also crowned as prince of Transylvania (ruled 1604–1606), and the principality voluntarily accepted Ottoman suzerainty.

More Attempts at Unification

During the next half-century, Transylvanian rulers made several unsuccessful attempts to unify the three Romanian principalities for reasons ranging from imperial ambitions to the desire to create a stronger defense against the Ottomans. Nevertheless, it helped to maintain momentum in the spirit of unification that started with Michael the Brave.

Gabriel (Gábor) Bethlen

In 1613, Gabriel Bethlen (ruled 1613–1629), one of the greatest of the Transylvanian princes, ascended to the throne. He brought improvements to the judicial and administrative systems, founded Bethlen College, and did much for education in general. He took side with Hungary against the Hapsburg attempts to force Catholicism on all its protectorates. On May 5, 1619, Bethlen formed an alliance with Wallachia and Moldavia that was to be the basis for a confederation of the three principalities. He had the ambition of becoming another "king of Dacia" through the union, and furthermore he aspired to the throne of Poland. Neither materialized, and he died prematurely in 1629.

The Rákóczi Family

The vision of unification carried on with Gabriel's successors, George Rákóczi I (son of Sigismund Rákóczi; ruled 1630–1648) and George Rákóczi II (son of George Rákóczi I; ruled 1648–1660). The latter, in his attempts to seize the Polish throne, was supported by both Prince Constantine Şerban (ruled 1654–1658) of Wallachia and Prince George Ştefan (ruled 1653–1658) of Moldavia. The Ottomans, however, intervened, and had all three princes ousted. Refusing to be banished, they initiated a number of confrontations with the Turks that lasted more than five years. There were some victories and some losses, but in the end the Ottoman armies won, and in 1662 the Porte once again was in control of all three principalities.

In 1683 Turkish armies laid siege to Vienna, but their attempt to capture it failed. With support from Poland and Germany, Austrian troops ended the siege in September and counterattacked, capturing Buda, which had been a major Ottoman stronghold for 145 years. In 1687 the imperial armies entered Mohács, and in 1688 Belgrade fell.

Hapsburg Rule

After the fall of Belgrade, the Transylvanian Diet, under pressure from the Hapsburg armies, decided on May 9 to accept Austrian protection. Emperor Leopold I issued a diploma in December 1691 that, while formally placing Transylvania under the Hungarian crown, guaranteed its separate administrative and judicial system. Under the Treaty of Carlowitz, signed on January 26, 1699, Sultan Mustafa II recognized Emperor Leopold I as suzerain over the principality, with the exception of the Banat. A movement of independence began in 1703, headed by Francis Rákóczi I. He was proclaimed Prince of Transylvania in 1704 by the Diet, but his rule and the struggle ended in 1711 when the Hapsburgs reestablished their authority.

At this time, while Moldavia and Wallachia were still under the yoke of the Ottoman Porte, Transylvania went through a relatively peaceful and prosperous period under the rule of the Hapsburg Empire. The conditions of the Romanians and the peasants, however, did not improve.

Act of the Union

During the seventeenth century and the rule of Transylvania by native princes, living conditions of the Romanian peasantry were deteriorating, while the Romanian Orthodox Church was still not recognized by the authorities. Under pressure by Calvinists, George Rákóczi I had encouraged the publication of Orthodox religious services and instructions in the Romanian language. The intent was to discourage direct influence from Eastern Orthodox churches across the Carpathians where liturgy was still in Slavonic. The result of this action, in fact, had the effect of strengthening the cause of Romanian nationalism.

At the close of the seventeenth century, a proposed union of the Roman Catholic and Romanian Orthodox churches was accepted with enthusiasm by the Orthodox synod as a means to official recognition. The union was confirmed by an imperial diploma issued on February

1616, which recognized the formation of the Uniate (or Greek Catholic) Church with the right to enjoy the same Christian freedom as the Roman Catholic Church. Although only a portion of the Romanian population embraced the new religion, the union played an important role in the rise of Romanian national identity.

Peasant Revolt Under Horea, Cloşca, and Crişan

During the eighteenth century, although Transylvania was enjoying peace and prosperity, the position of the Saxons and of the Romanian peasantry worsened. In 1784, as a result of visits to Transylvania by Emperor Joseph II, a decree of emancipation was issued, which permitted every serf to marry, practice a trade, or dispose freely of his property. It also forbade arbitrary eviction. Universal military conscription was also introduced. The direct result of this decree was a rush by serfs to enroll in the military to escape serfdom.

Vasile Nicula, a Romanian peasant known as Horea, was a serf on an imperial estate. He decided to travel to Vienna and plead for improved conditions for the oppressed Romanian peasants who made up more than 75 percent of the serfs in Transylvania. Horea returned from Vienna believing that he had had the emperor's backing in the abolition of all serfdom, but nothing came of it. In the meantime, a group of peasants led by a serf called Crişan left their work to enlist in the army. Unknown to them, the enlistment had been suspended. An attempt to arrest Crişan ended in the killing of three officials. The mood of the peasants turned violent and, led by Horea, Cloşca (Ion Oargă, a serf from Cărpiniş), and Crişan, they went on a rampage which, by the time it died down, caused the death of many nobles and the sacking of numerous castles and manors. The imperial army was ordered to squash the uprising. Horea, Cloşca, and Crişan were arrested. Crişan committed suicide in prison, while Horea and Cloşca were executed in public on the wheel. The following year, on August 22, 1785, Emperor Joseph II issued a further decree abolishing serfdom and giving peasants the right of free movement.

Horea and Closça

Courtesy of Romanian National Tourist Office

Transylvania remained under the sphere of influence of the Hapsburg Empire until 1867, when it became completely integrated with Hungary.

WALLACHIA AND MOLDAVIA

After the death of Michael the Brave in 1601, Wallachia and Moldavia fell back in the clutches of the Ottoman Porte, and the struggle for freedom continued. Political life in the principalities was dominated by the nobility, and any attempts by rulers to gain some authority were being thwarted. Princes bought their way to the throne and were changed frequently, undermining their authority and at the same time enriching the Ottoman Porte.

Radu Şerban

Michael the Brave's direct successor in Wallachia, Radu Şerban (ruled 1602–1611), continued to follow the same anti-Ottoman policies. In 1603, in the name of the Hapsburg emperor, he sent troops into Transylvania and deposed the anti-Hapsburg ruler, Moise Székély. In 1611, Transylvania's ruler, Gabriel Báthory, in turn, invaded Wallachia but was defeated by Radu Şerban. While the two armies battled each other, the Turks entered Wallachia and put their own candidate, Radu Mihnea, on the throne. Radu Şerban went to Vienna where he remained in exile.

Radu Mihnea

Radu Mihnea was ruler of Wallachia from 1611 to 1616 and again from 1623 to 1626. From 1616 to 1623, he was ruler of Moldavia. He is believed to be the first monarch to appoint Greeks from the Phanar district of Constantinople, known as Phanariots, to high government posts in the Romanian principalities. This started a trend that ultimately led to the period in Romania's history referred to as the Phanariot period.

The Greek families became landowners and caused much concern and resentment among the native landowners. A number of uprisings against the Greeks occurred in both states. The first outbreak of violence took place in Wallachia in 1617–1619, during which a number of Greek landowners and merchants were killed. A second anti-Greek uprising, in 1631, forced the ruler of Wallachia, Leon Tomşa, to issue a proclamation on July 15 stating that "all the needs and poverty in the country are due to the foreign Greeks who interfere in the affairs of court, sell our country mercilessly and thrive on usury." The decree ordered the expulsion of all Greeks from the country.

The political situation in Moldavia, which was similar to that in Wallachia, was exacerbated by a number of Turko-Polish wars, all of them fought on Moldavian soil. Prince Gaspar Graţiani (ruled 1619–1620) allied himself with the Poles against the Turks, and he ended up being assassinated by two members of the local nobility in Iaşi. Moldavia continued to be a theater of war for the Polish and the Turkish armies until peace was established with the Treaty of Carlowitz in 1699.

Matthew (Matei) Basarab and Basil the Wolf (Vasile Lupu)

During the first half of the seventeenth century two outstanding rulers emerged, reigning almost concurrently in the two principalities—Matthew Basarab (ruled 1632–1654) in Wallachia and Basil the Wolf (ruled 1634–1653) in Moldavia. Both princes succeeded in bringing a degree of independence and stability to their states by adept foreign diplomacy and military skill; both promoted the development of culture and the arts and provided funding for religious works.

During Matthew Basarab's tenure in Wallachia, landowners were permitted to bring soldiers (*dorobanţi*) and foreign mercenaries (*seimeni*) into serfdom by force. After Matthew's death, a bloody uprising, known as the revolution of the *seimeni*, took place, in which the soldiers were joined by a large number of peasants. It started in the

Matei Basarab

Courtesy of Romanian National Tourist Office

Basil the Wolf

Courtesy of Romanian National Tourist Office

country but quickly spread to principal towns, including Bucharest, causing many deaths on both sides, as well as the destruction of numerous mansions and castles. The revolt was finally put down by Matthew's successor, Constantine Şerban (ruled 1654–1658), aided by Transylvanian Prince George Rákóczi I.

Cantacuzinos and Cantemirs

Both principalities continued to be plagued by internal unrest, as well as by rivalries between various ruling families, which degenerated into aristocratic feuds and violent clashes. Gregory (Grigore) Ghica (ruled 1660–1664), a Wallachian prince, had Constantine Cantacuzino, a counselor of Matthew Basarab and married to Radu Şerban's daughter, killed. This led to an ongoing battle lasting fifteen years and four changes of rulers. It ended with the Cantacuzinos getting the upper hand with the crowning of Şerban Cantacuzino, Constantine's son. Şerban took measures to increase his authority over that of the nobility and continued the long struggle to liberate the principality from dependence on the Ottoman Porte.

After the siege of Vienna in 1683, in which both principalities supplied troops in support of the Turkish armies, Prince Cantacuzino entered into negotiations with the Austrians and established contacts in Poland and Russia, in an effort to form a Balkan alliance against the Turks. A treaty with Emperor Leopold I was concluded in 1688 under which Austria recognized Prince Şerban Cantacuzino's authority and right of succession in return for Wallachia's acceptance of Austria's suzerainty. However, Prince Cantacuzino died while his envoys were en route to Vienna to sign the accord.

Between 1683 and 1691 Moldavia was subjected to repeated attacks by Poland, Turkey, and the Tatars. Constantine Cantemir (ruled 1681–1693) signed the Treaty of Sibiu (1690) with Austria, under which Moldavia was to break relations and military cooperation with the Ottoman Empire as soon as the Austrian armies approached the Danube and Siret Rivers. The Austrians never made it that far.

Dimitrie Cantemir (ruled 1710–1711) turned to Russia for support. The Treaty of Lutsk (August 24, 1711) recognized the independence of the state of Moldavia as well as the succession to the throne of the Cantemir family. The Russo-Turkish War (1710–1711) ended in a Turkish victory, the Russians withdrew, and Prince Cantemir was forced to take refuge in Russia, where he remained in exile for the rest of his life. As a result, the Turkish government no longer trusted local princes in the two principalities and began to appoint rulers directly. As the Phanariots were previously used in many high positions in the government, as well as in foreign embassies, they were considered the best qualified to be appointed governors of the Romanian states. Dimitrie Cantemir was replaced by Nicholas Mavrocordat, who became the first of the Phanariot governors to be appointed by the Porte.

Constantin Brâncoveanu

Şerban Cantacuzino's successor to the throne of Wallachia was his sister's son, Constantin Brâncoveanu (ruled 1688–1714). He proved to be one of the greatest of Wallachian ruling princes, and his reign of twenty-six years was one of the longest in Wallachia's history. Under his leadership, there was significant economic progress and notable cultural development in Wallachia. In foreign diplomacy, he maintained the state's autonomy in the face of expansionist pressures from all sides, and without any military interventions. In fact, while concluding a treaty with Czar Peter the Great of Russia providing for Russia's support in ending Turkish suzerainty, he was named "prince of the empire" by Emperor Leopold I and was at the same time accorded the title of prince for the rest of his life by the Ottoman Porte. In the end, though, the agreements he entered into with the Russians brought about his demise. He was betrayed by the Cantacuzino family, and was swiftly taken to Constantinople, where he was imprisoned, tortured, and executed together with his two sons and son-in-law.

Constantin Brâncoveanu (r. 1688–1714), from a mural painting in the Horezu monastery

Private collection of Bogdan Ulmu

Brâncoveanu's successor, Stephen Cantacuzino (ruled 1714–1715), was also executed in 1716, and the governorship of Wallachia was given to the first of the Phanariot succession of governors appointed by the Turkish Porte, Nicholas Mavrocordat, the former governor of Moldavia.

CULTURAL DEVELOPMENT

The seventeenth century ushered in a remarkable period in the history of Romanian culture, including a profound artistic and architectural revival. Many splendid churches and monasteries were built during the reigns of Matthew Basarab and Basil the Wolf. One of the most striking monuments of seventeenth-century Romanian architecture, the Church of the Three Hierarchs, was built in Iaşi by order of Basil the Wolf. Prince Basil was a despot who introduced a penal code whereby rapists were to be raped and arsonists to be burned alive, but he also endowed Iaşi with churches and monasteries, founded a school, and had a printing press brought to Moldavia, which led to the blossoming of Moldavian literature. Both the school and the printing press were housed in the Church of the Three Hierarchs, which was originally a monastery. The church's entire exterior is carved with chevrons, meanders, and rosettes as intricate as lace. The basic design is classic Byzantine, with two octagonal drums mounted above the naos and pronaos in the Moldavian style. Presently it is a museum and contains the sarcophagi of Dimitrie Cantemir and of Alexandru Ioan Cuza, who concluded the unification of Moldavia and Wallachia in 1859.

Constantin Brâncoveanu promoted education and culture, opening schools and establishing printing presses. He also commissioned numerous churches and monasteries to be built in Wallachia, as well as other buildings of great beauty and artistic value that combine Oriental and Western styles into a unique Romanian style known as the "Brâncoveanu style."

Church of the Three Hierarchs, Iaşi
Courtesy of Romanian National Tourist Office

Constantin Brâncoveanu's palace at Mogosoaia, typical of the Brâncoveanu style
Courtesy of Romanian National Tourist Office

The history of Romanian literature can be divided roughly into three distinct periods: the Slavonic, from the middle of the sixteenth century to 1710, the Greek, from 1710 to 1830 (the Phanariot period), and the Modern, from 1830 to the present.

Change from Slavonic to Romanian was very gradual. Slavonic had been the language of the Church from the early middle ages, and all service books were in Slavonic. Medieval literature consisted of translations from Slavonic into Romanian, and these translations included service books. The first Gospels were translated in Braşov (Transylvania) in 1560 by a deacon of Greek origin named Koresi. He then translated the Homilies in 1570. At that time the Romanian language had not yet been introduced into the Church.

Braşov was one of the most important centers of Romanian culture during that period. Thanks to the printing press at Braşov, Romanian books spread throughout all three Romanian principalities, laying the basis for the Romanian literary language. During the reign of Basil the Wolf in Moldavia (ruled 1634–1653), a printing press was set up that published important religious books in the Romanian language. This press was later destroyed but printing was carried on in Poland by Dosoftei (Dositheiu), Metropolitan of Moldavia from 1610 to 1686. Dosoftei was also a poet and a highly educated man who was literate in Romanian, Greek, Polish, Old Slavonic, and Latin. His most important works were *Psalms in Verse* (1673) and *The Lives of the Saints* in four volumes (1682), which helped to promote the development of Romanian literature. In 1679, after he helped bring a new press to Moldavia from Russia, Dosoftei printed the first Liturgy in the Romanian language, and he was the first bishop to introduce it in the church service. However, the Liturgy that was eventually adopted in churches was a translation from Greek by Jeremia Kakavela (Iaşi, 1697). Romanian became the authorized language of the Church by the end of the seventeenth century.

Dimitrie Cantemir (ruler of Moldavia, 1693, 1710–1711) promoted the development of Moldavian literature. He himself was a prominent writer, historian, and philosopher, and authored numerous books. He wrote the first novel in Romanian literature, *The Hieroglyphic History (Istoria Hieroglifică).* His *History of the Rise and Decline of the Ottoman Empire* was written in Latin and translated into English, French, and German in the eighteenth century. Most of his writing was in Russian after 1711, which helped to make him well known throughout the world. He was elected a member of the Berlin Academy.

All books of this period in the Romanian language used the Slavonic Cyrillic alphabet. The Latin alphabet wasn't introduced until after 1830.

Baroque splendor in art and architecture dating to the seventeenth century is visible everywhere in Romania. During that time, the number of villages in both Wallachia and Moldavia increased in number, and towns grew into commercial centers. The towns of Bucharest (Bucureşti) in Wallachia and Iaşi in Moldavia became centers of commerce and culture. Under Constantin Brâncoveanu, Bucharest, with a then-estimated population of 50,000, was recognized as one of the important towns in southwestern Europe.

PHANARIOT REGIME

At the beginning of the eighteenth century, while Transylvania was part of the Hungarian kingdom and under the protection of the Hapsburgs, Moldavia and Wallachia were still vassal states of the Turkish Porte. With Dimitrie Cantemir's exile to Russia, and with Constantin Brâncoveanu and Stephen Cantacuzino's executions, the Turks no longer trusted native princes to remain loyal to the Porte. There were already a number of Greeks who resided in the principalities and had been serving in high government posts, some as rulers. In the Phanariots, the Turks believed that they would find more readily subservient rulers. Nicholas Mavrocordat, whose father had risen from a common laborer to the office of Dragoman to the Porte, was appointed governor of Moldavia on October 17, 1711, and later, on January 5, 1716, as governor of Wallachia. Thus began the Phanariot period in the two principalities, respectively—a period that was to last until the revolution of 1821.

The Phanariots were Greeks who came from the Phanar district of Constantinople. To facilitate contact with foreign countries, Turkish officials began, sometime in the seventeenth century, to employ them, first as secretaries, translators, and interpreters, and later in positions of responsibility such as those of Dragoman,[1] and as provincial governors of Moldavia and Wallachia. It was believed that the Phanariots were particularly well suited for this work because they were generally well educated, spoke several languages, and were Christians.

The Phanariot regime was characterized by a period of corruption, mismanagement, tax abuses, and decadence. It was also a period marked by a number of Austro-Turkish and Russo-Turkish wars, during which the Romanian principalities gained nothing and lost some of their territory, while the Romanian population suffered immensely from the battles that took place on their lands. The Phanariot rulers were changed frequently and were also moved from one principality to the other, thus enriching the Porte and limiting the opportunity of rulers to gain too much control. In the 106 years of the Phanariot regime, a succession of thirty-three governors in Moldavia and thirty-five in Wallachia were appointed from among twelve families. They and their families developed lifestyles of extreme luxury and decadence, which proved to be contagious, and before long the native nobility was copying them as well. Since the governors had an average of three years in which to recover the excessive outlays necessary to become rulers, and to build their own fortunes, the burdens carried by the native population were constantly increased until they reached an intolerable level.

Among the Phanariot governors, a few stood out as enlightened reformers. Nicholas Mavrocordat in Wallachia and Gregory Ghica II in Moldavia introduced some taxation reforms to help the overburdened peasants. From 1718 to 1739, Austria occupied Oltenia (western Wallachia), and introduced many reforms, ranging from curbing the power of the nobility to improving the administrative and judicial systems. Under the Treaty of Belgrade in 1739, Oltenia was returned to Wallachia. In 1741, Constantine Mavrocordat introduced wide-ranging reforms in Wallachia based on the Oltenian reforms, and when he was appointed as governor of Moldavia in 1742, he introduced similar reforms in that state. Between 1744 and 1749, Constantine Mavrocordat, who was shuttled back and forth between the two states, put an end to mass migration of peasants and abolished serfdom altogether. Further social and economic reforms were introduced by Gregory Alexander Ghica (ruled 1764–1767) in Moldavia and by Alexander Ypsilanti (ruled 1774–1782) in Wallachia. Under the last Phanariot governors, Alexander Suțu and Scarlat Callimachi, taxes were raised again, however, and this finally led to the 1821 revolution.

In 1736, under Empress Anne, the Russians tried to annex Moldavia and Wallachia. They invaded Moldavia and actually occupied it for a period in 1739 but were forced to abandon it. Under the Treaty of Belgrade in 1739, Moldavia was restored to Turkish control.

Another Russian military intervention in Poland led to the declaration of war by Turkey in 1768. With support from Romanian volunteers, the Russians defeated the Turkish armies and drove them south of the Danube. The two principalities were under Russian occupation from 1769 to 1774. At the Treaty of Focşani and Bucharest in 1772, Wallachian and Moldavian delegations demanded reestablishment of autonomy with guarantees of Austria, Prussia, and Russia. To pacify Austria, Russia agreed to return Moldavia and Wallachia to Turkish suzerainty in 1774, while Austria, who gave support to the Turks during the negotiations, was given the northern portion of Moldavia, called Bucovina, which remained under Austrian control until 1918.

Russian consulates were opened in Bucharest and Iaşi in 1782, followed by Austrian, Prussian, French, and British consulates in 1783, 1785, 1786, and 1803, respectively. Another war against Russia was declared by Turkey in 1787 to prevent Empress Catherine II's expansionist ambitions. Austria entered the war on the side of the Turks, and their troops advanced into Wallachia as far as Bucharest and the Siret River, while Russian troops invaded Moldavia.

The death of Emperor Joseph II and the outbreak of the French Revolution, however, diverted the attention of the powers. Catherine II was able to reach a favorable settlement in the Treaty of Iaşi in 1792 with Russia imposing the nomination of two chancellors chosen by its government in the states of Moldavia and Wallachia. She also obtained the Turkish government's promise to appoint governors in the principalities for a minimum of seven years, not to be removed without the express authorization of the Russian ambassador in Constantinople. Nevertheless, in 1806, Turkey ordered the deposition of the two chancellors, which directly led to another war, the Russo-Turkish War of 1806–1812. The war was brought to a close by a lightning and powerful offensive led by Russia's famous Field Marshal Mikhail Kutuzov, and the Treaty of Bucharest was signed on May 18, 1812, under which Bessarabia, an integral part of Moldavia until then, was annexed by the Russian empire.

The Turkish government, now at war with Greece, no longer supported the Phanariot rulers in the Romanian principalities. Taking advantage of this situation, an anti-Phanariot revolt took place in Wallachia under the leadership of Tudor Vladimirescu, with support from Moldavia, and in cooperation with the leader of the Greek uprising in Iaşi, Alexander Ypsilanti (ruled 1792–1828), the Phanariot regime was abolished. The Turkish government accepted the demands of the Romanians to once more have rulers of their own nationality, and on July 1, 1822, John (Ioniţă) Sandu Sturdza was appointed ruler of Moldavia. On the same day, Gregory (Grigore) Ghica IV became prince of Wallachia. Thus the Phanariot regime was abolished after 106 years of control.

NOTE

1. Dragoman of a foreign embassy had functions including the carrying out of the most important political negotiations between the Ottoman Porte and neighboring countries. There was also a Chief Dragoman to the Porte.

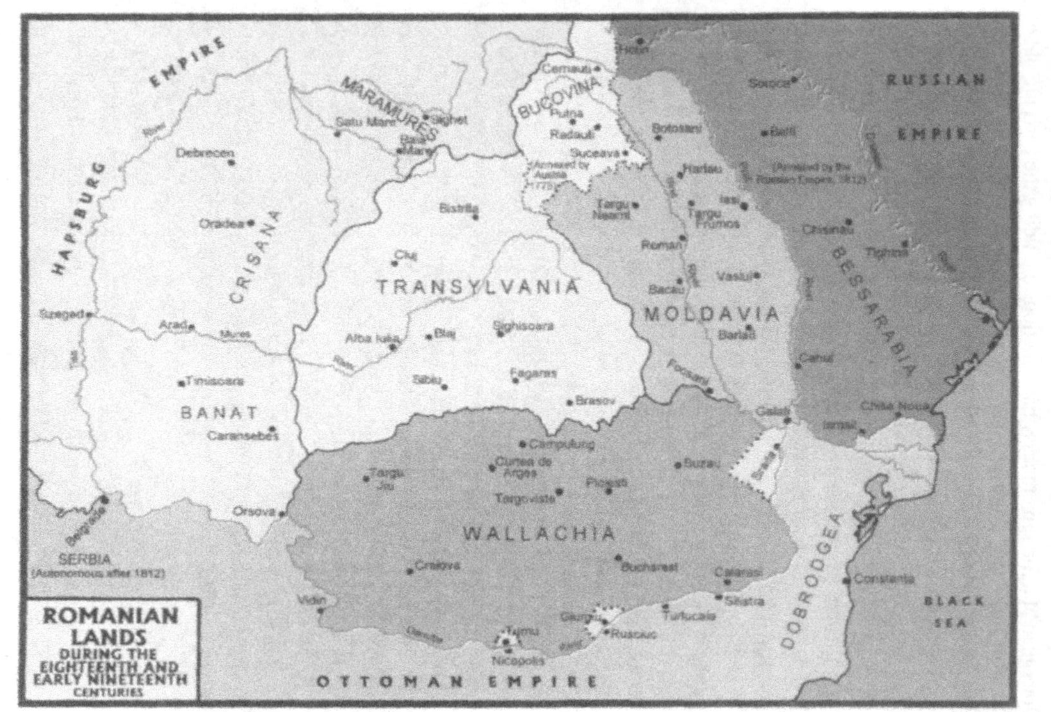

The Road to Unification

Reprinted with permission from the Center for Romanian Studies.

CHAPTER 6

The Road To Unification
(1821 to 1859)

PERSPECTIVE

Without a doubt, France played a dominant role in the historical events that unfolded during the first half of the nineteenth century in Europe: the French Revolution on July 14, 1789, the Declaration of the Rights of Man and Citizen, the Revolutionary Wars (1792–1802), the Napoleonic Wars, and the *Code Napoléon.* Changes in the map of Europe stimulated the movements for national unification throughout Europe. The French Revolution of 1848, which ended in the creation of the Second Republic, continued to have an effect on other revolutionary movements in Europe, including those in the Romanian principalities.

On May 14, 1804, Napolean was proclaimed emperor of the French; on August 11, Francis II, emperor of the Holy Roman Empire (ruled 1792–1806), assumed the title of Francis I, hereditary emperor of Austria (ruled 1804–1835). Two years later, on August 6, 1806, Francis formally renounced his title and functions of Holy Roman emperor, ending the era of the Holy Roman Empire. He was succeeded as emperor of Austria by his son, Ferdinand I (ruled 1835–1848).

The revolution of 1848 in Austria shook the Hapsburg Empire but failed in the end. Ferdinand abdicated on December 2, 1848 and was succeeded by his nephew Francis Joseph (Franz Joseph; ruled 1848–1916).

Germany's military humiliation during the Napoleonic wars stimulated nationalist fervor for a strong and unified state. The Congress of Vienna had redrawn the German map in 1814–1815, eliminating many small states and expanding Prussia and Bavaria. The German states were loosely linked in the German Confederation, and Austria obtained control of the confederation. German nationalism erupted into action in the Revolution of 1848, but failed. Prince Otto von Bismarck, who in 1862 took charge of Prussian policy, began to plan a German Confederation under Prussian leadership.

The office of regent of Hungary was held by members of the Hapsburg family until 1849, when it was abolished. Hungarian nationalism, influenced by the French Revolution, had been repressed by the Austrian Minister of Foreign Affairs Klemens Metternich until it burst forth in the Revolution of 1848. War broke out, and in 1849 Hungary was proclaimed an independent republic under the presidency of Louis Kossuth. It soon collapsed under military attacks by Austria with the aid of Russia. In 1866, the Austro-Hungarian Monarchy (dual monarchy) was set up.

The Greek War of Independence broke out in 1821, and as a result of the Conference of London (1832), an independent Greek state was established. On the Italian peninsula, the unification movement, which started during the Napoleonic era, continued unabated through the nineteenth century until political union was achieved in 1871.

TRANSYLVANIA

Following the uprising of 1784, the struggle continued for the Romanian population in Transylvania to be recognized as equals with the Hungarians, Saxons, and Szeklers. An association formed by Romanian intellectuals, which came to be known as the Transylvanian School, formulated a petition demanding equal rights for all Romanians in Transylvania. The petition was addressed to Emperor Leopold III and was sent to Vienna in March 1791. It bore the name of *Supplex Libellus Vallachorum* (Petition containing a Romanian request). The emperor forwarded it to the Transylvanian Diet, which rejected it outright. A second petition drawn up on March 30, 1792, was also rejected. The efforts having failed, the Romanian national movement passed through a transitional period, while the Transylvanian School turned its attention to cultural activities. During the first part of the nineteenth century, there was an increase in dialogue among Romanian students, intellectuals, and leaders from Transylvania and those in Moldavia and Wallachia. European events greatly influenced those that took place in all Romanian lands in 1848. It was the year of revolutions, and that of the Romanians in Transylvania occurred and overlapped with the Hungarian Revolution, which started on March 15.

During 1848 a number of manifestos were issued, including one published in the town of Blaj by Aron Pumnul, a Romanian Greek Catholic schoolteacher, stating the main objectives of the Romanian revolutionary program. It called for Romanians, both peasants and intellectuals, to gather in their villages and towns. The first such gathering took place on April 30, 1848, in Blaj under the leadership of Simion Bărnuţiu, who declared that the time had come for the Romanian nation to recover its ancient rights and to eliminate serfdom. As a result of this gathering, peasants began to revolt against landowners, occupying lands and refusing to perform the required hours of work. A second gathering in Blaj followed on May 14. The assembly approved a sixteen-point revolutionary program that was published as the National Petition of Blaj. A Romanian National Committee was established, to be located in Sibiu and to act as an interim government, and a Romanian national guard was to be created. Two days later, the Romanians in the Banat held an assembly in Lugoj and approved a similar program. The Hungarian Diet, which convened in Cluj, ignored the petitions and on May 29 approved the union of Transylvania with Hungary. The union was ratified by Emperor Ferdinand I on June 10.

Initially the Transylvanian Romanians were not opposed to a union with Hungary since they believed that once they were no longer subjected to the rule of the Hapsburgs, Romanians in Hungary and

Transylvania would be given equal rights. They were quickly disillusioned, however, as violent persecution of Romanians began. This created further revolutionary moves, and civil war was imminent. Bărnuţiu was elected president of a Committee of Pacification, and, under the leadership of Avram Iancu, a Romanian army was established. An offensive by the Hungarian Revolutionary Army against the Romanian legions and the Hapsburg forces ended in the occupation of the largest part of Transylvania by the Hungarian Revolutionary Army in March 1849. In the area that was still under the control of the Romanians, Iancu became the effective leader of the Romanian Revolution in Transylvania. After the defeat of the Hungarian Revolution in August 1849, Austria restored its rule of Transylvania, dissolved the Romanian legions, confirmed its national rights, and recognized the Committee of Pacification. Anton Puchner, the commander of the imperial army in Transylvania, was named ruler of Transylvania, and a civil war erupted between the Austrians and the Hungarians. Romanians joined the fighting on the side of the Austrians.

It was a war that set Romanians against Hungarians. In December, the Austrians appealed to the Russians for assistance and an army was sent across the Carpathian Mountains. On August 13, 1849, the Hungarians were defeated and Austria restored its rule of Transylvania. The Romanian legions were dissolved, and Transylvania remained under Vienna's rule.

Serfdom was abolished in all Austrian territories, but the rights of the Romanians still did not improve.

WALLACHIA AND MOLDAVIA

End of the Phanariot Regime

In 1815, an international revolutionary organization by the name of Philiké Hetaerea (Friendly Society) was founded by Greek merchants

Avram Iancu (1824–1872)

Courtesy of Regia Autonomă "Monitorul Oficial," Romanian Parliament

living in Russia. It had centers in Moscow, Bucharest, and other cities in the Balkans and in Mediterranean countries. Its aims were to incite Greek and other Christian uprisings against Ottoman domination and to achieve the independence of Greece. In 1820, the Friendly Society chose as their president Alexander II Ypsilanti, a former aide-de-camp of Czar Alexander I and eldest son of Constantine Ypsilanti, Phanariot governor of Moldavia and Wallachia. Both Constantine and his father, Alexander I Ypsilanti, were deeply involved in the struggle for freedom from Turkey. Alexander I Ypsilanti had been executed by the Turks for this, and Constantine was forced to flee to Russia where he spent the rest of his life.

In March 1821, a small force led by Alexander II Ypsilanti entered Moldavia. He allied himself with Tudor Vladimirescu, vice governor of a district of Oltenia. The plan was for Vladimirescu to seize Bucharest and there meet up with the Hetairia forces. Alexander Ypsilanti called for the Greeks, Serbs, and Bulgarians to rise against Turkey, and he let it be known that Russian military forces would join them. It soon became clear, however, that the czar did not approve of any uprisings. Ottoman troops entered Wallachia, and Tudor Vladimirescu began to negotiate with the Turks, but he was arrested by Ypsilanti and put to death as a traitor on June 8, 1821. Ypsilanti then fled to Austria, where he was arrested. The revolt was put down, and the principalities were occupied by Turkish troops for sixteen months. Their plundering devastated the economies of the Romanian states.

Although the uprising failed, it gave further stimulus to the struggle that led to the independence of Greece in 1829. It also made Russia and Turkey more cognizant of the Romanians' aspirations to be ruled by native princes. Thus, Gregory (Grigore) Ghica IV (ruled 1822–1828) became ruler of Wallachia and John (Ioniță) Sandu Sturdza (ruled 1822–1828) was installed as prince of Moldavia. In 1826, Russia and Turkey signed a protocol giving both principalities the right to elect their rulers from among local nobility, the elections to be confirmed by Russia and Turkey.

Bust of Tudor Vladimirescu (1780–1821)

Photo by author with approval of National Museum of History, Bucharest

Russian Occupation

In 1827, Czar Nicholas I declared war on Turkey in support of the Greek War of Independence. A combined British, French, and Russian naval task force engaged a Turko-Egyptian fleet in the Peloponnesian harbor of Navarino on October 20, 1827, destroying and sinking most of the warships. Russia continued to support the Greek cause and again declared war on Turkey in 1828. Its troops invaded Moldavia and Wallachia, advancing across Bulgaria to Constantinople. Turkey was forced to sign the Treaty of Adrianople on September 14, 1829. During the war, Wallachia and Moldavia had once more become a battlefield, and this time they remained under Russian occupation from November 1828 until March 1834.

Under the Treaty of Adrianople, the autonomy of the two principalities was recognized, princes were to be elected for life, and Turkey agreed to terminate its economic monopoly on them. Effectively, Ottoman domination over the Romanian states came to an end as a result of this treaty, and the principalities became a Russian protectorate.

Organic Regulations

The Russian occupation turned out to have a major effect on the two Romanian principalities. General Paul D. Kiselev (Pavel D. Kiseleff), who headed the Russian administration, took charge of repairing war damages and controlling a wave of famine and an outbreak of cholera, and he set up committees to organize political, economic, and social infrastructures. Two constitutions were drawn up, called Organic Regulations (Regulamente Organice), which gave identical structures to the two principalities. Princes were to be elected for life by the Extraordinary General Assembly made up of members of the nobility, clergy, and merchants. Each principality had a council of six ministers. The legislative branch of the government was called the National Assembly. It had 42 delegates in Wallachia and 35 delegates in Moldavia. The new structures were now the same in both principalities, which facilitated the eventual transition to a unified state. The Organic Regulations were put into effect in July 1831 in Moldavia and in January 1832 in Wallachia, and they remained in effect until the end of the Crimean War (1854–1856) and the Congress of Paris (1856).

During the occupation, Princes Alexander Ghica (ruled 1834–1842) and George Bibescu (ruled 1842–1848) in Wallachia, and Michael Sturdza (ruled 1834–1849) in Moldavia, introduced improved postal services, opened new schools, and upgraded the roads.

The first newspapers in the Romanian states appeared in 1828. In 1837 the Bucharest daily newspaper, *Românía*, began publication and was widely read in both states. Mihail Kogălniceanu, politician and historian and later the first prime minister of Romania, published a political and literary magazine in Iași called *Literary Dacia*.

During the first half of the nineteenth century, families from the Romanian nobility began to send their sons to Paris to complete their education. Some of these students formed a Romanian revolutionary circle where they discussed such topics as the unification of Wallachia and Moldavia, creating a constitutional government modeled after that of France under Louis Philippe, and ending foreign domination. Several of the members of the Romanian Circle took part in the Paris Revolution of 1848. Their ideas caught on, and soon secret societies emerged in Iași and in Bucharest.

Revolutions of 1848

The first revolutionary move occurred in Moldavia. On April 8, 1848, a petition to reform the Organic Regulations was submitted to Prince Michael Sturdza (ruled 1837–1849). The prince's response was to have the petitioners arrested, and that ended the movement in Moldavia for the moment. Not long after this event, on May 22, the

Revolutionary Committee of Wallachia was established in Bucharest under the leadership of Nicolae Bălcescu, Alexandru G. Golescu (both of them just back from Paris), and Ion Ghica. On June 21, a group including Ion Eliade-Rădulescu, Christian Tell, Ştefan Golescu, and Gheorghe Magheru met in the village of Islaz (near Corabia) in Oltenia, and there set up a provisional government, issued a twenty-two-point manifesto, and called for Prince George Bibescu (ruled 1842–1848) to enact reforms. It demanded autonomy of Wallachia under Ottoman suzerainty, with European guarantees of the abolition of serfdom and of privileges of nobility, an elected ruler, an assembly elected by universal suffrage, freedom of the press, and emancipation of the Jews. It did not call for union with Moldavia, however. Prince Bibescu was caught by surprise. In Bucharest, Wallachian revolutionaries forced him to accept the manifesto and to name a provisional government. The prince, decidedly motivated by a bullet that grazed one of his uniform epaulets, and by the hasty departure of the Russian consul, abdicated two days later.

On June 26, the two provisional governments merged. A blue, yellow, and red flag bearing the words "Justice and Brotherhood" was adopted, titles of nobility were revoked, a national guard was established, and the death penalty was abolished. The revolution had thus prevailed in Wallachia. The new government assured the Ottoman Porte of its continued loyalty, while it asked for French, British, and Austrian support.

Russia, who was openly hostile to the new government, insisted on her right to intervene and restore order in the principality. When, on September 25, a large crowd gathered in Bucharest and burned a copy of the Organic Regulations in front of the Russian consulate, Turkish troops entered Bucharest. Two days later, Russian troops entered Wallachia. The revolutionaries went into exile, and the 1848 revolutions came to an end.

Crimean War

Under Russian and Turkish occupation, order was restored and the Organic Regulations, burned by the revolutionaries, was once again put into effect. On June 22, 1849, under a Russo-Turkish agreement, Barbu Ştirbei (ruled 1849–1853) was appointed ruler of Wallachia, and Gregory Alexander (Grigore Alexandru) Ghica V (ruled 1844–1853) was made ruler of Moldavia. A period of calm followed, brought to an end in 1853 with the outbreak of the Crimean War (1853–1856).

In 1853, Czar Nicholas I gave orders for the occupation of the two principalities as a guarantee to be held until Turkey complied with a series of Russian demands. On July 2, Russian troops crossed the Prut River into Moldavia. Turkey, with British support, demanded the retreat of the Russian forces. Upon Russia's refusal, Turkey declared war. The Western powers became involved in diplomatic maneuvers to settle the dispute. On June 3, 1854, Austria demanded the immediate evacuation of the Romanian principalities by Russia. Reluctantly, the czar ordered his troops to retreat, but no sooner did they begin to pull back than Austrian troops invaded and occupied Moldavia and most of Wallachia. This move actually prevented a full-scale invasion of the principalities by the Turks, supported by the Western Allies. Instead, the action moved to Crimea.

By the end of 1855, France became the center of peace negotiations between Turkey and Russia, and a treaty was signed on March 30, 1856, at the Congress of Paris.

During the Crimean War, Wallachia and Moldavia were under continuous foreign occupation, either by Russian forces, Turkish armies, or joint forces, as well as by Austrian troops.

Union

In July 1856 the occupation of the two states ended. The Ottoman government removed princes Ghica and Ştirbei, who had returned briefly to their thrones, and installed two regents, Theodor Balş (ruled 1856–1858) in Moldavia and Alexander (Alexandru) D. Ghica (ruled 1856–1858) in Wallachia. As a result of pressure from France, Russia, Prussia, and Sardinia, the Porte authorized elections to be held by electoral committees for union of the principalities. They were held in Iaşi and Bucharest, and the results were overwhelmingly in favor of a union. Two assemblies and state councils were formed. Mihail Kogălniceanu submitted a proposal for the union of the two principalities into a single state to be called Romania, to be ruled by a foreign prince chosen from a reigning European family. He proposed a representative constitutional government, its existence to be guaranteed by the seven great powers (France, Britain, Austria, Prussia, Russia, Turkey, and Sardinia). The proposal was voted on and was approved unanimously in Bucharest and 81 to 2 in Iaşi. The results were submitted to a conference of the seven powers held in Paris by Napoleon III. On August 19, 1858, a convention was signed, which, although it did not approve a complete union, stipulated that the two principalities were to be known as the United Principalities of Moldavia and Wallachia. There would be two rulers, two capitals, two assemblies, and two governments; a unified army, a central committee, and a supreme court of justice and cassation would handle common problems and develop uniform legislation. The convention represented an important step forward toward a complete union.

The election for the Elective Assembly took place in Iaşi in December 1858. The unionists who had formed a political party called the National Party won thirty-four deputy seats out of fifty-four. Their candidate was Colonel Alexandru Ioan Cuza, the minister of war, and he was unanimously elected prince of Moldavia on January 17, 1859.

The Wallachian Assembly met on January 24, 1859, and also elected Alexandru Ioan Cuza as prince of Wallachia. Thus, although the convention of Paris stipulated that each principality was to elect its own ruler, it did not specifically oppose the separate election of the same ruler by the two assemblies.

Of the seven powers, only Austria and Turkey opposed the election, and thus Cuza was recognized by the powers in September 1859 as ruler of both states. It took two years from his election, and with tacit support from France, for Cuza to make the United Romanian Principalities an officially recognized reality.

MEANWHILE, THE OTHER ROMANIAN LANDS

Bucovina

Bucovina, as part of Austrian Galicia since 1775, had no separate autonomy and was used by the Austrians as a territory for settlement of Ukrainians, Poles, Germans, and Jews to replace the majority Romanian population. Nevertheless, a Romanian sense of national consciousness began about the same time as that in Transylvania and the Banat. In 1844, an imperial decree introduced Romanian as the language of instruction in some Orthodox schools, and in 1848 a pedagogical school opened in Cernăuţi for Romanian-speaking teachers.

The outbreak of the revolution in Vienna in March 1848 had its effect on the Romanians in Bucovina as well. An assembly was held in Cernăuţi, where a twelve-point program was developed and then expanded as the "Nation's Petition." This was sent to Vienna, and other petitions followed. They resulted in a constitution issued in March 1849. It separated Bucovina from Galicia and made it an autonomous dukedom with its own Diet. A Romanian high school was established in 1860, and the Society for Romanian Culture and Literature was founded in 1862.

Bessarabia

At the time when Wallachia's unification was achieved by Voievod Basarab I, in 1310, the principality included an area in the Danube Delta that came to be known as Bessarabia. The name was later extended to cover the rest of the area between the Prut and Dniester Rivers, previously under the control of Moldavia. In the fifteenth century, the southern Budzhak area became part of the Ottoman Empire, while the rest of Bessarabia remained part of Moldavia until 1812, when it became part of the Russian empire under the Treaty of Bucharest. After Russia's defeat in the Crimean War, a southern strip of Bessarabia was ceded to Moldavia, but it was lost again in 1878 under the Treaty of Berlin.

The Revolution of 1848 did not spread to Bessarabia because of the presence of the Russian army, but manifestations by the Romanian population did take place. The Peace Conference of Paris in 1856 returned the southern Bessarabian counties of Cahul, Ismail, and Bolgrad to Moldavia, a region populated mostly by Romanians. Under his rule, all of Alexandru Ioan Cuza's reforms were put into effect in these counties.

Dobrogea

The despotate of Dobrogea (Romanian, Dobrogea; Bulgarian, Dobritch), located between the Danube and the Black Sea, probably acquired its name toward the end of the fourteenth century during the rule of Dobrotch (Dobrotici; Dobrotitch), who reigned over that region under the suzerainty of Byzantium. It came under Ottoman domination in 1411 and remained under its rule for over 400 years, until 1878.

CHAPTER 7

The Road To Independence
(1859 to 1881)

PERSPECTIVE

Revolutions that Transformed Europe

The French Revolution had a major effect upon the history of Europe in the nineteenth and twentieth centuries, resulting in an outbreak of revolutions across the continent, the creation of larger political entities, and movements toward an increase in human rights.

The second far-reaching development affecting European and World history was the Industrial Revolution. The French Revolution was the result of an effort to apply human powers of reason to human institutions and to politics. The Industrial Revolution was the result of an effort to apply reason to the force of nature in order to harness it for use in the fulfillment of humanity's desires.

The Industrial Revolution began in Britain during the eighteenth century and early nineteenth century and spread to the rest of Europe as the benefits of industrialization began to be felt. It is generally accepted that the Scottish inventor James Watt's improved steam engine in 1769 marked the high point in this development. It drove the change from a stable agricultural and commercial society to a modern industrial one, relying on complex machinery rather than on tools. The steam engine provided power to an ever-increasing number of new machines, including the steam locomotive with its dramatic change in transportation, changes in metallurgy, and the design of new warfare-related equipment.

The Industrial Revolution also created a new social class, the industrial workers. It gave rise to urban centers requiring vast municipal services. Relations between capital and labor were aggravated, and Marxism was one of the results.

As new and larger countries emerged, and as war equipment became increasingly more efficient and lethal, defensive alliances began to be formed. These blocks of countries, armed to the teeth and suspicious of each other, inescapably led to World War I.

Ottoman Empire

A steady weakening of the Ottoman Empire marked the period from 1859 until World War I. The evacuation of Turkish garrisons from Belgrade in 1867; rebellions in Crete and Bosnia and Herzegovina; the Russo-Turkish War and Austrian occupation of Bosnia and Herzegovina; the creation of Greater Bulgaria and that of Romania, with its subsequent declaration of independence; internal strife, oppression, and economic bankruptcy—all these added to the empire's difficulties and steady decline.

ALEXANDRU IOAN CUZA

The ruler under whom Romania became a state, who made it happen, was Alexandru Ioan Cuza (ruled 1859–1866). He was born in Galați, Moldavia, on March 20, 1820, and belonged to an ancient noble family. His education began at a French *pension* (boarding school) in Iași, as was the custom with the children of the local aristocracy in those days. He was then sent to Pavia, Bologna, and Athens to complete his secondary education. After a brief stage in military service, Cuza enrolled in the Faculty of Law at the Sorbonne, in Paris, but left

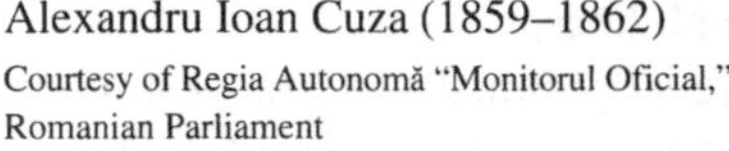

Alexandru Ioan Cuza (1859–1862)
Courtesy of Regia Autonomă "Monitorul Oficial," Romanian Parliament

Statue of Alexandru Ioan Cuza, Piața Unirii, Iași
Photo by author

before he completed his degree. In 1845 he married Elena Rosetti who, in 1862, founded the Princess Elena Refuge for Orphans in Bucharest.

On March 27, 1848, at the age of twenty-eight, Cuza was arrested by Russian authorities for participating in the Revolutionary Assembly held in Iași, but he escaped to Vienna. He returned to Moldavia in July 1849 and became prefect of Galați. In 1857 he rejoined the army and became minister of war, as well as the representative of Galați in the Moldavian Assembly. Cuza was an eloquent speaker and strongly advocated the complete union of Wallachia and Moldavia.

The Paris Convention signed on August 19, 1858, was the result of a compromise between those powers favorable to the union and those adverse to it. It stipulated that each principality would elect its own prince, but did not specifically oppose the separate election of the same prince by the two assemblies. On January 17, 1859, in the Moldavian Assembly, the unionists led by Mihail Kogălniceanu, Costache Negri, and others unanimously elected Alexandru Ioan Cuza as prince. In Wallachia, an electoral confrontation between the conservative non-unionists and the unionists ended in a deadlock that was finally resolved by selecting a candidate they both could support, Alexandru Ioan Cuza. He was elected on January 24, thus achieving the union of the principalities under one ruler. The double election was approved by five of the great powers but opposed by the Ottoman and Hapsburg empires.

As negotiations between Turkey and the other European powers were not making any headway, Cuza began to take measures toward a complete unification, establishing a common currency and integrating custom services and telegraph lines.

In June 1860, Cuza decided to travel personally to Constantinople, where he successfully negotiated the terms of the Paris Convention with the Turkish authorities. Members of the Paris Convention were summoned to Turkey, and on December 4, 1861, the Conference of Constantinople issued a declaration recognizing the union, but only for the duration of Cuza's reign. Prince Cuza chose to interpret this limitation purely as a face-saving device and moved rapidly to complete the union.

Two days before the legislature of the two principalities were to meet, on January 24, 1862, Cuza appointed the conservative leader, Barbu Catargiu, as prime minister to head the first government of the united principalities. On February 5, 1862, the national assemblies were merged into one, located in Bucharest, and a single ministry was formed for the two principalities. The term *România* (Romania) began to be used in official acts.

Political Parties

Once the government's administrative infrastructure was in place, political parties began to form. The first such body had appeared with the introduction of the Organic Regulations in 1831. It was the National Party in Moldavia, led by Ion Câmpineanu. During the 1848 revolution, the National Party split into separate conservative, moderate, and radical groupings. After the union, the liberals organized under three main factions—the Radicals, led by Ion C. Brătianu and Constantin A. Rosetti; the Moderates, under Ion Ghica; and the Free and Independents, led by Nicolae Ionescu. There were also several factions under Mihail Kogălniceanu. The leaders of the conservatives were Barbu Catargiu, Dimitrie Ghica, Gheorghe Ştirbei, Lascăr Catargiu, and M. C. Epureanu. The liberals favored progressive changes, while the conservatives believed in the pre-revolution status quo. As the middle class grew in importance in Romania, so did the liberal factions.

POLITICAL PARTIES (1831–1881)

1831		**National Party** Ion Câmpineanu	
1848	**Radicals**	**Moderates**	**Conservatives**
1859–1862	**Liberals**		**Conservatives** Barbu Catargiu Dimitrie Ghica Lascăr Catargiu
Radicals Ion C. Brătianu C. A. Rosetti Mihail Kogălniceanu	*Moderates* Ion Ghica	*Free & Independent* Nicolae Ionescu	
After 1866	**National Liberal Party** (Partidul Naţional Liberal)		**Conservative Party** (Partidul Conservator)

Ion C. Brâtianu, leader of the National Liberal Party. This cut-out from an NLP New Year's greeting card reads, "2000—You, too, can be liberal!"
Private collection of Bogdan Ulmu

Attempts to form a united liberal party during Prince Cuza's reign failed, although all the factions believed that a modern society is based on its industrial and commercial classes and not on the landed aristocracy. They also depended on the peasant class for support. Neither were the conservatives able to form a united political party, even though they all agreed on basic principles, such as continuation of property ownership and opposition to electoral and agrarian reforms.

Reforms

Prince Cuza was able to introduce a series of reforms, including a modernized legal system, a modern university-level education system, and new fiscal policies. Unfortunately, his aggressive effort to introduce reforms and dictatorial style of leadership alienated all classes of Romanian society, and opposition to his rule mounted. The point was reached where an unlikely coalition of liberals and conservatives introduced a resolution in February 1863 to demand Cuza's abdication in favor of a foreign prince. The resolution was not approved, but a vote of censure against the prince was passed.

Cuza realized that before any major agrarian or other reforms could be achieved, the electoral system needed to be changed. On October 23, 1863, Cuza formed a new government and appointed Mihail Kogălniceanu as prime minister. Cuza and Kogălniceanu presented major electoral and agrarian reforms to the National Assembly, but neither of the bills were passed. On May 14, 1864, Cuza summoned the assembly to convene in an extraordinary session to reconsider the reform bills, and when the majority refused, he dissolved the assembly and had the opposition deputies physically removed by military force. The National Assembly was replaced by a Senate and a Chamber of Deputies, and under a new constitution, the prince took control of the government, with the Senate appointed almost solely by him. On August 26, 1864, his agrarian reform was passed by decree and put into effect in April 1865. Peasants were no longer required to devote a number of hours of work for the landowners, and could purchase their allocated holdings. Under the law the state compensated the landowners for sold property and allowed peasants to reimburse their debt in thirty-six yearly payments. Cuza also held a referendum for a constitutional reform which gave him powers to increase the electorate base.

In 1865 Cuza granted a concession to an Anglo-French consortium to establish the Bank of Romania (Banca României). This was to be an important banking act. Cuza was certain that the new bank would not only bring capital investment into Romania but would also strengthen financial ties with Great Britain and France. However, neither result materialized.

Despite his success in bringing about the union of the principalities, creating the state of Romania, and introducing his legislative and social reforms, opposition to his leadership style was mounting. Conservatives were not pleased with the abolition of forced labor; peasants were disappointed because agrarian reforms did not go far enough; and the clergy was unhappy with the confiscation of monastic estates. In February 1865 tensions came to a head when Cuza asked for the resignation of his prime minister, Mihail Kogălniceanu, suspecting him of ambitions to become prince, and thus losing his most ardent supporter. A new coalition led by Ion C. Brătianu and Constantin A. Rosetti, with military support, ousted Prince Cuza. He abdicated on February 22, 1866, and left for Vienna. He spent the rest of his years in Vienna, Paris, Wiesbaden, and Heidelberg, where he died on May 15, 1873. A provisional ruling council was formed and undertook preparing the way for the arrival of a foreign prince.

PRINCE CAROL OF HOHENZOLLERN-SIGMARINGEN

As early as 1802 the unionists in the principalities of Wallachia and Moldavia planned to invite a foreign prince to rule over the united principalities in order to put an end to all of the internal power struggles, as well as to create closer ties with the West. Following Cuza's abdication, the majority of conservatives and liberals still favored a ruler chosen from European royalty outside Romania, and their first choice was Philip of Flanders, the brother of Leopold II, king of Belgium. However, the prince declined, and it was their second choice who accepted the invitation, with support from Napoleon III. It was Karl Eitel Friedrich von Hohenzollern-Sigmaringen, a cousin of Napoleon III. Ion C. Brătianu was assigned the tasks of proposing the throne to Karl and gaining support for him in Romania.

Mihail Kogălniceanu by Dan Mihail

Courtesy of National Museum of History, Bucharest

Although Karl knew little about Romania and spoke no Romanian, he had excellent qualifications for the job. Through his father, who was minister-president of Prussia, the young prince had formed close relationships with Prussian and German royalty. Throughout his reign as a prince and later as king of Romania, Karl took a leading role in internal and international affairs, and he enjoyed a great deal of parliamentary support. The first challenge he had to face, however, was the logistics of getting to Bucharest. As a Prussian officer, passage through Russia, Austria, or Turkey was impossible. It was decided that he should travel incognito. He journeyed as a Swiss traveling salesman, complete with a Swiss passport in the name of Karl Hettingen. After long hours in overcrowded second-class rail cars across Austria and Hungary, he was met by Brătianu, and together they traveled first on a Danube steamer, then overland in an open carriage, finally reaching Bucharest on May 22, 1866. The same day he was led to the Chamber of Deputies, where he took the oath as Prince Carol of Romania (ruled 1866–1881). He appointed the conservative Lascăr Catargiu as prime minister to lead a coalition government.

Once he was sworn in, Prince Carol moved quickly to set up the operating machinery of the new country. A new constitution was adopted and ratified on July 11, 1866, patterned after the Belgian constitution of 1831. It was a relatively liberal document, designed to create a modern constitutional government. It referred to the country as România (Romania); it made no reference to any Ottoman suzerainty; it provided for a modern parliamentary government structure; it guaranteed protection of personal property and individual freedom. Under the constitution, the title of ruling prince was made hereditary; Carol was named commander of the army and retained the right of absolute veto over bills passed by the legislature.

Formal recognition of Prince Carol by the Ottoman Porte and the European powers was given on October 19, 1866.

In 1869, Carol married Princess Elizabeth of Wied. Their only child, a daughter, died in childhood, and Elizabeth sought refuge from her grief in literary activity. She identified herself completely with her adopted people and devoted herself to their cultural development. Under the pseudonym of Carmen Sylva, she wrote extensively in English, German, French, and Romanian. Her books number over fifty volumes. It was through her efforts that many unknown Romanian artists, such as George Enescu, got their start. She also brought Carol great domestic happiness.

Although Romania was now recognized as an autonomous state ruled by one prince, it still remained a vassal state of the Ottoman Empire and was even considered to be an integral part of the empire. Prince Carol accepted this for the moment but began to plan and work toward gaining complete independence for Romania.

Internally, continuous power struggles between liberal factions and conservatives brought a degree of instability to Romania during the first five years of Carol's reign. Friction was also developing between Parliament and the prince. When war broke out between France and Prussia on July 19, 1870, most liberals and some of the conservatives tended to side with France, whereas Carol naturally favored Prussia. Carol also opposed the introduction of too much Western style liberalism into a country that he considered not yet ready for it.

On March 22, 1871, Carol dissolved Parliament, which was then headed by Ion Ghica, and asked Lascăr Catargiu to form a new government. The new conservative administration put an end to the early period of instability and began to concentrate on the task of achieving full independence. By June 1875, with the conservatives still in power, the liberals decided to unite and formed one party, the National Liberal Party (Partidul Naţional Liberal; NLP). On May 9, 1876, the National Liberal Party won a majority vote, and a new liberal government headed by Manolache Costache Epureanu took over, with Ion C. Brătianu as finance minister and Mihail Kogălniceanu as foreign minister. On August 5, Epureanu resigned, and a liberal government headed by Brătianu remained in power until 1888. In 1885, the conservatives formed the Conservative Party (Partidul Conservator).

Efforts by Prince Carol and the government toward achieving independence intensified from 1876 on. In May 1876, Mihail Kogălniceanu, as foreign minister, sent a note to Romanian diplomatic agents demanding recognition of Romania's independence under joint guarantee of the European powers. The note was ignored. The same year, two notes were sent to the Ottoman Porte, which were both ignored. In September, Brătianu traveled to Crimea to negotiate a military convention with Czar Alexander II and his minister of foreign affairs, Alexandr Gorchakov, to allow Russian troops passage across Romania in case of war against Turkey. In December, a Romanian delegation traveled to Constantinople, where a conference of the Treaty of Paris members was being held. The members of the conference refused to discuss Romania's independence. On April 16, 1877, Romania and Russia signed the military convention, and on April 24 Russia declared war on Turkey. Its troops crossed into Romania and headed toward the Danube. Turkish troops bombed the town of Brăila, and Romanian artillery responded by bombing Vidin.

A state of war now existed between Romania and Turkey. On May 9 Parliament passed a resolution proclaiming the independence of Romania, and Romania's army and navy went into action in support of the Russian forces. The war ended in an armistice on January 31, 1878, and on February 19 the Treaty of San Stefano officially recognized the independence of Romania. Dissatisfied with the terms of the treaty, which tended to greatly increase Russia's influence in southeastern Europe, the Western powers called for its review. A conference was convened in Berlin on July 13, which resulted in the Treaty of Berlin confirming Romania's independence and providing for the return to Russia of southwestern Bessarabia in exchange for handing over to Romania the Danube Delta, Snake Island, and Dobrogea. France, Germany, and Britain withheld official recognition until the beginning of 1880, when Romania's Parliament implemented a required change in the constitution of 1866 that eliminated all religious restrictions on the exercise of civil and political rights.

On February 20, 1880, after some 400 years of Ottoman suzerainty, the independence of Romania was officially recognized by all the European powers, and diplomatic relations were established. Prince Carol, who in the fall of 1878 had taken the title of Royal Highness, became king on March 26, 1881, when Parliament proclaimed the Romanian Kingdom. King Carol I declared at his coronation: "It is not just for me personally that I accept the title, but for the glory of my country."[1]

NOTE

1. Carol I, trans. Dan Berindei, *Cuvântiri şi scrisori,* vol. 2 (Bucharest, 1909), 427.

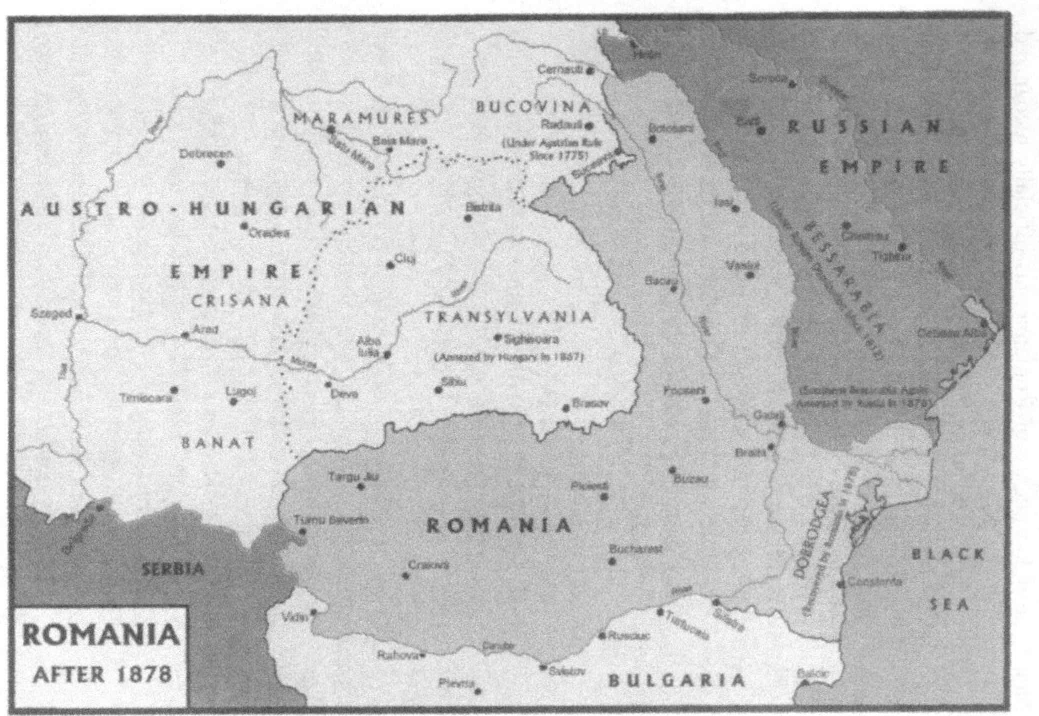

Into the Twentieth Century

Reprinted with permission from the Center for Romanian Studies.

CHAPTER 8

Into The Twentieth Century
(1881 to 1918)

PERSPECTIVE

Ententes and Alliances

The Crimean War that ended with the Treaty of Paris in 1855, the acquisition of Nice and Savoy in 1859, the completion of the Suez Canal in 1869, all helped France reach the pinnacle of its prestige in Europe. The Franco-Prussian War (1870–1871) in which a coalition of German states defeated France, threatened French supremacy and had far-reaching results. With the loss of Alsace-Lorraine, France and Germany entered the twentieth century in an atmosphere of animosity.

In the meantime Russia, under Czar Nicholas I, suffered the loss of southern Bessarabia and, with it, direct access to the mouth of the Danube. Then, in 1875 under Czar Alexander II, the revolt of Bosnia and Herzegovina led to a war with Turkey (1877–1878), ending in a diplomatic setback at the Congress of Berlin in 1878. Since 1872, Russia had been a member of the so-called Three Emperors' League, an informal alliance between Austria-Hungary, Germany, and Russia. Such was the animosity between Russia and its partners after the Congress of Berlin that Germany and Austria-Hungary formed a secret defensive alliance, the Dual Alliance, leaving Russia out on a limb. In 1881, Italy joined the Dual Alliance, thus creating the Triple Alliance (1882–1913), and in 1883 Romania also joined this group.

Faced with a hostile alliance, Russia and France began a process of rapprochement, and in 1895 they formalized a dual alliance between them. Britain, also finding itself isolated from the other European countries, signed the Entente Cordiale with France, and in 1907 came to an understanding with Russia, thus creating the Triple Entente (1907–1913). Two powerful European blocs, members of the Triple Entente and those of the Triple Alliance, were now facing each other, distrustful of one another, literally waiting for the slightest of incidents, a spark, to ignite and turn it into a major conflagration. That incident occurred unexpectedly on June 28, 1914, at Sarajevo, in Serbia.

World War I

At the Congress of Berlin in 1878, greater Bulgaria was divided into three parts—Bulgaria, Eastern Bumelia, and Macedonia. Bulgaria and Eastern Bumelia were united in 1885. Serbia and Montenegro were guaranteed their independence, while Austria-Hungary was given the right to occupy Bosnia-Herzegovina, which it annexed in 1908. This created increasing tension with Serbia, where nationalistic movements considered Bosnia-Herzegovina as rightfully belonging to Serbia. When Archduke Franz Ferdinand, the heir to the Hapsburg throne, was assassinated in Sarajevo, Serbia, by a Serbian nationalist on June 28, 1914, most European governments believed that the incident could be localized. However, this time a series of threats, ultimatums, and mobilizations was set in motion that resulted in a general war between the two major alliances.

At the onset of the war, Italy and Romania declared their neutrality, leaving the Triple Alliance with only Germany and Austria-Hungary, which became known as the Central Powers. Turkey joined them in July 1914, and Bulgaria followed in 1915.

The Triple Entente, which had been comprised of Britain, France, and Russia, was joined by Italy in 1915, by Romania and Greece in 1916, and by the United States in 1917. The Triple Entente was now generally referred to as the Allies.

Although World War I was fought principally in Europe, eventually it involved all the continents of the world. A bloody war of attrition from trenches on both sides, mostly on French soil, was fought on what was called the Western Front and resulted in a deadlock. In the east, Russian forces fought against German and Austrian troops but, despite enormous casualties, were unable to break through German defenses. Other fronts involved Britain, Turkey, Persia, Mesopotamia, Egypt, Italy, and Austria and also resulted in huge losses and human suffering. On the high seas, the war was fought mainly between Britain and Germany; the first submarine, introduced by Germany, was put into combat. The arrival of American troops on the Western Front, numbering some 1.2 million by 1918, had a decisive effect on the outcome of the war. By October 1918 Allied forces recovered most of occupied France and part of Belgium. Widespread unrest in Germany resulted in the abdication of William I, and two days later an armistice was signed, ending World War I.

Russian Revolution

Toward the end of the nineteenth century, during the reign of Czar Alexander III, the backward agricultural system in Russia led to famines, unrest, and revolutionary movements. Under Nicholas II (ruled 1895–1917), the eldest son of Alexander III, conditions worsened to such an extent that an uprising occurred in 1905 and strikes broke out in St. Petersburg, Moscow, Warsaw, and Baku in 1913. A period of two years after the outbreak of World War I followed without any major uprisings, but with Russia's poor performance and great losses of life fighting the Central Powers, a full-scale revolution erupted, ending with the abdication of Czar Nicholas on March 14, 1917. It was followed by the Bolshevik Revolution in November. By Lenin's order, Russia unilaterally ceased hostilities on November 26 and signed a formal armistice with Germany. Civil war continued in Russia until the Soviet Union was created in 1922.

KING CAROL I

Political Parties

Ion C. Brătianu's liberal government, in power since August 1876, continued its leadership until April 4, 1888. In the meantime, the two major parties, the National Liberal Party and the Conservative Party, began to split into various factions. The first split in the Conservative Party occurred when the "Junimists," members of the Junimea Literary Society (see chapter 9), took a favorable position toward joining the Triple Alliance in opposition to the majority who leaned toward France and the Triple Entente. Within the National Liberal Party, there were the Radicals led by Constantin A. Rosetti and Gheorghe Pann, and the Conservative Liberals under Gheorghe Vernescu and Petre S. Aurelian. In 1882, Constantine Dobrescu-Argeş with Vasile M. Kogălniceanu (son of Mihail Kogălniceanu) and Ion Mihalache founded the Peasants' Party. In 1893, a Romanian Social Democratic Workers' Party was founded but collapsed in 1899 to be reorganized in 1910 as the Social Democratic Party; and in 1909, the well-known historian, Nicolae Iorga, and Alexandru C. Cuza formed the Democratic Nationalist Party. Although Romania now had a multiparty system, governments continued to be led by one of the two major parties.

Peasant Revolts

By 1885 many politicians were ready for a change in government. Although some reforms had been put into effect, most peasants still owned no land, and most of the crops were being exported without economic benefit to them. Electoral reforms were still insufficient, leaving the majority of the population with no real voting power. A peasant uprising in 1888 prompted King Carol to bring the conservatives back to power, and then he set up a system of rotation between the two major parties, which continued until 1914. The Conservative Party under Junimists Theodor Rosetti and Petre P. Carp attempted to pass a number of reforms to improve the peasants' conditions, but it

POLITICAL PARTIES (1881–1918)

National Liberal Party	Conservative Party
Radicals – C. A. Rosetti Gh. Pann	Junimists Democratic Conservatives (1908) – Take Ionescu
	Pro-French
Conservative Liberals – Gh. Vernescu P. S. Aurelian	Pro-German

1882	Peasants' Party (Partidul Ţărănesc) – Constantin Dobrescu-Argeş
1909	Nationalist Democratic Party (Partidul Naţionalist Democrat) – Nicolae Iorga A. C. Cuza
1910	Social Democratic Party of Romania (Partidul Social Democrat Român)
1917	Labor Party (Partidul Muncii)

was not able to obtain agreement between the various party factions on an effective program. In 1891, a new conservative cabinet under Lascăr Catargiu did get a law enacted that allowed the sale of state-owned property to peasants who had none. However, inefficiency, economic and financial difficulties, and lack of real effective reforms continued to plague the country.

In February 1907 one of the most violent uprisings in the history of southeastern Europe started in northern Moldavia and spread to the rest of the country. It lasted until mid-April, when Dimitrie Sturdza's liberal government, with military backing, crushed it by brute force. A few makeshift laws were passed to pacify the peasants, but it was not until January 1914 when Ion I. C. (Ionel) Brătianu's liberal cabinet came to power that the electoral and agrarian issues began to be tackled seriously. A constituent assembly was elected to vote on the

1907 by Octav Băncilă

Courtesy of National Museum of History, Bucharest

necessary constitutional amendments to allow the expropriation of land for peasants and to establish universal suffrage. The outbreak of World War I, however, brought this effort to a temporary halt.

Neutrality

On October 30, 1883, King Carol signed a defensive treaty with Austria-Hungary. This treaty was kept a secret, and not even the Romanian Parliament was privy to it, as sympathies were running high on the side of France. Also to be considered were the large number of Romanians still struggling for recognition in Transylvania, Banat, and Bucovina under Austro-Hungarian rule. However, King Carol believed that Russia posed a danger to the new state, while Germany and Austria-Hungary would guarantee Romania's frontier. Thus Romania effectively joined the Triple Alliance.

As the condition of the Romanians in Transylvania worsened in 1907, and as Austria-Hungary annexed Bosnia-Herzegovina in 1908, opposition grew against membership in the Triple Alliance. In October 1912, when the First Balkan War erupted, Titu Maiorescu (1840–1917) whose conservative Junimist cabinet had just come to power, kept Romania out of the conflict, hoping that by its neutrality Romania would be awarded southern Dobrogea. However, Bulgaria refused to cede this territory, and, as a result, when Bulgaria attacked Serbia in June 1913, triggering the Second Balkan War, Romania joined Serbia and Greece to defeat it. By the Treaty of Bucharest on August 10, 1913, Bulgaria was forced to cede Southern Dobrogea, south of Romania's present border, from Silistra to the Black Sea, south of Mangalia.

On June 28, 1914, Archduke Franz Ferdinand was assassinated by Serbian nationalists, and a month later, on July 28, Austria-Hungary declared war on Serbia, triggering World War I. When Germany declared war on Russia on August 1 and on France on August 3, King Carol and Petre Carp, the Conservative Party leader, advocated entering the war as members of the Triple Alliance, but Ion I. C.

King Carol I

Courtesy of the Photo Archive of the Academia Civică Foundation, Bucharest, and Mircea Carp

Brătianu, joined by other Conservative Party leaders, favored neutrality, and for the time being, Romania stayed out of the war.

On October 10, King Carol I died. His death ended a forty-eight-year reign, the longest in Romanian history and a period of relative stability, economic growth, and unprecedented cultural development. It was also a period during which Romania won its independence from the Ottoman Empire and became a kingdom with a structured political system. In 1913, Romania ranked fourth in the world as a wheat exporter and second in Europe as an oil producer.

KING FERDINAND I

Carol, whose only daughter had died in childhood, designated his nephew, Prince Wilhelm von Hohenzollern as heir to the throne, but he renounced his rights and his brother, Prince Ferdinand, was chosen in his place on March 18, 1889. In 1893 Ferdinand married Marie Alexandra Victoria, daughter of Alfred, Duke of Edinburgh, granddaughter of Queen Victoria and of Czar Alexander II. Following the death of Carol I, Ferdinand became king of Romania on October 11, 1914 (ruled 1914–1927).

WORLD WAR I

After Germany declared war on Russia and on France, Great Britain declared war on Germany, Montenegro and Japan joined the Allies, and Turkey joined the Central Powers, thus setting off the goriest, costliest, and largest-scale war the human race had ever before unleashed. Brătianu, who controlled Romania's foreign policy since the death of Carol I, was determined to stay out of the war as long as he could. However, Romania's geographical location meant that it was inevitable that it would be drawn into the conflict. A number of both liberal and conservative statesmen supported joining the Allies

King Ferdinand I

Courtesy of the Photo Archive of the Academia Civică Foundation, Bucharest, and Mircea Carp

Queen Marie

Courtesy of National Museum of History, Bucharest

in May 1915, when Italy declared war on Austria-Hungary, but Brătianu preferred to wait until the course of the war was more predictable and until he could negotiate the best terms and conditions for Romania's contribution.

In the spring of 1916, the Allies were planning a major offensive on both the Western and Eastern Fronts and were therefore interested that Romania join in attacking Austria-Hungary. They agreed to conditions brought to the negotiation table by Brătianu's delegation. Foremost among them were guarantees of the union of Transylvania, Banat, Maramureş, Crişana, and Bucovina with Romania; protection of Romania's southern frontier against a Bulgarian invasion; the supply of sufficient ammunition for the duration of the war; and Allied offensives on all fronts to coincide with a Romanian military action against Austria-Hungary. It was also a propitious moment to enter the war because Austrian army units were being moved from Hungary in preparation for an offensive against Italy, and German troops had been halted at Verdun.

On August 17, a favorable treaty was signed in Bucharest between Romania and the Allied powers, followed by Romania's declaration of war on Austria-Hungary on August 27. Germany declared war on Romania the next day, followed by Turkey and Bulgaria. Romanian troops crossed the border into Transylvania, and by September 25 they had reached Sibiu and Sighişoara but had to stop there. The offensive that the Allies were to initiate from Salonika was being delayed, with the result that Bulgarian and German troops were able to begin an offensive in Dobrogea, necessitating reinforcements to be sent from the Transylvanian front to the Danube. At the same time, a powerful counteroffensive by Austro-Hungarian forces drove the Romanian troops back across the Carpathians, while German troops were crossing the Danube at Zimnicea. Despite heroic resistance, the Germans advanced toward the capital, and on December 6, they entered Bucharest. Romania was cut in two; some quarter-million Romanian soldiers were killed, wounded, or taken prisoner; most weapons were captured; and the Ploeşti oil fields were ablaze, set on fire by British agents to prevent them from entering into the hands of the enemy.

King Ferdinand and the Romanian government left Bucharest before it was captured and set up a government of resistance and unity in Iaşi. They were followed by masses of Romanian refugees making their way to Moldavia in the bitter cold and snow of winter, without shelter or food. In Moldavia, living conditions were not much better. With the influx of people from Wallachia and the continuing war, there was a shortage of housing, food, fuel, and medical supplies. That winter was exceptionally long and severe, and an epidemic of typhus added to the suffering of the population.

That winter, the government in Iaşi, with the assistance of a French military mission, began training and reorganizing the available troops, while a supply of new military equipment that had been purchased from the Allies arrived in Moldavia. The Germans now planned to launch a major offensive in Moldavia in the summer of 1917 to smash the last vestige of Romanian resistance and open the way to Ukraine. On July 24, however, the Second Romanian Army under General Alexandru Averescu, supported by the Fourth Russian Army, hindered their plans with an offensive at Mărăşti. Then German forces went on the offensive advancing on Iaşi, but on August 6, at Mărăşeşti, north of Focşani, Romanian troops, determined to preserve the last unoccupied region of their country, fought a fierce battle lasting thirteen days, and brought the Germans to a halt. Some 27,000 Romanians and 60,000 Germans lost their lives there.

These battles saved the Romanian kingdom, and no further German offensives took place on that front. Late in 1917, however, the Bolshevik Revolution changed the situation. The new Soviet government declared a unilateral cease-fire, and Romania thus lost the needed support of the Russian armies, making further resistance demanded by the Allies unattainable. Ion I. C. Brătianu was forced to conclude a provisional armistice with the Central Powers on December 11, after which he resigned. General Alexandru Averescu, the new prime minister, prepared a peace draft under which the Central Powers annexed

Dobrogea, and then he too resigned. A new Conservative Party cabinet under Alexandru Marghiloman renegotiated the peace terms and ended up signing a humiliating treaty in Bucharest on May 17, 1918.

In the meantime, an Allied counteroffensive on the Western Front and an offensive from Salonika were gaining momentum. On November 6, Marghiloman's cabinet resigned and a new Liberal Party government was formed, led by General Constantin Coandă. On November 10, Allied troops under the French General Henri Berthelot crossed the Danube into Romania at Zimnicea, and on the same day, the Romanian government declared that Romania was resuming military operations on the side of the Allies and that it was entitled to all territorial claims included in the Treaty of Bucharest on August 17, 1916. The following day, on November 11, an armistice was signed between the Allies and the Central Powers, ending World War I.

King Ferdinand and Queen Marie, accompanied by General Berthelot, entered Bucharest on November 30, at the head of a battered but victorious army. Between 1918 and 1920, under various World War I peace treaties, Romania's territory more than doubled in size.

CHAPTER 9

Cultural Development in the Nineteenth Century

The remarkable cultural development in the Romanian principalities of Wallachia and Moldavia during the seventeenth century (see chapter 5) became stagnant for the next 100 years, during the Phanariot regime. The Phanariot rulers were Greek and were placed in their position by or with the approval of the Ottoman Porte. Neither they nor the Turks had a great deal of interest in sponsoring or promoting the development of Romanian literature, art, and music. This development only reawakened after the 1821 revolution. After 1848, original writings in the Romanian language became more prevalent, and by 1860 the Latin alphabet had replaced the Cyrillic. It was between 1866 and the beginning of World War I that cultural development in Romania blossomed.

Chapter 9 covers the early and late nineteenth century, and chapter 13 continues with the cultural development in the twentieth century. However, the work of many of the literary, artistic, and musical figures overlap this arbitrary division.

EARLY NINETEENTH CENTURY

The revolutionary spirit of Europe during the first half of the nineteenth century bolstered the national consciousness of the Romanians and gave support to their effort to achieve unity and independence. The period also witnessed the birth of Romanian literature. The expression of poets and writers sharpened the Romanians' awareness of their Latin heritage and was a source of inspiration in the cause of unity.

George (Gheorghe) Lazăr (1779–1823), a Transylvanian by birth, started a movement in Transylvania that had as its object arousing the Romanians' awareness of their Latin roots. In 1818 Lazăr became head of a new school in Bucharest named St. Sava, in which Romanian replaced Greek as the language of instruction, and in 1819 the students of St. Sava staged the first theatrical performance in Romanian to be performed in Bucharest. The driving force behind Lazăr's movement was Ion Heliade-Rădulescu (1802–1872), considered by some as the "father of Romanian literature." Lazăr's movement was behind the publication of a dictionary of the Romanian language, produced by August Laurian, in which all the words of non-Latin origin were simply eliminated.

Toward the end of the eighteenth century and beginning of the nineteenth century, ideas of the Enlightenment influenced a group of Transylvanian intellectuals who had taken up the struggle for equal rights of Romanians in Transylvania. They came to be known as the Transylvanian School (Şcoala Ardeleană). Influenced by the Transylvanian School, George (Gheorghe) Asachi (1788–1869) established the first school of higher education where students were taught in the Romanian language (1813). In 1816, he organized in Iaşi the first theatrical performance in Romanian. Asachi was a cofounder with Rădulescu of the Romanian National Theater.

Literature

Many of Romania's literary figures of the nineteenth century had studied in France, and after 1830, Romanian literature was increasingly influenced by Western Romanticism. This movement toward the West also tied in with the rise of the Romanians' national consciousness and awareness of their Latin roots. Heliade-Rădulescu, Vasile Alecsandri (1819–1890) and Mihail Kogălniceanu (1817–1891) are associated with this national renewal movement, as well as the cultural opening toward the West.

Alecsandri, a participant in the Revolution of 1848, a statesman, diplomat, poet, and writer, founded the journal *România Literară*, wrote lyric poetry, and collected Romanian folk ballads. From an early age, Alecsandri took an interest in ancient Romanian oral popular poetry, ballads that were recited or sung by various regional groups. He began collecting them, and in 1852 his first collection was published in Iaşi.

The final collection, his greatest work, was published in 1866 as *Poezii Poporale* (Popular poems). It contains, among many others, a pastoral ballad called *Mioriţa* (The ewe-lamb), one of the most beautiful and best-known Romanian ballads. Many versions of this ancient ballad have been recited, but the best is that of Alecsandri. It recounts the story of a shepherd who was warned by one of his ewes that two of his companions who were envious of his sheep were planning to kill him. The shepherd does not run away but accepts death with equanimity. Mircea Eliade (1907–1986), Romanian historian and philosopher of comparative religion, writes that *Mioriţa* is one of the folk creations that help one best understand the attitude of the Romanian soul in front of death:

> It is seen as a mystical marriage by which man is reintegrated in nature. Death is not a diminution of the human being, on the contrary, it is an increase, from the metaphysical point of view, of course. Man should not run away from death and even less so should he lament upon its arrival: death is a fact of cosmic size that has to be accepted with equanimity and even joy, because due to it the individual frees himself from his limits.[1]

Together with Costache Negruzzi (1808–1868) and Mihail Kogălniceanu (1817–1891), Alecsandri served as director of the National Theater in Iaşi in 1842 and in 1855.

Among other well-known writers and poets of this period were Grigore Alexandrescu (1812–1885), Andrei Mureşanu (1816–1863), Nicolae Filimon (1819–1865), and Alecu Russo (1819–1859).

Art and Architecture

The same period also marked the beginnings of pictorial art in Romania, which until then had been devoted almost exclusively to religious subjects. The first artists were sons of the nobility who were studying in Rome and Paris during the revolutionary period. Among them were Constantine Lecca (1810–1887), Carol Pop de Satmari (1813–1888), and J. Negulici (1812–1851).

Architectural development had reached a high during the seventeenth century in Wallachia with the distinct Romanian style developed in the reigns of Princes Matthew (Matei) Basarab and Constantin Brâncoveanu. The process of Europeanization that followed the gradual decline of Turkish domination influenced Romanian leaders and architects, who began to build in the neoclassical style.

LATE NINETEENTH CENTURY

Stimulated by the unification of Wallachia and Moldavia and by Romania's independence from the Ottoman Empire, this period witnessed an unprecedented proliferation of cultural activity.

Literature

Junimea Literary Society

Titu Maiorescu (1840–1917), professor of logic and the history of philosophy at the universities of Iaşi and Bucharest was the leading Romanian literary critic of his time, and a Moderate Conservative Party leader. In Iaşi in 1863, he founded a cultural and literary association named Junimea (Youth). Its original members were mostly young Moldavians who had returned from studies in Western universities and who met regularly to discuss cultural and literary issues, as well as the direction their newly founded nation should be taking.

As it grew in importance, Junimea became the forefront of cultural reform, and its literary journal, *Convorbiri Literare* (Literary conversations), edited by Jacob Negruzzi (1842–1932), attracted the best of Romania's writers. Junimea was responsible for promoting the work of three great literary figures: Mihai Eminescu (1850–1889), the great poet whose lyrical, romantic, and revolutionary poems had a profound influence on Romanian literature; Ion Creangă (1837–1889), the national storyteller; and Ion Luca Caragiale (1852–1912), the foremost Romanian playwright. Some of Junimea's other leaders were Vasile Pogor (1833–1906), Petre P. Carp (1837–1918), and Theodor Rosetti (1837–1923). Although Junimea initially avoided politics, it did ultimately become an influential political determinant as a faction of the Conservative Party.

Mihai Eminescu

To appreciate Romanian culture, it is necessary to become acquainted with the works of Mihai Eminescu (1850–1889). He was one of the leading cultural figures of nineteenth-century Romania. Born on January 15, 1850, in Botoşani (Moldavia), he ran away from home at the age of fourteen, joined a theater company, and traveled with it throughout Romania and Transylvania. At the age of sixteen he became deeply interested in the Romanian language and culture and published his first poem. In 1859, Eminescu left to study at the University of Vienna. Briefly back in Romania in 1872, he published much of his literary work, and then he left again to obtain his doctorate at the University of Berlin. There he became interested in mythology, the history of religion, law, and history, and even the Sanskrit language. He also translated Kant's *Critique of Pure Reason* into Romanian, but he lost interest in his doctorate.

Returning to Romania, he held a number of positions, including editor of the newspaper *Timpul* (The Times), a position that brought him fame and a reputation as an insightful journalist. Meanwhile, he continued to write and publish poetry. Aside from his work, poems, and ideas, he was mostly indifferent to the material world, events around him, social conventions, wealth or the lack of it, class distinction, and even love affairs. At the age of thirty-three Eminescu's health deteriorated, and he began to suffer from periodic fits of madness. He spent the last six years of his life in and out of sanitariums until his death on June 15, 1889.

Among the best-known poems by Mihai Eminescu are *Luceafărul* (Lucifer, the morning star) considered by critics as one of the most beautiful poems of nineteenth-century European poetry, and *Doina*, a nationalistic poem written on the occasion of the unveiling of a statue of Stephen the Great.

Mihai Eminescu (1850–1889)
On grounds of Church of the Three Hierarchs, Iaşi. Photo by author.

Doina

From Tisa to Dniester's tide
All Romanians to me cried,
That they could no longer dwell
Amidst the foreign swell.
From Hotin until the sea
Rides Muscovite cavalry,
On their way they're always seen
From the seashore to Hotin,
And from Dorna to Boian
Plague is spreading on and on.
The foreigner is everywhere
Like you were no longer there;
Up to mountains, down to valley
Enemies on horses rally,
From the seashore to Hotin,
They as flooding waters are.
Oh, the poor Romanians all
Like the crab they backwards crawl;
A cruel fate to them begotten
Autumn is no longer autumn,
No more summer in their hand,
Now all strangers in their land.
From Dorohoi to Turnu
Enemies in steady strew
All, together overcome you,
As they arrive by railway
All our songs they drive away,
All the birds fly out of sight
From wretched foreign plight.
Over shadows of a thorn
Are the poor Christians born,
Ravaged is the country's face
Forests – our refuge place
Bending, their axe bide,
Even pure springs are dried,
Poor in poor countryside.
He who loves the foes about
May his heart the dogs rip out,
May desert his home efface,
May his sons live in disgrace!
Rise, O'Stephen, mighty Prince,
From sacred Putna come hence,
Let the holy Prelacy
Guard alone the monastery,
Let the saints and their deeds
In the trust of pious priests,
Let them ring the bell with might
All the day and all the night,
And may mercy grant thee Lord
Redeem thy people from the horde.
Rise, O'Stephen, from the ground
So I may hear your horn sound
And gather all Moldavia 'round.
If you blow your horn one blare
All Moldavia will be there,
If you sound a second time
All the woods will fall in line,
If your horn is blown again
All the enemies will be slain
And our borders we regain,
That the crows may hear their cry
Above gallows trees so high.

—MIHAI EMINESCU, 1883

Translation by Kurt W. Treptow and Irina Anadone, from *Selected Works of Ion Creangă and Mihai Eminescu*

Ion Creangă

Kurt W. Treptow writes:

> [Ion Creangă], the peasant sage, ranks among the leading story tellers in world literature. His works have been translated in over twenty languages. . . . Creangă's stories and tales are all extracted from the rural society in which he grew up and demonstrate different aspects of peasant mentality, as well as elements of traditional Romanian folklore. As such, Creangă's writings are an irreplaceable part of Romania's culture.[2]

Ion Creangă (1839–1889) was born on March 1, 1839, in Humulești, which is now a picturesque suburb near the Moldavian town of Târgu Neamț. In his childhood it was a village of whitewashed houses, surrounded by dense forests and cool, pure streams—forests inhabited by wild boar, bears, lynx, wildcats, fox, and wolves. Much later, having left his beloved village to complete his studies, he often reminisced about his childhood. He thought about the long, dark winter nights when the family was gathered around the wood-burning stove, listening to his mother tell stories—stories that were handed down from generation to generation.

Ion Creangă (1837–1889)
Courtesy of Romanian National Tourist Office

Creangă's mother aspired to priesthood for Ion. He became a deacon in 1858. In 1861 he married the daughter of a priest, and they settled in Iași. In 1864, at the age of twenty-five, he renewed his education to become a teacher. For such unholy behavior as frequenting the theater, he was defrocked in 1872 and suspended as a teacher. His wife abandoned him, leaving him alone with his young son. Fortunately, with the help of Titu Maiorescu, who was at the time head of the school, he was reinstated in 1874.

The following year he met Mihai Eminescu, and a lasting friendship developed. It was Eminescu who encouraged Creangă to write down the stories that he had heard in his childhood. He joined the literary circle Junimea, to which he recited his tales. They were published in Junimea's *Convorbiri Literare.* Creangă is best known for his work *Amintiri din Copilărie* (Memories of my childhood). It is his recollections of childhood in Humuleşti. Between 1880 and 1882 the first three parts appeared, while the last part was to be published posthumously. He portrays his native village and its inhabitants, presenting vivid character studies. His narratives are notable for their irony and humor.

At the age of forty-four, Creangă began to suffer from health problems and died two years later, on December 31, 1889, in the same year as his friend Eminescu.

Visual Arts

Three great painters—Theodor Aman, Nicolae Grigorescu, and Ioan Andreescu—dominate the fine arts of this period.

Theodor Aman

Theodor Aman (1831–1891) was born at Câmpulung (Argeş) on March 20, 1831. He studied under Constantin Lecca and Carol Wahlsteiner. In 1850 Aman settled in Paris, where he became associated with participants in the Revolution of 1848. In 1952, he opened his first studio, painting indoors in the style of the Flemish and Dutch masters. He made his debut in Paris in 1853 with *Self-portrait*, which was favorably received by critics.

Returning to Romania in 1858, Aman produced major historical paintings and many portraits. Alexandru Ion Cuza appointed him as principal of the new Romanian School of Fine Arts in 1864. He was impressed by the work of Nicolae Grigorescu, and in 1870, as president of the jury of the "Living Artists" exhibit, he awarded Grigorescu the First Class Medal. While being treated for an ailment, Aman died prematurely at the age of sixty on August 19, 1891. He was considered to be the founder of the Romanian school of art and the forerunner of modern Romanian painting.

Winter Landscape by Ioan Andreescu
Courtesy of Regia Autonomă "Monitorul Oficial," Romanian Parliament

Nicolae Grigorescu

Nicolae Grigorescu (1838–1907) was born in Pitaru on May 15, 1838. He trained in Bucharest with various church painters, producing icons and religious murals, becoming well known for his royal icons, which were distinguished for the elegance of their figures. In 1861, Grigorescu was awarded a government grant to study abroad. He left for Paris and was admitted to the Ecole des Beaux Arts.

After graduating, he established himself in Barbizon, where he became a friend of Millet and produced his first *plein-air* paintings. He was profoundly influenced by Barbizon School masters such as Corot and Courbet. Romanian artists such as Ioan Andreescu, Ştefan Luchian, and Gheorghe Petraşcu, who were founders of the modern Romanian school of painting, were, in turn, influenced by Grigorescu's art. Grigorescu died in Câmpina on July 21, 1907.

The Merry Peasant Girl by Nicolae Grigorescu

Courtesy of Regia Autonomă "Monitorul Oficial," Romanian Parliament

Ioan Andreescu

Ioan Andreescu (1850–1882) was born on February 27, 1850. He studied at Theodor Aman's Academy of Fine Arts in Bucharest, where he attended Aman's drawing classes. After graduation, he was appointed teacher of drawing and calligraphy at the Episcopal Seminary in Buzău. Andreescu made his debut in December 1874, and his paintings attracted Nicolae Grigorescu's attention. With Grigorescu's assistance, the young painter obtained a year's grant to study in France. He took courses at the Julian Free Academy and also painted at Barbizon and Fontainebleau.

Andreescu developed a passion for artistic expression but was never to enjoy the rewards for his gift of painting, maturity, and creative genius. He lived a life close to poverty; often in poor health, he died in Bucharest on November 13, 1882, at the early age of thirty-one, just when he was beginning to acquire the prestige and appreciation he deserved. Today many consider him Romania's greatest artist.

Music

In music, two outstanding masters during this period should be mentioned: Ciprian Porumbescu and Eduard Caudella.

Ciprian Porumbescu

Ciprian Porumbescu (1853–1883) was born in Şipota (now Şipota Sucevei) near Suceava, on October 14, 1853. Composer, conductor, and choirmaster, he studied the violin and then continued his studies at the Vienna Conservatory, where he was a pupil of Anton Bruckner. Settling in Braşov, he concentrated on composing. Porumbescu is best known for his *Crai Nou* (The new emperor), written in 1882, which by 1900 became the most popular Romanian operetta, his *Balada* for violin and piano, and *Rapsodia Română*. Porumbescu was one of the founders of the Romanian School of Instrumental and Vocal Music. He died on June 6, 1883.

Eduard Caudella

Eduard Caudella (1841–1924) was born in Iaşi on June 3, 1841. A composer, violinist, and teacher, he studied the violin in Berlin, Frankfurt, and Paris. He worked as a violinist at the court of Alexandru Ioan Cuza and was director at the Conservatory and the National Theater.

During his early career he spent much time as a concert violinist in Romania and abroad. As a composer, he played an important part in the development of Romania's best-known and loved composer, conductor, and violinist, George Enescu (1885–1955; see chapter 13). After only two meetings, Caudella advised him to send young George to Vienna for studies. Caudella composed numerous musical works of different kinds. He was particularly attached to his native land and incorporated much of the rich popular Romanian music into his classical compositions. His *Petru Rareş* was the first nationalist Romanian opera. (Peter Rareş was a sixteenth-century Moldavian ruler.) Eduard Caudella died in Iaşi on April 15, 1924.

Other Major Musical Events

The Romanian Philharmonic Society Orchestra was founded in 1868 and the Romanian Opera House was founded in 1877. Between 1885 and 1888, an exquisite concert hall, the Ateneul Român (Romanian Atheneum), was built in Bucharest, designed by the French architect Albert Galleron.

Education and Historiography

This period also witnessed a significant development in the field of education. The University of Iaşi (1862) and the University of Bucharest (1864) became respected centers of learning.

The development of a Romanian national consciousness in the nineteenth century created a situation whereby intellectuals also became patriots, and the cultural advancement was inextricably linked with the movements for unification and independence. From

Ateneul Român (Romanian Atheneum) Concert Hall (1886–1888)
Courtesy of Regia Autonomă "Monitorul Oficial," Romanian Parliament

this, a new historical profession emerged and grew rapidly, especially after the 1870s. Alexandru D. Xenopol (1847–1920) produced the first major chronicle of Romanian history, which became an international standard reference. He was followed by such leaders in the field as Ioan Bogdan (1864–1919), Nicolae Iorga (1871–1940), Constantin Giurescu (1825–1918), Dimitrie Onciul (1856–1923) and Vasile Pârvan (1882–1927). Historiography played an important role in the developing Romanian civilization in the nineteenth century and into the twentieth century.

Architecture

Architecture during the nineteenth century continued to be influenced by the early Brâncoveanu style but, affected by the cultural revolution associated with the Enlightenment and Romanticism, it now began to blend with neoclassicism.

During the latter part of the nineteenth century, architecture flourished, evolving from neoclassicism to classical eclecticism and Second Empire French. Magnificent and imposing buildings such as the University of Bucharest (1869), the Romanian Atheneum (1888), and the Central Library of the University of Bucharest (1893) sprang up, not only in Bucharest but in other cities such as Iași, Constanța, and Craiova.

NOTES

1. Eliade, *The Romanians, A Concise History*, 48.
2. Treptow, *Selected Works of Ion Creangă and Mihai Eminescu*, VIII.

Greater Romania Between World Wars

Reprinted with permission from the Center for Romanian Studies.

CHAPTER 10

Greater Romania
(1918 to 1940)

PERSPECTIVE

On November 11, 1918, World War I, the largest conflict the world had yet seen, came to an end with victory for the Allies. Ten million dead and twenty million wounded is a conservative estimate. Starvation and epidemics raised the total in the immediate postwar years. People called it "the great war," the war "to end all wars." The League of Nations was created to "promote international cooperation and to achieve peace and security." Yet only twenty-one years later, mankind was to face the horrors of another global conflagration, World War II.

Aftermath of World War I

At the end of the war, four empires had foundered, two new nations emerged, and the map of Europe had been altered once again.

Separate armistices and treaties were signed between 1918 and 1920 by the Allies on the one side and members of the defeated Central Powers on the other.

Austria

The Austro-Hungarian empire was totally fragmented. Austria was declared a republic—a small, economically unviable nation, without its sources of fuel and raw materials, with no access to the sea, and surrounded by unfriendly neighbors on three sides. It lost its affiliation with Hungary, which was declared an independent state; Bohemia, Moravia, and part of Silesia became a constituent of the new state of Czechoslovakia; South Tyrol, Trieste, Istria, Friuli, and some islands were given to Italy; Bucovina was incorporated into Romania; and West Galicia became a part of Poland, which regained its independence on November 9, 1918.

Hungary

Hungary lost one-third of its territory and population. Slovakia and Ruthenia became part of Czechoslovakia; Transylvania and part of Banat were integrated into Romania; and Croatia, Slavonia, and western Banat were incorporated into the Kingdom of Serbs, Croats, and Slovenes, which in 1929 changed its name to Yugoslavia.

Bulgaria

Bulgaria ceded part of West Thrace to Greece and some border areas to Yugoslavia.

Ottoman Empire (Turkey)

World War I liquidated what was left of the Ottoman Empire and practically eliminated the state altogether, leaving in its control only Constantinople and its immediate surroundings. It was only after the declaration of the republic of Turkey under Kemal Ataturk in 1923 that a new treaty was negotiated under which Turkey recovered some of its territory.

Germany and the Road to World War II

The Treaty of Versailles, signed on June 28, 1919, by Germany on the one side and the Allies (without Russia) on the other, was a humiliating treaty for Germany and was deeply resented by German nationalists; it was the principal treaty among the five peace treaties that ended World

War I. Germany had to give up all its colonies, Alsace-Lorraine was returned to France, and some border territories were lost to Belgium and Denmark. Parts of Upper Silesia and most of West Prussia were integrated into Poland, including a strip of land, the "Polish Corridor," which gave Poland access to the sea but cut East Prussia off from the rest of Germany. The Saar was put under French administration for fifteen years, and the Rhineland was to remain under occupation for the same number of years. Danzig was declared a free city. Germany was also burdened down with massive war reparations.

The first four postwar years were accompanied by economic instability and hardship for defeated Germany. The country was thrown into chaos when, in 1923 French troops marched into the Ruhr claiming that Germany was not abiding by the reparations agreement. The country's workforce went on strike, bringing commercial and industrial activity to a halt. By November, inflation became rampant and all confidence in the Weimar Republic vanished.

In 1913, a twenty-four-year-old Austrian, the son of a poor farmer, having failed in school as well as in his ambition to be an artist, moved to Munich and joined the army at the outbreak of World War I.

The war had a profound influence on young Adolf Hitler. He was wounded and decorated for bravery. After leaving military service in 1920, he became affiliated with a small nationalist party whose name later became the National Socialist German Workers' Party. Hitler was jailed for instigating an attempted coup during the crisis of 1923. While in prison, he wrote *Mein Kampf* (*My Battle*). In his book Hitler argued that Germans are a superior race that is threatened by liberals, Marxists, and Bolsheviks, who, he believed, were all manipulated from behind by Jews. Relief would only come from a dictatorship capable of fighting against these foes, and for that, Lebensraum (living space) had to be conquered to make Germany impregnable.

In April 1925, Field Marshal Paul von Hindenburg was elected president with the support of Prussian conservatives. A period of four years followed in which Germany's economy stabilized and a series of financial reforms set it on the road to recovery. Then the crash of the New York stock market in 1929, which plunged the whole world into depression, hit Germany's budding industry very badly, resulting in massive unemployment and staggering inflation.

Extreme right-wing parties, including the National Socialist Party led by Adolf Hitler, began to agitate against the republic and against democracy. In 1933, aging von Hindenburg appointed Hitler as chancellor and head of government. From 1933 to 1939, Hitler completely transformed Germany into a one-party National Socialist (Nazi) state and an instrument for waging international war. The ruthlessness with which this was carried out was unique in Prussia's or Germany's history.

Early in March 1933, the first concentration camps were established, and on April 1, the Nazis initiated their anti-Semitic policies by a nationwide boycott of Jewish shops. By terror strategies, they suppressed labor unions and all other political parties. On October 14, Hitler withdrew Germany from the League of Nations, and in March 1936, he moved troops into the Rhineland.

In October and November of that year he established the Berlin-Rome Axis and signed a pact with Japan. A year later, Hitler announced his determination to start a war of supremacy in Europe.

The first step was the annexation of Austria. Assisted by widespread German nationalism in Austria, German troops crossed the border on March 13, 1938, and Austria was proclaimed a part of the German Reich. Under the pretext of protecting German minorities in Sudetenland, Hitler convinced France and Great Britain to pressure Czechoslovakia into ceding that territory to Germany in the interest of keeping the peace. Having accomplished this, Hitler's armies nevertheless invaded the rest of Czechoslovakia on March 15, 1939. When, on September 1, 1939, German troops invaded Poland, Britain and France declared war on Germany and World War II became a reality.

GROWING PAINS: THE UNION OF 1918

Ion I. C. Brătianu, leader of the National Liberal Party, who was prime minister in Romania during the war years, and who had resigned rather than accept the humiliating peace terms offered by the Central Powers, regained his position on December 12, 1918. His first major task was the integration of the newly acquired territories. Although the liberal government under General Constantin Coandă had notified the Allies that Romania was entitled to all the territorial claims negotiated in 1916, there were those who believed that Romania's treaty with Germany invalidated these rights.

In a speech on September 27, 1918, Woodrow Wilson stated that self-determination was the best means of resolving territorial disputes in central and southeast Europe. Accordingly, Romanians began the process of unification without waiting for the end of the war or the results of the various peace treaties between the Allies and the member states of the Central Powers.

Bessarabia

One of the unexpected results of the February 1917 Russian revolution and the abdication of Nicholas II was the intensification of the Romanian national movement in Bessarabia. While Romania was still under partial German occupation, a National Assembly (Sfatul Ţării) was established in Chişinău. On December 15, 1917, the assembly declared Bessarabia to be the independent Democratic Republic of Moldavia. As roaming Russian army deserters were creating chaos in Bessarabia, the Russian army occupied Chişinău in January 1918. The National Assembly called on Romania's government in Iaşi to give them support, and an army division was dispatched to Bessarabia. Order was reestablished, and on March 27 the National Assembly voted for unification with the Kingdom of Romania.

Bucovina

On October 27, 1918, just weeks before the end of World War I, Romanians living in Bucovina, led by Iancu Flondor, ex-president of the Romanian National Party of Bucovina, set up the Romanian National Council in Cernăuţi. Its primary objective was to promote the union with Romania. Immediately after the end of the war, local Ukrainians attempted to incorporate northern Bucovina by force, with the support of Ukrainian troops, into the Ukrainian Democratic Republic. Romanian troops were dispatched to Bucovina, and they took control of the province. On November 28, the Romanian National Council of Bucovina declared the "unanimous and unconditional" union with the kingdom of Romania.

Transylvania, the Banat, Crişana, and Maramureş

In Transylvania, Romanians were also beginning to agitate for self-determination. The two Romanian political organizations, the Romanian National Party of Transylvania and the Romanian Social Democratic Party, each issued similar declarations demanding the right of Romanians to self-determination. A Romanian National Council made up of representatives from both parties was created in Budapest. On the eve of the armistice, November 10, it called for a Grand National Assembly to convene in Alba Iulia. The assembly took place on December 1, 1918, and a decree was issued, uniting all Romanians and all territories inhabited by Romanians with the kingdom of Romania. Romanian troops began moving into Transylvania, and military guards were set up throughout the province.

The situation in Transylvania, however, became much more complex than in Bucovina. A Bolshevik, Béla Kun, born in Transylvania, returned from Russia in December and founded the Hungarian Communist Party. Count Mihály Károlyi, president of the new Hungarian republic, after trying unsuccessfully to obtain favorable peace terms from the Allies, with Transylvania occupied by Romanian troops, and with the threat of communism, decided to resign. On March 20, 1919, the Communists and the Social Democrats formed a coalition government under Kun, who set up a "dictatorship of the proletariat."

Hungary was thrown into revolution, and Kun's new Red Army even overran Slovakia.

Concerned with the developments in Hungary and the threat of communism on both east and west borders, Brătianu ordered the troops in Transylvania to advance to the Tisa River. After repelling a Hungarian attack, the troops moved west and by May 1 reached the river, where they took defensive positions.

But Kun's plans also included discussions with Soviet Russia on a common strategy to recover Bessarabia and Transylvania and eventually to turn Romania into a Soviet state. Hungarian armed forces went on the offensive on July 20 and crossed the Tisa River. After a week of fighting, Brătianu ordered Romanian troops to enter Hungary and put an end to Kun and to Communism in that country. When Romanian troops entered Budapest on August 4, Béla Kun had already flown to Vienna, and Hungary was in the hands of a socialist government. The Romanian troops pulled out in November 1919, when Admiral Miklós Horthy's counterrevolutionary army entered the city.

With the threat gone, Transylvania was now safely integrated with the rest of Romania. The occupation of Budapest and the loss of Transylvania left a bitter taste in Hungary, however, and deepened the hostility that was already widespread between Hungary and Romania. It was to continue well into the 1940s.

On December 29, 1919, the Romanian Parliament under the presidency of Nicolae Iorga issued acts that formally ratified the union of Bessarabia, Bucovina, Transylvania, Crişana, Maramureş, and the Banat with Romania. The union was officially sanctioned in the various treaties after World War I.

Prewar Romania consisted of 53,000 square miles and a population of seven-and-one-half million, of which 92 percent were ethnic Romanians. Greater Romania's land surface was now 114,000 square miles, and its population of eighteen million consisted of 71.9 percent ethnic Romanians.

KING FERDINAND'S POSTWAR ROMANIA

Greater Romania was not only a larger country with a greater population. It also acquired a different ethnic makeup, as well as new and complex political issues. New political leaders from Transylvania—such as Alexandru Vaida-Voevod, Iuliu Maniu, and Octavian Goga—encroached on the old established parties, while the Conservative Party became inactive after the death of its leader, Take Ionescu, in 1922.

On June 28, 1919, the Allies signed the Treaty of Versailles with Germany without taking into consideration Romania's request to negotiate war reparations for the great human and material loss sustained while fighting the Germans during 1916 and 1917. The Romanian delegation, led by Ion I. C. Brătianu, as well as those of other small countries were nevertheless forced to sign the treaty. Brătianu sent a memorandum to Georges Clemenceau, the president of the peace conference, requesting that in future treaties Romania should be consulted beforehand. On September 10, the Treaty of St. Germain was signed between the Allies and Austria without giving the Romanian delegation an opportunity to object to unfavorable conditions, such as provisions allowing the Allies to intervene in Romania's internal affairs and giving the Allies rights of free passage of goods and personnel for five years. When Brătianu's objections were rejected, he resigned.

The first postwar elections took place on December 1, 1919. A coalition between the newly formed Peasant Party and the National Party of Transylvania, under Alexandru Vaida-Voevod won the majority. An effort was made to bring about badly needed agrarian reforms, but a series of social and economic crises with resulting strikes impeded these efforts. King Ferdinand (ruled 1919–1927) dismissed the cabinet in March 1920 and called for General Alexandru Averescu, the war hero and leader of a new nationalist right-wing movement, to form a new government. Averescu created a political party called the People's

Party and proceeded to dissolve the Parliament. He put down a general strike in October 1920 and prepared an agrarian reform that was introduced by royal decree in November. On the international scene, Averescu signed a cooperation and non-aggression pact with the neighboring countries of Poland, Czechoslovakia, and Yugoslavia, known as the Little Entente, as protection against the perceived threat of communism and Soviet Russia.

Romania's sudden swing to the right encouraged a consolidation of left-wing parties and the creation of new parties and splinter groups.

By the end of 1921, King Ferdinand was convinced that Romania needed a more Western-type democratic system. He dismissed Averescu and, on January 19, 1922, asked Ion I. C. Brătianu, who had remained a close confidant of the king, to form a new government. With only brief interruptions, Brătianu and his Liberal Party government led the country until 1927, when both he and King Ferdinand died.

Under the liberals, important agrarian and electoral system reforms were introduced. A new liberal and democratic constitution was adopted in 1923 and remained in effect until 1938. It provided for universal suffrage and granted additional rights to minorities, including Jews. During this period, foreign investment in crude oil production and processing, positive economic policies, and a favorable tax structure helped create political stability, economic growth, and prosperity.

At the age of sixty-two, King Ferdinand's health began to fail. At the Peleş Palace on July 20, 1927, he succumbed after a lengthy battle with cancer. Reserved and withdrawn in character, Ferdinand was not a popular figure. Nevertheless, with the support of Brătianu, he maintained political stability in Romania and was able to obtain the Allies' agreement to Romania's territorial claims. He promoted agrarian reform and universal suffrage and supported the introduction of the new constitution. Brătianu, certainly the most influential figure in post-World War I Romania, with whom Ferdinand had always kept a close working relationship, died himself only a few months after the king's death.

THE REGENCY

King Ferdinand and Queen Marie's eldest son, Crown Prince Carol, had renounced his rights to the throne in favor of living with his mistress, Elena (Magda) Lupescu. So when Ferdinand died, Carol's son, Michael, was designated heir to the throne. Michael was only six years old, and a three-member regency headed by Carol's younger brother, Prince Nicholas, the Romanian patriarch Miron Cristea, and the president of the supreme court, Gheorghe Buzdagan, was appointed. The regency lasted from 1927 to 1930.

KING CAROL II

National Peasant Party

At the end of World War I, a schoolteacher named Ion Mihalache founded a new party, the Peasant Party, whose platform was extensive agrarian reforms, expropriation of lands, establishment of peasant cooperatives, and better credit facilities for the peasants. In October 1925, the Peasant Party and the Romanian National Party of Transylvania merged and became the National Peasant Party. Iuliu Maniu was elected chairman of the new party. After Brătianu's death in 1927, his brother, Vintilă I. C. Brătianu, took over the leadership of the government, but in the election of December 1928 the National Peasant Party won 77.76 percent of the electoral vote. The regents asked Iuliu Maniu to form a new cabinet, and the National Peasant Party remained in power until October 1930.

There are differences of opinion among historians regarding the achievements of Iuliu Maniu during these two years. Some believe that he was not strong enough to carry out effective political changes and improved social conditions. He was certainly hampered in his efforts by increasing external influences such as the rise of fascism and Nazism, the spread of communism, and, finally, the financial crash of October 1929. Economic collapse was followed by political

LEFT: Iuliu Maniu (1873–1953), leader of the National Peasant Party

RIGHT: Ion Mihalache (1882–1963), World War I hero and founder and president of the Peasant Party and the National Peasant Party

Private collection of Mircea Carp

crises, strikes by miners, and violent clashes. Conditions were rapidly deteriorating.

Meanwhile, Michael's father, Carol, was living in France and Great Britain with his mistress, having agreed not to return to Romania for ten years. However, in 1930 Iuliu Maniu offered to help Carol by rescinding the disinheritance act if he would return to Romania and claim the throne. He believed that this would reinforce his party and stabilize conditions in Romania. Carol promised Maniu to abide by the constitution and to return without Mme Lupescu. Carol returned to Bucharest on June 6, 1930, but brought his mistress with him. Maniu felt betrayed and resigned the following day in protest. In another attempt at reconciliation, Maniu formed another government, but resigned again on October 10 finding it too difficult to work with Carol.

Carol II's Rise to Power

Born in 1893, Carol was the eldest son of the then Prince Ferdinand and Princess Marie. At the age of twenty-five he deserted from the army and married a commoner, Zizi Lambrino, in Odessa. The marriage created an international scandal and was dissolved by the Romanian supreme court in 1919. In 1921 Crown Prince Carol married Princess Helen, daughter of King Constantine of Greece. Their son, Michael, was born on October 25, 1921. Just as Carol and his family settled down, he formed a romantic relationship with Elena Lupescu (née Magda Wolff) and went with her to live in Paris. In 1925 he renounced his rights to succession in favor of his six-year old son, Prince Michael, but in 1930 he took advantage of Iuliu Maniu's invitation to return to Romania, and became king on June 8, 1930 as Carol II. His wife, Princess Helen, had divorced him in 1928. His reign lasted until September 6, 1940, when he was forced to abdicate by his prime minister, Ion Antonescu, in favor of his son, Michael.

On April 18, 1931, King Carol appointed Nicolae Iorga to form a government. It stayed in power a little over a year. From Carol's return in 1930 until February 1938, when he introduced a royal dictatorship, Romania had eleven governments, of which only one stayed in power for the full four years as specified by the constitution—that of Gheorghe Tătărăscu's Liberal Party (ruled 1934–1937).

National Liberal Party

After the death of Ion I. C. Brătianu, several splinter groups appeared. In 1930 a new National Liberal Party was founded by Gheorghe I. Brătianu, Ion's son. In 1931, another splinter group called itself the Liberal Democratic Party, while the rest of the party split between the

King Carol II

Courtesy of the Photo Archive of the Academia Civică Foundation, Bucharest, and Mircea Carp

old liberals led by Constantin "Dinu" I. C. Brătianu and the young liberals led by Gheorghe Tătărăscu, the minister of industry and commerce. Finally, in 1938 the Gheorghe Brătianu liberals and the Dinu Brătianu liberals reunited, while the Gheorghe Tătărăscu group became inactive.

Legion of the Archangel Michael and the Iron Guard

The right-wing legionary movement began at the University of Iaşi, where a student, Corneliu Zelea Codreanu, participated widely in anti-Communist and anti-Semitic activities. In 1922 he helped found the Association of Christian Students that he affiliated with the League of National Christian Defense (LANC), headed by university professor Alexandru C. Cuza. Codreanu was imprisoned in 1923 for threatening to kill "traitors"; he was arrested again in 1925 on a murder charge, but he was acquitted. In June 1927 he broke with the LANC and, together with four prison friends, founded the Legion of the Archangel Michael. Its basic characteristics, as described in Codreanu's memoirs, were (1) faith in God, (2) faith in the mission, (3) love for each other, and (4) songs as the chief manifestation of the legion's state of mind. The legion had no program: "The country is dying for lack of men, not programs." He then established, in spring 1930, the so-called Iron Guard (Garda de Fier), a militant political section of the legion. His legionary movement would eventually be referred to as the Iron Guard. Its mission was highly nationalistic, anti-Communist, anti-Semitic, and anticorruption, with a mystical religious undertone.

The Iron Guard was declared illegal in 1933 by Liberal Party Prime Minister Ion Gheorghe Duca, and, in retaliation, Duca was murdered on December 31, 1933, by three members of the guard. Despite being declared illegal, the movement flourished. In 1934, Codreanu and General Gheorghe Cantacuzino-Grăniceru, a hero of World War I, founded a political party under the name of All for the Fatherland

Gheorghe I. Brătianu in military uniform, beginning of WWII

Courtesy of the Photo Archive of the Academia Civică Foundation, Bucharest, and Mircea Carp

Party (Totul Pentru Ţară). Between 1934 and 1937 the Iron Guard began to work within the legislative system, and Codreanu himself turned his movement into an organization dedicated to anticorruption and civic responsibility. This gave the legion a sense of respectability, and it gained considerable popular support. Duca's assassination and subsequent acquittal of the Iron Guard assassins by a military tribunal, coupled with increasing external pressures from Nazi Germany and Fascist Italy, convinced King Carol that it was no longer possible to pursue a middle-of-the-road policy.

In August 1936, Carol asked Nicolae Titulescu, his minister of foreign affairs and one of the most brilliant of Romania's diplomats, to resign because he advocated the signing of a mutual assistance pact with the Soviet Union. In February 1937, King Carol met secretly with Codreanu and asked him to form a government, offering to give him full dictatorial powers. Codreanu refused, and in the December 1937 elections the All for the Fatherland Party received 15.58 percent of the electorate vote. This party successfully advocated both national rebirth and social reform, and it opposed Romania's traditional foreign policy in favor of closer relations with Germany and Italy as a means of defending the country against the threat of communism. Codreanu's popularity and his anticorruption drive eventually put him in direct conflict with the king and led to his arrest and imprisonment on trumped-up charges. In March 1938, Carol abolished all political parties to establish the National Renaissance Front and thus assumed dictatorial powers. On the night of November 29, 1938, while Codreanu was being shuttled between prisons, he and thirteen of his associates were assassinated, supposedly while trying to escape. In turn, Prime Minister Armand Călinescu was assassinated by members of the Iron Guard on September 21, 1939. In retaliation, Carol ordered the killing without trial of 252 members of the Iron Guard. Their leaders were exposed in the public squares of several cities in Romania. Many of the Iron Guard members fled to Germany and were trained there by Nazi SS troops in terrorist tactics.

Nicolae Titulescu

Nicolae Titulescu (1883–1941) studied law in France. Returning to Romania in 1904, he taught at the University of Iaşi, where he received his doctorate in civil law in 1905. His resignation in 1936 ended a brilliant career as a politician, statesman, and diplomat. In 1917, in the government of Ion I. C. Brătianu, he became minister of finance. He was a delegate to peace negotiations at St. Germain and Trianon and was one of the signatories of the Treaty of Trianon in June 1920. The following year he was sent to London as Romanian ambassador and held that post until 1927, when he became minister of foreign affairs. In that capacity, for more than seven years, Titulescu acted as a relentless defender of the principles laid down by the League of Nations. King Carol supported his policies, and under his guidance worked toward establishing a "peace zone" in the Balkans. Titulescu was the permanent representative of Romania to the League of Nations and became the only diplomat to be twice elected president of the League (1930, 1931). After his forced resignation, Titulescu went into exile to France, where he continued to use his extensive contacts and influence in diplomatic circles to work in the interests of Romania.

National Christian Party

General Alexandru Averescu's People's Party broke up into several splinter groups after 1927. The most important group broke away in 1932, led by the poet Octavian Goga, who founded the National Agrarian Party, which, in turn, merged in 1935 with A. C. Cuza's right-wing anti-Semitic League of National Christian Defense. In the elections of December 1937, thirteen major political parties and fifty-three minor groups ran for office, with the result that none of the parties won a majority. King Carol decided to name Goga to form a new government, even though the National Christian Party only received 9.15 percent of the electorate vote. Democracy was on its way out.

During the month-and-a-half that Goga's cabinet stayed in power, it closed many newspapers and adopted a series of anti-Semitic bills that caused outrage and concern in the banking and industrial sectors and discouraged foreign investment in Romania. When Western powers protested against Goga's anti-Semitic measures, Carol abruptly dismissed the cabinet and on February 24, 1938, submitted a new constitution based on the Royal Dictatorship to a public referendum. It was overwhelmingly approved, as anyone opposing the new constitution was subject to arrest. On March 30 all political parties were dissolved, and on December 16 the National Renaissance Front (Frontul Renaşterei Naţionale) was founded, the only legal political formation allowed. Carol's constitution eliminated practically all of the democratic institutions introduced by King Carol I and King Ferdinand.

Octavian Goga (1881–1938)
Courtesy of Regia Naţională "Monitorul Oficial," Romanian Parliament

Royal Dictatorship

Between February 10, 1938, and September 4, 1940, six separate governments led the country. It was a period of political uncertainty but the economy blossomed. Industrial production reached its highest peak, partially as a result of Germany's imports in preparation of war.

In November 1938, Carol went to London and Paris in search of more substantial support but received no tangible promises. Neville Chamberlain told Carol that it was inevitable that Germany should dominate the area economically.

On March 15, 1939, Germany invaded and occupied Czechoslovakia. Tension grew in Romania. King Carol signed a trade agreement with Germany on March 24, putting the country's entire economy and oil production at the disposal of Germany. On April 13, Britain and France promised to guarantee Romanian territorial integrity, but, pressured by Germany, the Royal Dictatorship swung further to the right instead. On June 1, Romania repudiated the British and French guarantees, and on July 10 it withdrew from the League of Nations. When German troops invaded Poland and World War II broke out on September 1, 1939, Romania declared itself neutral.

By the end of 1939, King Carol felt that his Royal Dictatorship was not receiving the popular support he had counted on. He recalled Gheorghe Tătărăscu to form a new government, and he appealed to all parties to support him in defending the nation against dangers from abroad. When both Iuliu Maniu and Constantin I. C. Brătianu refused to participate in the new government, Carol concluded a reconciliation with the Iron Guard, releasing the guard leaders from prison. By the end of April 1940, the guard pledged allegiance to the National Renaissance Front. Horia Sima (who had taken over the Iron Guard leadership from Codreanu) and other guard members (who had taken refuge in Germany) were allowed to return to Romania, and three cabinet posts were given to Iron Guardists.

As Germany proceeded with its lightning offensives, Stalin took advantage of the general confusion to give Romania an ultimatum on

June 27, 1940, to evacuate Bessarabia and northern Bucovina. Under pressure from Germany, Tătărăscu and Carol were forced to relent. Tătărăscu took the blame for this loss and resigned on July 4. The Soviet Army invaded and occupied the provinces, eventually deporting between 100,000 and 500,000 Romanians to Siberia and Central Asia. Unlike Finland in 1940, however, Moscow avoided concluding an international treaty establishing a new Soviet-Romanian border in hopes of further gains at Romanian expense. With the fall of France in June, the king decided to take another step closer to the Berlin-Rome Axis. He changed the name of the National Renaissance Front to the Party of the Nation (Partidul Naţiunii) under his own leadership, and on July 4, he appointed Ion Gigârtu to form a far-right government, under which anti-Semitism became official policy. In a series of acts, Jews were forbidden to hold any public office, to practice law, or to serve in the military forces. Marriage between ethnic Romanians and Jews became illegal, and public education at all levels was severely restricted. Horia Sima was made minister of education. He later became minister of art and culture.

By taking these pro-Axis steps, Carol was hoping to gain Nazi Germany's support in protecting Romania's borders. Events proved otherwise. The loss of Bessarabia and northern Bucovina without resistance to the Soviet Union triggered a movement in Budapest for war with Romania to recapture Transylvania. Bulgaria, too, was intent on repossessing southern Dobrogea. A war in the Balkans was the last thing that Hitler wanted to face at a time when he was preparing for an offensive against the Soviet Union. Under German pressure, Romanian-Hungarian negotiations took place at Turnu Severin, but no agreement was reached. On August 29, 1940, a Romanian delegation headed by the foreign minister, Mihail Manoilescu, was told that to avoid war it must accept a decision taken by the Axis arbitrators, the foreign ministers Joachim Ribbentrop and Galeazzo Ciano. When shown the portion of northern Transylvania given to Hungary, Manoilescu fainted on the spot. On August 30, 1940, the Axis awarded northern Transylvania to Hungary, and in September Romania was forced to return southern Dobrogea to Bulgaria. This was a final blow to King Carol. Having given up one-third of Romania's territory and population without a struggle, Carol lost what little support he had managed to retain.

On September 4, the king suspended the constitution entirely, dissolved Parliament, and asked General Ion Antonescu, the chief of general staff and minister of national defense, to govern the country, granting him full dictatorial powers. Within twenty-four hours of his new appointment, with full backing from the National Liberal Party and the National Peasant Party, Antonescu gave Carol an ultimatum to abdicate and leave the country. On September 6, 1940, King Carol II officially turned the throne over to his son, Michael, now nineteen years old, and left Romania the day after with his mistress, Mme Lupescu.

ROMANIA IN 1940
HUNGARY
SOVIET
UNION
YUGOSLAVIA
BULGARIA
ROMANIA
BLACK SEA
Northern Transylvania
(Awarded to Hungary by the Diktat of Vienna, 30 August 1940)
Northern Bucovina
Bessarabia
(Occupied by the Soviet Union 28 June 1940)
Southern Dobrodgea
(Ceded to Bulgaria 7 September 1940)
Debrecen
Satu Mare
Baia Mare
Oradea
Bistrita
Cluj
Turda
Targu Mures
Blaj
Sighisoara
Arad
Timisoara
Sibiu
Cernauti
Hotin
Siret
Radauti
Suceava
Vatra Dornei
Botosani
Soroca
Balti
Iasi
Chisinau
Tighina
Tiraspol
Piatra Neamt
Husi
Vaslui
Barlad
Cetatea Alba
Miercurea Ciuc
Sfantu Gheorghe
Brasov
Focsani
Galati
Buzau
Curtea de Arges
Targu Jiu
Ploiesti
Belgrade
Turnu Severin
Bucharest
Craiova
Constanta
Turtucaia
Mangalia
Balcic
Danube River

World War II

CHAPTER 11

The Antonescu Regime
(1940 to 1944)

PERSPECTIVE

In the conflict that is generally referred to as World War II, more than fifty nations participated on one side or another, and most of the people inhabiting the earth were directly or indirectly involved. Although many of the countries and their citizens made incalculable sacrifices and endured great suffering, only the United States and Great Britain can be said to have fought a global war.

The portion of World War II that directly or indirectly affected Romania was the one fought in Europe and was directly attributable to Adolf Hitler and Nazi Germany. However, Nazism would probably never have had the opportunity of taking root had it not been for the humiliating peace treaties of World War I.

After Hitler's occupation of Austria and Czechoslovakia, Great Britain and France reluctantly declared war on Germany three days after its troops crossed the border into Poland on September 1, 1939.

Before attacking Poland, Germany first signed a non-aggression pact with its archenemy, the Soviet Union, with an understanding that Poland would be divided between them. By the end of 1939 this was accomplished. During the last two weeks of September, the Soviet Union forced the three Baltic states of Estonia, Latvia, and Lithuania to grant it rights to station Soviet troops and build bases on their territory. On November 30, Soviet forces attacked Finland. The war with Finland lasted until March 1940, with heavy losses on both sides. Finland lost the war but managed to remain independent.

On April 9, 1940, Germany began the invasion of Norway. Assisted by British and French troops, Norway put up resistance, but as the French and British armies were collapsing in France, an armistice was signed between Norway and Germany. In the meantime, German troops occupied Denmark and overran Holland, which surrendered in five days after the destruction of Rotterdam. On May 10, the German troops advanced into Belgium, and, after a lightning offensive, on June 22 they entered Paris. France surrendered and signed an armistice with Germany, dividing the nation into occupied and unoccupied zones.

Italy, which at first remained neutral, intervened on Germany's behalf on June 10, 1940. During August and September 1940, Germany launched massive air bombardments on Great Britain in preparation of an invasion. The Battle of Britain was won by the Royal Air Force, and the invasion never took place. Hungary, Romania, and Slovakia joined the Axis in November.

Hitler regarded control of the Balkans as a necessary step before invading the Soviet Union, which he originally planned for May 15, 1941. On March 1, 1941, Bulgaria joined the Axis, and shortly after that Germany invaded Yugoslavia. Its troops met up with the Italian forces, and both moved toward Greece. By April 27, Yugoslavia and Greece were occupied. On June 22, Hitler abandoned the non-aggression pact of 1939 and launched a massive invasion of the Soviet Union.

Within fewer than two years, almost all of Europe was at war, and concentration camps were being built in occupied countries for the main purpose of exterminating the world's Jewish population. An estimate of close to six million men, women, and children died in these camps before the end of the war.

Throughout 1941 and 1942, the German offensive against the Soviet Union met up with fierce resistance. Soviet counteroffensives and severe winter conditions brought the Germans to a halt on the outskirts of Moscow in December 1941 and at Stalingrad (Volgograd) in November 1942. By February 2, 1943, the last of the German forces surrendered.

Meanwhile, the United States, which made every effort short of entering the war to support Great Britain militarily, finally declared war on Japan after the devastating strike on Pearl Harbor in the Hawaiian Islands on December 7, 1941; three days later, President Franklin D. Roosevelt declared war on Germany and Italy, too.

The invasion of Europe by the Allies began when British-American troops from North Africa landed in Sicily on July 10, 1943. After disastrous losses in North Africa and the Eastern Front, Italy surrendered on September 3, 1943, and Allied forces landed on Italy's mainland. The Italians found themselves fighting with the Allies against Germany. Rome was captured on June 4, 1944, and by May 1945 the Germans surrendered in Italy.

The Allies landed on the beaches of Normandy on June 6, 1944 (D-Day), and began the advance eastward toward Germany, while U.S. troops landed in southern France near Cannes. The crossing of the Rhine River began on March 23, 1945, while Soviet forces drove the Germans out of the Soviet Union into Germany, Poland, Czechoslovakia, Hungary, and Romania. With Berlin surrounded, Hitler committed suicide, and on May 7, 1945, the German government surrendered to the Allies at Rheims, France.

The war continued in the Pacific for another four months, until Japan surrendered on September 2, 1945, after two atomic bombs were dropped by the United States over Hiroshima and Nagasaki.

Thus ended a war that resulted in an estimated thirty-five to sixty million deaths, of which eighteen million were Soviet military and civilians alone, as well as incalculable suffering and destruction. The United Nations was established on October 24, 1945.

ION ANTONESCU

Time and time again, throughout the history of Romania and its people, from the formation of the principalities, back in the fourteenth century, rival foreign powers endangered Romania's independence and territorial integrity. Rulers often had to resort to astute diplomatic and military tactics for the nation's survival. It was the same in World War I, and no different during World War II. When Ion Antonescu (ruled 1940–1944) took over the leadership of the country on September 4, 1940, Romania was again in great danger. Great Britain was being bombarded by the German Luftwaffe, France had surrendered; Nazi Germany was in control of central Europe, and the might of the Soviet Red Army was a constant threat on Romania's eastern borders. Romania was still neutral, but one-third of its territory had been lost to the Soviet Union, Hungary, and Bulgaria; it was economically dependent on Germany, and it depended on Germany to dissuade further Soviet incursions. It was Antonescu's turn, for better or for worse, to steer the nation through these troubled and dangerous waters.

Ion Antonescu was born in 1882 in Piteşti, of a military family, and he carried on this tradition. He attended military schools where he graduated at the top of his class. As a captain he distinguished himself during the Balkan War in 1913, and again as a major in World War I, where he played an important role in the defense of Moldavia during the 1917 German offensive. Strongly anti-German, he opposed the separate peace with the Central Powers. Antonescu earned the respect of France and Great Britain while serving as military attaché in Paris in 1922 and in London from 1923 to 1927. Promoted to chief of general staff with the rank of general in 1934, he became minister of national defense under the short-lived Goga government in 1937.

When at an audience with King Carol in July 1940, he protested the king's intention to cede Bessarabia and northern Bucovina to the Soviet Union without military resistance, and asked for a mandate to form a new government, Carol had him arrested. Diplomatic

Marshal Ion Antonescu, leader of Romania from 1940–1944

Private collection of Mircea Carp

intervention from Germany, where Antonescu was also highly regarded as a man of integrity, capable of taking control of Romania, forced the king to offer him the mandate after all. Carol counted on Antonescu's good relations with the Germans, and the Iron Guard leadership, as well as with the leaders of the National Liberal Party and the National Peasant Party, to preserve his Royal Dictatorship. In less than twenty-four hours after he was appointed as leader, Antonescu, with full support of the German legation, Iuliu Maniu, and Constantin I. Brătianu, asked Carol to abdicate and leave the country. On September 6, 1940, the king turned the throne over to his son, Michael, who once again became King Michael (Mihai) I (ruled 1940–1947).

National Legionary State

On September 6, 1940, the day King Michael was inaugurated, he issued a decree giving Ion Antonescu full dictatorial powers as the leader of the Romanian state (Conducătorul Statului Român). Antonescu also took the titles of chief of state and president of the council of ministers.

His initial intention was to set up a government composed of all major parties, and while both Maniu and Brătianu agreed that an authoritarian regime was necessary under the circumstances, neither agreed to join formally such a regime. Although both offered their services in an advisory capacity and declared their willingness to allow members of their parties to accept ministerial positions, only Brătianu's liberals actually did so. When this project failed, and as the result of German insistence, Antonescu formed a government composed mainly of Iron Guard leaders, military officers in the Ministry of National Defense, and some nonpolitical finance specialists in the Ministry of National Economy. Horia Sima was named vice president of the council, and Mihai Antonescu (no relation), a professor of law at the University of Bucharest, was appointed minister of justice. Romania was declared a National Legionary State.

It soon became evident that the political alliance between Antonescu and Sima's Iron Guard was not going to work out. Sima accused Antonescu of being too lenient and of preventing the establishment of "the new order" in Romania. Antonescu accused Sima of brutalizing and robbing the Jewish population and sabotaging his attempt to rebuild the Romanian state. This situation came to a head when, on November 26, members of the Iron Guard broke into a prison and murdered sixty-four former political leaders and officers who had been jailed for their involvement in the assassination of Corneliu Zelea Codreanu. Guard members also dragged Virgil Madgearu, a National Peasant Party leader and Nicolae Iorga, historian and former leader of the Democratic Nationalist Party, out of their homes and shot them. They held Iorga responsible for the arrest, imprisonment, and ultimately assassination of Codreanu.

Antonescu met Hitler on January 14, 1941, to obtain his support in dealing with the Iron Guard. He accused the Guard of creating anarchy in Romania and proposed that the National Legionary State be under his own leadership. He told Hitler that he would either remove legionnaires from all governmental positions and create a military dictatorship, or he would completely reorganize the Iron Guard under his control. While Hitler was still supportive of the legionary movement, he also needed a stable Romania for his future plans, and he assured Antonescu of his support. Reassured, Antonescu set in motion his plan by dismissing the minister of the interior and other security officials. Concurrently, with the assistance of the German SS and Nazi Party, Sima was organizing a coup to oust Antonescu. On the night of January 21, a full-scale revolt broke out in Bucharest. Throughout the city, shops were burned, synagogues were desecrated, the radio station and other public buildings were occupied, and people were assaulted. By the end of the next day, Antonescu received Hitler's consent, assuring him that he was "the only man capable of guiding the destinies of Romania."[1] With full support of the army and of the German military mission in Romania, the rebellion was crushed and the Iron Guard surrendered. Some 240 people were dead, 124 Jews among them. During the following months, over 9,000 guard members were arrested. Many others escaped to Germany, aided by German Legation officials.

A new government composed almost entirely of generals was formed on January 27, and on February 14 the National Legionary State was officially abolished.

Romania at War

Ion Antonescu had served as military attaché in both Paris and London, and he was fundamentally pro-British and pro-French. However, he did not trust the Soviet Union, communism being anathema to Antonescu's nationalist upbringing and principles. Furthermore, the Soviet Union had occupied Romanian territory and was still pressing Germany to allow its further expansion into southern Bucovina and part of Dobrogea. The Allies were in no position to give support to Romania at that stage of the war, while Nazi Germany was already in military and economic control of central Europe and appeared willing to prevent further Soviet encroachments in Romania in order to protect its access to Romanian oil resources. In his view, Antonescu had no other option but to play the German card. On October 8, 1940, a German "military mission" composed of over 20,000 men and equipment set up headquarters in Romania.

During Antonescu's meeting with Hitler on January 14, 1941, he was informed of Operation Barbarossa, the planned invasion of the Soviet Union that was to take place on June 22, 1941. On that date, Antonescu declared war on the Soviet Union and ordered Romanian troops to cross the Prut River. He appointed Mihai Antonescu vice president of the Council of Ministers, and he himself became commander-in-chief of Romania's armed forces. By July 27, both Bessarabia and northern Bucovina were captured, at a cost of 10,486 Romanian dead.

Up to that point, Antonescu had the nation's full support in his undertaking, with the exception of the Romanian Communist Party. Once Romania regained its territories, King Michael, as well as Maniu and Brătianu, urged him to disengage and bring his troops back home. But Antonescu, now promoted to the rank of marshal, did not heed their advice, believing that his political leverage within the "alliance" with Germany, as well as Romania's sovereignty could not be maintained without further military effort. He therefore continued to lead his troops alongside the German armies. After confronting fierce resistance, the combined German-Romanian troops captured Odessa on October 16. Over 27,000 Romanian soldiers died in that offensive, in addition to 89,000 wounded and 14,000 missing in action.

As a reward, Germany gave Romania control over a Ukrainian territory extending from Bessarabia to the Bug and Dniester Rivers, including Odessa. This region was named Transnistria, and became known for its detention camps where Jews and other "non-Romanians" from Bessarabia and Bucovina were subsequently deported. At the time Romania took over the administration of Transnistria, the population of the region was two and one-half million, the majority of whom were Ukrainians and Russians. Among them were 300,000 Jews, 290,000 Romanians, and 125,000 Germans.

After Odessa, Antonescu once again ignored pleas to end hostilities, arguing that the Germans would react by occupying Romania. Aside from causing additional loss of Romanian blood, such an act would threaten the country's independence. Meanwhile, as the Soviet Union was an ally of Great Britain, Stalin urged Winston Churchill to take action against Romania. On November 28, the British government sent an ultimatum to Romania to cease all military operations against the Soviet Union by December 5. When Britain officially declared war on Romania on December 7, 1941, Antonescu, in a radio broadcast, expressed regret that Romania's centuries-old struggle to preserve its existence was not understood. Although Romania declared war on the United States five days later, Washington did not reciprocate until June 5, 1942, immediately after the Anglo-Soviet Treaty was concluded. One of the central sticking points of that treaty had been Stalin's insistence that the British accept the territorial gains made as a result of the Soviet invasion and occupation of Romania (and Finland, the Baltic states, and Poland) from 1930 to 1940.

During the next year, both the government and the leaders of the National Liberal Party (NLP) and the National Peasant Party (NPP) made contacts with the Allies through diplomatic channels, offering to stage a coup against a guarantee by the Allies of Romania's independence and its borders, but they had no success. As early as March 1943, Anthony Eden, Great Britain's foreign secretary and Winston Churchill's principal negotiator, made Britain's policy toward Romania clear. He said that no commitments and no action would be considered without the full consent of the Soviet Union.[2] The offensive against the Soviet Union continued. The major objectives of the German summer offensive in 1942 were the capture of Stalingrad and the conquest of the Caucasian oilfields. The Romanian armies were deployed to protect the German flanks. As the bitter cold winter approached, the Soviet army broke through the front of the Third Romanian Army on the Don and through the Fourth Romanian Army, south of Stalingrad. German and Romanian troops continued to put up stiff resistance in a desperate effort to hold Stalingrad, but by January supplies were running out, and Soviet forces went on the offensive.

The Romanian government began renewed negotiations with the Allies to pull out of the war. On March 26, 1944, the Soviet Red Army reached the Prut River. While the British and Americans refused to negotiate, steadfastly insisting on an unconditional surrender, the Soviet Union offered terms that eventually included the immediate end of hostilities against the Soviet Union, the expulsion of German troops from the country, official recognition that Bessarabia and northern Bucovina were Soviet territories at the time of Romania's entrance into the war, and free passage of Soviet troops through

Romania. In exchange, all or the major part of northern Transylvania would be returned to Romania.

The Antonescu government flatly refused to provide Moscow with a legal justification for its invasion and occupation of Romania by granting an after-the-fact recognition of Bessarabia and northern Bucovina as Soviet territory in 1940. Aside from robbing Romania of the protections offered by the Atlantic Charter, it would cast Romania into the role of aggressor state with everything that implied at the peace conference. Antonescu also refused to accept the principle of free passage unless it included the safeguard of a designated territory in and around Bucharest to where Romanian troops could withdraw and where no foreign (Soviet) forces would be permitted to enter.

In June of 1944, the NPP, the NLP, the Social Democratic Party (SDP), and the Romanian Communist Party (RCP) agreed to found the National Democratic Bloc (NDB), and Iuliu Maniu communicated to the Allies the new bloc's intention to overthrow the Antonescu dictatorship if the Romanian leader did not withdraw from the war and accept an armistice in accordance with the Allied terms at the right time. On August 20, an anticipated Soviet offensive was launched on the Romanian front. On the evening of August 22, the bloc's leaders met with the king and agreed that if Antonescu did not withdraw from the war by August 26, the opposition and palace would overthrow him and withdraw themselves. On August 23, the palace decided to take unilateral action and arrested Antonescu, a move that was later supported by the rest of the opposition. That evening, the king announced in a radio broadcast to the nation that Antonescu's dictatorship was terminated and that a new government composed of members of the NDB would be formed. He also announced a break of diplomatic relations with Germany and an armistice with the Allies. General Constantin Sănătescu, an aide to the king who played an important part in organizing the coup, was appointed prime minister. The two Antonescus were subsequently turned over to Romanian Communists who, in turn, handed them over to Soviet military forces that entered Bucharest a week later.

JEWS OF ROMANIA*

In the region that is now Romania, there were very few Jews before the nineteenth century. During the seventh century B.C., a small number of Jewish traders and merchants settled in Greek colonies along the shore of the Black Sea, such as Tomis, now Constanţa. Others came with the Romans during the second century A.D., when Dacia was being colonized. An estimated 1,000 to 5,000 Jews who emigrated from Spain during the crusades and inquisition of the fifteenth and sixteenth centuries, settled in Moldavia and Wallachia. It was only in the nineteenth century that the Jewish population in Romania increased dramatically. Violent pogroms against the Jews in southern and southwestern Russia during the period of the Czars forced many to flee to Romania, particularly to Moldavia. In 1899 there were 269,000 Jews in Romania—200,000 in Moldavia and 69,000 in Wallachia.

By 1939, at the beginning of World War II, Greater Romania's Jewish population peaked at around 800,000, over half of them in Bessarabia, Bucovina, and Transylvania, which united with Romania at the end of World War I. In 1940, after the loss of Bessarabia, northern Transylvania, and northern Bucovina, the total Jewish population in Romania was 312,972.[3]

Jewish Holocaust

In Germany the Nazis initiated their anti-Semitic policies on April 1, 1933, following up in 1935 with the Nuremberg Laws, which effectively eliminated the German Jews legally and economically. The

*Figures given in this section on the number of inhabitants, deportations, and deaths are a result of tabulating data from the following sources: Dr. K. Treptow, Radu Ioanid, Associate Director of the International Pogroms Division of the United States Holocaust Memorial Museum, and the following books: *Eichmann in Jerusalem*, *Genocide and Retribution*, *The Destruction of Romanian and Ukrainian Jews*, *The Silent Holocaust*, *The Destruction of the European Jew*, and *The Holocaust in Romania*. (See Bibliography.)

tragedy that befell the rest of Europe's Jews began only after the outbreak of World War II, as Germany invaded and occupied one country after another.

In Romania, most restrictions imposed on those considered as non-Romanians, including Jews, were removed under the constitution of 1866 and confirmed by the Treaty of Berlin in 1878. In 1923, under Ion I. C. Brătianu, a revision of the 1866 constitution became even more liberal and democratic.

Anti-Semitism was present in Romania since the eighteenth century, but sporadic anti-Semitic riots became a regular phenomenon only during the first decades of the twentieth century. Bowing to increasing anti-Semitism with the rise of Hitler, King Carol II authorized the "revision" of Jewish citizenship. At the very end of 1937, the so-called Goga-Cuza government had already enacted heavy anti-Semitic legislation. *Numerus clausus*, a law that would strip approximately 200,000 Jews of their citizenship, was to become a fact. On February 24, 1938, the king rescinded the 1923 constitution and replaced it with one that eliminated practically all of the democratic institutions introduced by King Carol I and King Ferdinand. As Carol moved the country closer to the Berlin–Rome Axis, so anti-Semitism also increased.

On August 8, 1940, under Ion Gigârtu's far-right government, Law No. 2650 was enacted and approved by King Carol II. It defined who was to be considered a Jew. Under this law, Jews lost many of their rights (including rural property), were excluded from military service, and were obliged to report for compulsory labor. Another law forbade marriages between Romanians "by blood" and Jews.

Meanwhile, Nazi Germany proceeded methodically to introduce new steps toward the "final solution" of the "Jewish question." First came expulsions, then emigration, followed by the displacement of whole Jewish populations into ghettos. Finally, on July 31, 1941, Hermann Gring issued orders to Gestapo's Reinhard Heydrich to prepare a comprehensive plan for the final solution. Six months later, at the Wansee Conference, the plan was put into effect, and shortly thereafter the first extermination camp was installed in Poland. But even before this last step was initiated, with the invasion of the Soviet Union on June 22, German killing squads called Einsatzgruppen, totaling 3,000 men, were ordered to follow the German troops and systematically kill all Jews and Soviet political commissars.

Iași Pogrom

On the same date that Germany began Operation Barbarossa, Romania declared war on the Soviet Union. Since Bessarabia was annexed by the Soviet Union, Iași, the former capital of Moldavia, had become a border town, only ten miles away from the front line. According to available statistics, on the eve of the war some 100,000 people inhabited the city, 50,000 of them being Jewish. While Jews and Christians had long lived together peacefully, Iași was also the city where such extreme-right leaders as A. C. Cuza and C. Z. Codreanu began their political careers.

Just before Romania's entry into the war, the first operational echelon of the SSI (Secret Intelligence Service) was created "to defend the rear against sabotage, espionage, and acts of terror." On June 18, 1941, this unit traveled to Moldavia to prepare the ground for deportation of Jews and Communists from border areas. After a second Soviet air raid, on June 26, it was reported that Russian paratroopers landed behind lines and that they "had accomplices among 'Judeo-Communist' suspects in Iași."[4] The same day, the first Jewish inhabitants were killed. On June 27, the chief of police accused the Jewish population of involvement with Soviet agents and warned the leaders of the Jewish community that 100 Jews would be killed for each Romanian or German soldier killed. Hysteria built up to such a degree that on June 28 and 29, thousands of Jews were dragged out of their homes by military and police personnel and massacred. Another 4,332 survivors were hauled onto sealed railcars and shuttled back and forth until they died of hunger, thirst, and the intense summer heat.

The total number of Jews who died during the Iaşi massacre was estimated at 3,000 to 5,000, although a 1943 census published by the Jewish Center of Romania puts the figure at 8,751, and a document issued by the SSI in the same year, based on lists prepared by the synagogues of Iaşi, indicates that 13,266 Jews perished during that tragic event.

Romania as a Whole

While Jews in Romania as a whole suffered severe persecution, and atrocities such as the Iaşi pogrom were committed, they fared better than those in Bessarabia, Bucovina, and northern Transylvania. No systematic deportation to Nazi death camps took place despite Nazi insistence. Synagogues were closed and then opened again; Jews were ordered to wear the Star of David badges, and then the decree was rescinded. Jewish high schools stayed open throughout the war, and in Bucharest a Jewish theater and orchestra continued to function. At the end of 1942, the Romanian government began to facilitate Jewish emigration to Palestine. An estimated 20,000 Jews within truncated Romania were killed during that period.

Bessarabia, Bucovina, and Northern Transylvania

The Jewish population of Bessarabia and Bucovina, while under Romanian occupation, suffered the brunt of the Romanian Jewish holocaust. The full statistical picture of the human carnage in these reoccupied provinces may never be accurately determined. Between 45,000 and 60,000 Jews were killed by Romanian and German troops in 1941. At least 75,000 died as a result of deportations to Transnistria. During the postwar trial of Romanians accused of war crimes, Wilhelm Filderman, former head of the Federation of Unions of Jewish Congregations, declared that at least 150,000 Bessarabian and Bucovinian Jews died during the Antonescu regime. Other estimates are as high as 270,000.

In northern Transylvania, while under Hungarian occupation, 148,172 Jews were deported to the Auschwitz death camp in March 1944. Only 29,405 survived.

END OF THE WAR

In September 1944, the Jewish population of Romania that survived the Holocaust was estimated at 300,000 persons. According to data furnished by the Jewish World Congress of 1947, there were 428,312 Jews in Romania in 1945. A large number of displaced persons who had escaped from Hungary, Poland, and Transnistria accounts for the difference in numbers.

Where does responsibility lie for the atrocities committed in Romania and the Romanian-occupied territories of Transnistria, Bessarabia, and northern Bucovina during the Antonescu regime? Although there is much documentation available that tends to imply active or passive involvement of the Antonescus, it has not been established exactly who gave the first orders, how they were transmitted, or what ranks of military and police personnel took part, or whether the orders were given on the Romanians' own initiative or with the support or assistance of the German Einsatzgruppen.

Nevertheless, the mass deportation of Jews to Nazi extermination camps was twice postponed by direct intervention of Wilhelm Filderman and Dr. Ştefan Antal, another Jewish leader, with Metropolitan Nicolae Bălan and Ion Antonescu. In fact, it was completely abandoned, as Romanian authorities began to prepare measures authorizing emigration of Jews to Palestine.

There is also ample documentation regarding the innumerable humanitarian acts by Romanian officials, military officers, and civilians who helped thousands of Jews survive the Holocaust.

NOTES

1. Andreas Hillgruber, *Hitler, König Carol und Marschall Antonescu, Die deutsch-rumänishen Beziehungen 1938–1944*, (Wiesbaden, Germany: F. Steiner, 1954), 117–119.
2. Georgescu, *The Romanians–A History*, 218.
3. Matei Dogan, *Analiza statistică a democrației parlamentare din România,* (Bucharest: Federaţia Comunităţilor Evreieşti; Monografie., 1946), XXI. & several other unpublished sources.
4. Matatias Carp, *Cartea Neagră*, vol. 2, (Bucharest, Romania: Diogene, 1996), 102.
5. Cristian Troncotă, *Eugen Cristescu, asul serviciilor secrete românești*, (Bucharest, Romania, 1996), 118–119; archival source: USHMM/SRI, folder 11314, 28.

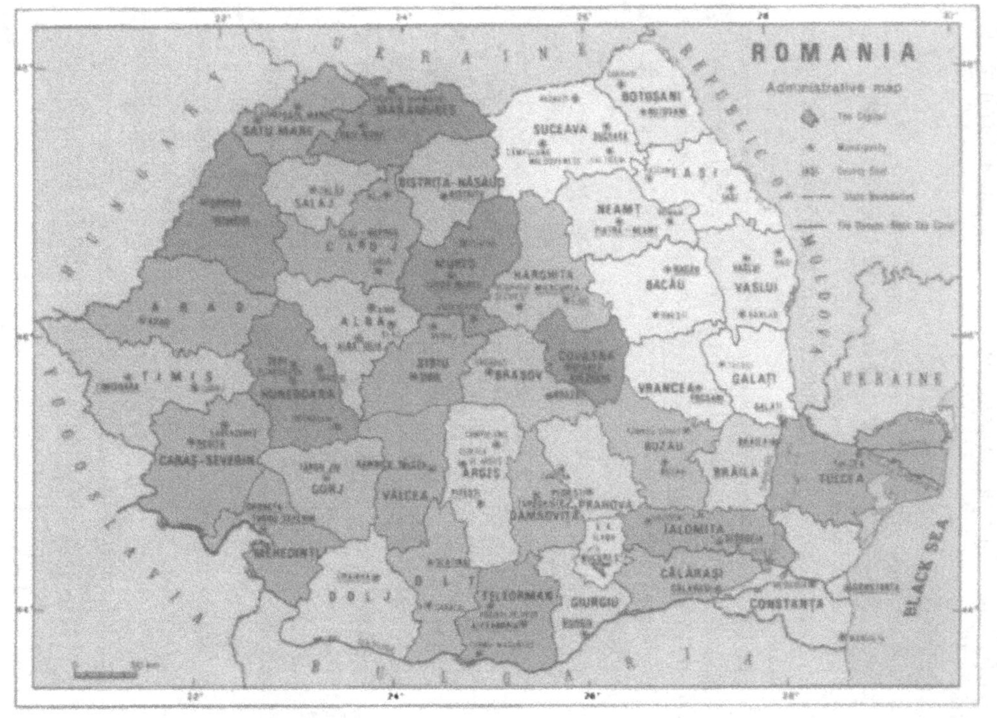

Into and Out of Communism (administrative map after 1965)

Reprinted with permission from the Center for Romanian Studies.

CHAPTER 12

Romania Under Communism (1944 to 1989)

PERSPECTIVE

In the aftermath of World War II, western European countries began the process of recovery from the staggering loss of lives and destruction of their economic wealth. Two major world-class powers emerged, the United States of America and the Soviet Union. As the Red Army overran eastern Europe and fought its way into Berlin, the Soviet Union established control over the occupied countries, where they installed and supported Communist governments. In response, the nations of western Europe allied themselves with the United States, thus creating two sharply divided political and military blocs on the continent.

By 1947, the failure to revive industrial and agricultural production in western Europe demonstrated that closer economic cooperation between states was necessary. The United States offered large-scale direct economic and military aid to all European countries by means of the Marshall Plan, named after its creator, then U.S. Secretary of State George Marshall. The Soviet government and the other eastern European Communist countries refused to participate in this scheme. The aid plan was put into effect in April 1948, when the U.S. Congress passed the Economic Cooperation Act and sixteen recipient countries set up the Organization for European Economic Cooperation (OEEC). The aid plan proved to be a very effective scheme, and in the postwar decades western Europe enjoyed an unprecedented period of prosperity and economic growth. In turn, eastern bloc countries set up the Council for Mutual Economic Assistance (Comecon) in January 1949.

In March 1947, the United States announced a change in its international policy toward the Soviet Union. The object of the Truman Doctrine was to contain Communist expansion by supporting "free people who are resisting attempted subjugation by armed minorities or outside pressure."[1] Hostility built up between the two superpowers, and Stalin lowered the "Iron Curtain" between the Communist bloc countries and the West. The Soviet Union tested its first nuclear fission bomb in 1949 and the first thermonuclear device in 1953. Fear of a nuclear war prevented direct military confrontation, and the "Cold War" was fought on economic, political, and ideological fronts.

In April 1949, the North Atlantic Treaty Organization (NATO), a mutual defense pact, was signed by the United States, Canada, and ten western European countries. In response to NATO, the Communist bloc countries signed the Warsaw Pact in May 1955. The Cold War reached its peak with the Cuban missile crisis in 1963.

After Germany's defeat, the country was first divided into British, French, Soviet, and U.S. occupation zones, and then into two separate states, East Germany and West Germany. East Germany, or the German Democratic Republic, was formed from the Soviet-occupied zone, and it became an independent Communist republic in 1954. Berlin remained divided into four zones: in 1948, it became two separate administrative units—Soviet-controlled East Berlin and French-, British-, and U.S.-controlled West Berlin. During the same year, the Soviet Union cut off all road, rail, and water links with Berlin in an attempt to force their former allies to abandon their rights in West Berlin. Far from abandoning Berlin, an operation by the Allies was put into effect, referred to as the Berlin Airlift, which kept a steady flow of planes flying across Soviet air space to drop vital supplies to the isolated West Berlin population. The blockade was finally lifted as a result of an embargo on exports from East European states. In 1961, the Berlin Wall was erected by East Germany to prevent the steady flow of refugees to West Germany.

Détente between the two superpowers began in the 1970s but the Cold War was renewed after the Soviet invasion of Afghanistan in 1979. It lasted until in 1989 when, as a result of more liberal policies adopted under Mikhail Gorbachev (Glasnost), the Cold War ended officially by a joint declaration by Gorbachev and U.S. president George Bush. Aided by Gorbachev's new policies, the overthrow of Communist regimes in eastern Europe followed one after another in rapid succession in 1989 and 1990. With the exception of Romania, all were achieved peacefully without bloodshed. In 1991, Communist Party rule in the Soviet Union collapsed. The constituent republics asserted their independence, and the Soviet Union ceased to exist in December 1991.

ROMANIAN COMMUNIST PARTY

The Romanian Communist Party (Partidul Comunist Român; RCP) was founded on May 13, 1921. It was a member of the Third Communist International (Comintern), whose executive committee established its policies.

In December 1923, the Comintern advised the RCP to support the self-determination and separation of Bessarabia, Bucovina, Transylvania and southern Dobrogea from Romania. This was followed by a directive from the fifth Comintern congress held in June and July 1924 calling for the union of Bessarabia, northern Bucovina, and the western Ukraine with the Soviet Union, and for Transylvania and Dobrogea to be made independent states. Understandably, the adherence of the RCP to this policy made the party generally unpopular, and its membership remained insignificant between 1923 and 1937, varying between 300 and 1,600 members. Alexandru Averescu's government ordered the delegates to the first RCP Congress arrested, and on April 11, 1924, the party was banned because of its support of the Soviet Union's refusal to recognize Romanian control over Bessarabia. The ban, which lasted twenty years, weakened its effectiveness as a political organization considerably. In the 1930s, to a great extent leadership was composed of intellectuals, 78 percent of whom were non-Romanians.

The party was split between moderates and hard-liners, the latter being totally committed to Soviet guidelines, while the moderates opposed any policy that they considered detrimental to Romanian interests. The hard-liners staged strikes, blew up the Senate building in Bucharest, and eventually were forced to operate from the Soviet Union for their own safety. They came to be known as the "Odessa Group." Among the leaders of this group were Ana Pauker, Vasile Luca, Teohari Georgescu, and Emil Bodnăraş. Between 1934 and 1937, following directions from Moscow, the RCP began a campaign against right-wing parties and proposed the creation of an antifascist front.

Under Antonescu's National Legionary State in 1940, anticommunism intensified, and by the end of World War II, most of the RCP leaders were either in Moscow or in prison. Only three of them were still free: the secretary-general of the party, Ştefan Foriş; Romus Kofler; and Lucreţiu Pătrăşcanu. In 1943, the RCP, the Union of Hungarian Workers in Romania, the Plowmen's Front led by Dr. Petru Groza, and the Social Democratic Party (SDP), jointly founded the National Patriotic Front (NPF). Bodnăraş returned to Romania under the assumed name of "engineer Ceauşu" to take control of the NPF and to maintain contact with the RCP leaders who had been jailed, including Gheorghe Gheorghiu-Dej, Gheorghe Apostol, I. Chişinevski, Miron Constantinescu, Chivu Stoica, and Nicolae Ceauşescu. Notwithstanding RCP's activities, it remained on the fringes of Romanian politics until the end of the war.

At a meeting held between Bodnăraş and Gheorghiu-Dej in the Târgu Jiu prison infirmary in April 1944, the decision was taken to replace Foriş as secretary-general with Gheorghiu-Dej. Later that year, on August 9, according to RCP records, Gheorghiu-Dej's lawyer, Ion Gheorghe Maurer, dressed as an army officer and bearing forged documents, smuggled him out of prison. Shortly thereafter Ceauşescu was officially released.

END OF THE WAR

On August 23, 1944, General Constantin Sănătescu, the new prime minister, formed a multiparty government composed of members of the National Democratic Bloc (NDB). He then appointed a delegation headed by Lucreţiu Pătrăşcanu to travel to Moscow, where an armistice, announced by King Michael, was to be negotiated between Romania and the Soviet Union (representing the Allies). By August 28, German forces began to retreat from Romania, while Soviet troops occupied Bucharest on August 31.

The armistice, which the Romanian delegation was forced into accepting since the western Allies left the decisions entirely in the hands of the Soviets, was signed on September 12. Its terms gave the Soviet Union practically complete political and economic control over Romania. To ensure themselves of Romanian military support, the Soviets included a promise to return northern Transylvania to Romania, although the final agreement was to be ratified at a general peace conference at the end of the war. The armistice also recognized Romania's entry into the war on August 24 on the side of the Allies against Germany and Hungary. Sănătescu's government continued the war effort on the side of the Allies until the cease-fire in May 1945.

It was at great human loss, human suffering, and economic cost that Romania came out of the war, confident of its future as an independent, democratic nation, with northern Transylvania regained, with a multiparty government, and its king. Over 300,000 Romanian refugees fled Soviet forces in Bessarabia and northern Bucovina during 1940–1941, and over 200,000 fled from Hungarian forces in northern Transylvania. Romanian casualties in World War II were estimated at 625,000 killed, wounded, and missing. But Romania's future had already been decided upon by the Allies during a secret high-level conference, code-named "Tolstoy," held in Moscow on October 9–19, 1944. Present were Winston Churchill and Joseph Stalin with their military and diplomatic advisors. W. Averell Harriman, the U.S. ambassador to the Soviet Union, was also present as an observer. An agreement was reached over the degree of influence Britain and the Soviet Union would have in the Balkans. They agreed upon a 50/50 split in most countries, but Britain insisted on keeping Greece within its zone of influence, and Romania was traded for Greece. The final agreement gave Britain 90 percent influence in Greece and gave the Soviet Union 90 percent in Romania. On that occasion, Churchill later wrote to his foreign secretary Anthony Eden: "Remember, Anthony, the Bolsheviks are crocodiles."[2]

GHEORGHIU-DEJ ERA

Born in the Moldavian town of Bârlad on November 8, 1901, Gheorghe Gheorghiu-Dej (served 1944–1965) was an electrician by trade. Interested in politics as a young man, it is said that he belonged for a time to the Social Democratic Party and later also to the National Peasant Party. He joined the Communists in 1930, by which time he had become a respected leader of the railwaymen. Posted to the Transylvanian town of Dej (where he acquired his hyphenated name), he achieved national prominence when he was elected as secretary general of the National Committee for Action of All Railwaymen in March 1932. Under his leadership, the railwaymen called a strike

Gheorghe Gheorghiu-Dej
Courtesy of Romanian National Tourist Office

on February 1933, for which Gheorghiu-Dej was arrested. The strike ended in a clash with troops called in by the government, and a number of railwaymen were killed. Overnight Gheorghiu-Dej became a Communist hero. He remained imprisoned until just before Romania changed sides in the war, when, on August 9, 1944, he was smuggled out of the Târgu Jiu detention camp and was elected first secretary of the RCP.

Transition

After the formation of the new government led by General Constantin Sănătescu, Gheorghiu-Dej, with the backing of Moscow and the Red Army, decided that it was time to put into effect the first step toward Romania's change to a full-fledged Communist country, the takeover of the Romanian government. The transition lasted from 1944 to 1947. Rather than support the National Democratic Bloc (NDB) coalition government, he opted to set up another coalition of Communist-friendly political parties. On October 12, 1944, the National Democratic Front (NDF) was founded, consisting of the RCP, the SDP, Groza's Plowmen's Front, the Union of Patriots, the Patriotic Defense, and the Union of Hungarian Workers in Romania. The NLP was now the only opposition party left in the NDB coalition government, since the NPP decided to work on its own platform. Sănătescu formed a new cabinet on November 4 in which the NLP had ten seats and the NDF had seven seats. Groza was named vice premier, Gheorghiu-Dej became minister of communications, and Pătrăşcanu took the post of justice minister.

It soon became evident that with the growth of Communist influence, the government was no longer able to function effectively, and Sănătescu decided to resign on December 2. King Michael replaced him with General Nicolae Rădescu, former chief of general staff, who had spent time in the Târgu Jiu prison for not cooperating with the Germans. Another Communist leader, Teohari Georgescu, joined the new cabinet as undersecretary in the ministry of the interior.

Dr. Petru Groza
Courtesy of Romanian National Tourist Office

In January 1945, Gheorghiu-Dej and Ana Pauker, one of the Odessa Group leaders, went to Moscow, where they had high-level meetings including, according to some historians, Stalin and his foreign minister, Vyacheslav Molotov. At these meetings, a power struggle between the "Odessa Group" and Gheorghiu-Dej was settled when the latter was assured of Soviet support in a government takeover. Since he preferred to work behind the scenes and to choose others to front him, Gheorghiu-Dej convinced Moscow to support the appointment of Dr. Petru Groza as prime minister.

Upon Gheorghiu-Dej's return to Bucharest, the Communists began to put into effect a carefully planned program designed to lead to the disruption of the government and the elimination of the historical political parties. On February 28, Andrei Vyshinsky, the Soviet first deputy foreign minister, met with King Michael and demanded that Rădescu's government be replaced with one headed by Groza. With no effective support from the western Allies, the king had no other choice than to give in to Soviet pressure. The British and American delegations to the Potsdam Conference in July–August 1945 refused to recognize the Groza government on the basis that it did not meet the requirements of the Yalta Declaration on Liberated Europe. At another conference of the Allies in Moscow on December 16–26 the Soviet Union agreed to support a multiparty government in Romania. A delegation, including W. Averell Harriman (U.S. ambassador to the Soviet Union), Sir Archibald Clark-Kerr (British ambassador to the Soviet Union), and Vyshinsky went to Bucharest and met with King Michael and Groza on January 2, 1946. On the insistence of the delegation, Groza agreed to include NLP and NPP members in the cabinet at the next elections, whereupon the

Allies recognized the Groza government. The elections were actually postponed, and when they eventually took place, on November 19, NCP's newly formed Bloc of Democratic Parties (BDP) received 79.86 percent of the votes, or 378 of the 414 seats in Parliament. International observers generally agreed that the elections were faked, but then Stalin used to have an adage that what counts is not who votes or how, but who counts the votes. A popular joke among Romanians after the elections was that each time Maniu goes into the ballot box, out comes Groza. The Communists had now achieved effective control of the government, and the western Allies made no further attempts to protest. Romania's fate had already been sealed at the "Tolstoy" conference in October 1944.

The Communist-controlled government now began to consolidate its power over the press, the military, and cultural activity. On December 1, 1946, they achieved control over the economic and financial sectors by the appointment of Gheorghiu-Dej as minister of national economy.

The peace treaty with Romania was signed on February 10, 1947, in Paris. It annulled the Vienna Award, officially returning northern Transylvania to Romania, while it approved the Soviet annexation of Bessarabia and northern Bucovina, and Bulgaria's annexation of southern Dobrogea. The Soviet Union agreed to withdraw its army from Romania. During the following year, a series of new laws was introduced, some of which effectively centralized control of all branches of the economy, others on the sale of private property and currency reforms.

It was time to eliminate opposition parties. In July 1947 the NPP leaders, including Iuliu Maniu and Ion Mihalache, were arrested on charges of treason for conspiring to overthrow the government. They were sentenced to life in prison, where they died of neglect and starvation in solitary confinement. King Michael was distressed by his inability to prevent this tragedy. He himself had by now become a powerless figurehead.

Ana Pauker, before December 1947 (to the left is Dr. Petru Groza, to the right, King Michael)

Courtesy of the Photo Archive of the Academia Civică Foundation, Bucharest, and Mircea Carp

The next step was to eliminate Gheorghe Tătărăscu, whose Liberal Party was the only party not controlled by the RCP that was left in the government. Tătărăscu was accused of negligence and given a vote of no confidence. He and his ministers resigned on November 5, 1947. Ana Pauker became foreign minister, and Vasile Luca took the ministry of finance. This added still more Communist leaders to the Groza government.

It was now felt that a kingdom was incompatible with a Communist government. When, in December 1947, King Michael returned to Bucharest from attending the wedding of Prince Philip and Princess Elizabeth in London, and announced his own engagement to Princess Anna Marie of Bourbon-Parma, instead of being welcomed, he was asked to abdicate. He resisted, but when faced with the threat of possible bloodshed, and with arrest and imprisonment, he abdicated on December 30. Shortly thereafter he left Romania with his mother Helen and twenty-eight members of his court. On the same day the Deputies' Assembly passed a law that proclaimed the Romanian People's Republic.

Romanian People's Republic

On December 30, 1947, the government of the Romanian People's Republic was restructured. Dr. Constantin I. Parhon, internationally known as one of the founders of endocrinology, became president of the Grand National Assembly, while Dr. Petru Groza was appointed president of the Council of Ministers, effectively retaining his function as prime minister. The only other changes in administration were the appointment of Gheorghe Vasilichi as minister of national education, replacing Ştefan Voitec, who became a member of the Presidium.

King Michael (Mihai) I, London, 1948 (shortly after he was exiled by the Communists)
Private collection of Mircea Carp

ROMANIAN PEOPLE'S REPUBLIC
GOVERNMENT STRUCTURE
(effective December 30, 1947)

PARLIAMENT

Parliament
Grand National Assembly (Marea Adunare Națională)

The Grand National Assembly was considered the supreme organ of state authority.

PRESIDIUM

Presidium
The Presidium of the Grand National Assembly (Prezidiul Marii Adunări Naționale)

The Presidium was composed of the president, the secretary, and seventeen members. It acted on behalf of the assembly when the latter was in recess. The president was the head of state.

On March 21, 1961, the Grand National Assembly approved a major reshuffle and set up a State Council to replace the Presidium. The State Council consisted of a president, three vice-presidents, and thirteen members as a supreme body. The president was the head of state.

COUNCIL OF MINISTERS

Council of Ministers
Council of Ministers (Consiliul de Miniștri)

The Council of Ministers was considered the supreme executive body. The president of the council was effectively the prime minister.

ROMANIAN HEADS OF STATE, GOVERNMENT, AND PARTY (1944–1989)

Heads of State

<u>Transition Period</u>

King Michael I	September 6, 1940–December 30, 1947

<u>Romanian People's Republic</u>

President of the Presidium of the Grand National Assembly

Constantin I. Parhon	December 30, 1947–June 2, 1952
Dr. Petru Groza	June 2, 1952–January 7, 1958
Ion Gheorghe Maurer	January 11, 1958–March 21, 1961

President of the State Council

Gheorghe Gheorghiu-Dej	March 21, 1961–March 19, 1965
Chivu Stoica	March 23, 1965–December 9, 1967
Nicolae Ceaușescu	December 9, 1967–December 21, 1989

(President of the Socialist Republic of Romania, from March 28, 1974)

Heads of Government (Prime Minister)

<u>Transition Period</u>

Dr. Petru Groza	March 6, 1945-December 30, 1947

<u>Romanian People's Republic</u>

Dr. Petru Groza	December 30, 1947–June 2, 1952
Gheorghe Gheorghiu-Dej	June 2, 1952–October 4, 1955
Chivu Stoica	October 4, 1955–March 21, 1961
Ion Gheorghe Maurer	March 21, 1961–February 27, 1974
Manea Mãnescu	February 27, 1974–March 30, 1979
Ilie Verdep	March 30, 1979–May 20, 1982
Constantin Dãscãlescu	May 21, 1982–December 22, 1989

HEADS OF RWP PARTY (General Secretary or First Secretary)

Gheorghe Gheorghiu-Dej	October 22, 1945–April 19, 1954
Gheorghe Apostol	April 4, 1954–October 1, 1955
Gheorghe Gheorghiu-Dej	October 1, 1955–March 19, 1965
Nicolae Ceaușescu	March 22, 1965–December 22, 1989

Metamorphosis of a Nation

During the 1944–1947 transition period, the Communists had achieved control of the government and eliminated the major opposition parties, as well as the monarchy. They also began the process of consolidation of power and centralization of the economy, the military, the media, and cultural activity. Between 1948 and 1952, the Communist government effectively dismantled Romania's traditional heritage and values and patterned the new society according to the Soviet Stalinist model. Any opposition to this transformation was labeled "fascism" and was handled with a brutality typical of Stalinist methods. All religious organizations other than the Orthodox Church were outlawed, while the Orthodox Church was turned into a government-controlled institution.

On February 21–23, 1948, at the Congress of the Communist Party, the only surviving political party, the Social Democratic Party, was incorporated into the RCP, whose name changed to the Romanian Workers' Party (RWP, Partidul Muncitoresc Român), and became the only legal political organization in the country. Gheorghe Gheorghiu-Dej was elected secretary-general, while Ana Pauker, Teohari Georgescu, and Vasile Luca became secretaries.

In April, the government adopted a new constitution, which was then replaced by another one in 1952, both of them being patterned after the 1936 constitution of the Soviet Union. On May 24, an organization was set up under the Ministry of the Interior specifically to arrange several trials of industrialists on trumped-up charges. It was named the Directorate of the People's Security (Direcţia Generală a Securităţii Poporului; DGSP), or Securitate for short. Lt.-Gen. Gheorghe Pintilie, a former Soviet secret agent, known by the name Pantiuşa, was appointed head of the DGSP, which became the dreaded vehicle of Communist state dictatorship terror until the revolution of 1989.

On March 2, 1949, land was completely removed from private ownership and collectivization of farms was slowly, and brutally, accomplished by 1962. Tens of thousands of families lost their homes and were resettled, and an estimated 80,000 peasants who resisted collectivization were imprisoned. On June 8, 1950, a Directorate of Labor Units was set up under the Ministry of the Interior, and forced labor was introduced. It was operated on the Soviet system of so-called reeducation through labor. Over 180,000 people branded as elements hostile to the People's Republic were forced into slave labor, many of them being sent to work in the most appalling conditions on the infamous Danube–Black Sea Canal. The canal was to be forty miles long, and to link Cernavodă on the Danube with Năvodari, north of Constanţa. It was conceived by the Soviet Union and financed by the Council for Mutual Economic Assistance, to allow Russian seagoing vessels up to 15,000 tons easy access to the Balkans for both military and commercial usage. Romania was to provide the labor and pay any budget deficits. In 1953 the project was abandoned. It claimed the lives of over 100,000 slave laborers and became known as the Canal of Death. The work was resumed in 1973 by Nicolae Ceauşescu, using a modified route to Agigea, south of Constanţa, and was successfully completed in 1984.

Beginning in 1950, the Cold War between the United States and the Soviet Union led Stalin to change his pro-Israeli stance to an anti-Zionist, anti-imperialist policy. He began the purge of high officials suspected of Zionism in the Soviet Union and other Communist-bloc states. Ana Pauker, who was Jewish and had a brother who lived in Israel, fell out of Stalin's favor and provided just the right opportunity for Gheorghiu-Dej to consolidate his party position by initiating a purge of not only Ana Pauker but her associate, Vasile Luca, as well as Teohari Georgescu. After a series of charges by the Central Committee involving currency reform, Luca was dismissed from the party and Georgescu was removed from his post as minister of the interior. Ana Pauker was allowed to remain foreign minister.

Gheorghiu-Dej, now in full control of the party, was appointed president of the council on June 2, 1952, retaining his position as first secretary of the RWP. A new series of accusations were now instigated, designed to totally eliminate Pauker, Luca, and Georgescu from the political arena. Stalin's death on March 5, 1953, saved Pauker's life. She was released from prison after Molotov's direct intervention and lived the rest of her life in secluded retirement.

With the Soviet Union now under Nikita Khrushchev, Gheorghiu-Dej decided to eliminate Lucreţiu Pătrăşcanu, the last of the Communist leaders who might have proven to be favored by the new regime. He had been in prison and often interrogated since 1948. In April 1954, he was tried on fabricated charges of espionage and sentenced to death.

Education, Science, and Culture

Under the Law for Educational Reform passed in August 1948, a purge of students and faculty was followed by closure of all foreign schools. At the same time, schools were opened to the masses, new vocational training centers were created, and illiteracy gradually ended in Romania. Following the Soviet Union model, the Communist regime encouraged the development and popularization of the sciences and culture, provided that they did not deviate from the Communist ideology.

Romania's Emancipation from the Soviet Union

After Stalin's death, on March 5, 1953, the Khruschev administration began a process of de-Stalinization in the Soviet Union, but in Romania, Gheorghiu-Dej continued his Stalinist hard-line rule. It was the relationship with the Soviet Union that began to change after 1953.

During 1954 and 1955, the Soviet Union sold its shares in the eighteen joint Soviet-Romanian companies known as Sovroms and set up on May 8, 1945. These joint ventures were supposed to assure a mutually beneficial economic relationship, but in fact were intended as vehicles to exploit Romania's natural resources. At the Fourth Congress of the RWP, in December 1955, Gheorghiu-Dej was reelected

Gheorghe Gheorghiu-Dej and Nicolae Ceauşescu, heads of state of the Romanian People's Republic (Caricature by V. Baciu)
Private collection of Bogdan Ulmu

first secretary, the post he had temporarily relinquished in April 1954 in favor of Gheorghe Apostol at a time when Soviet propaganda was accusing Stalinists of promoting a "personality culture." Two new members were elected to the party's political bureau, Nicolae Ceauşescu and Alexandru Drăghici. Drăghici became minister of the interior while Ceauşescu was given the post of central committee secretary for organization and cadres. That position offered Ceauşescu the perfect opportunity for rapid advancement since he controlled all promotions within the party.

During the following ten years, between 1956 and 1965, major changes took place in Romania's internal and external affairs, mainly driven by shifts in the post-Stalinist Soviet policies, but also by other international events. These changes gradually led to Romania's emancipation from the Soviet Union.

Khruschev's de-Stalinization presented a serious problem to Gheorghiu-Dej, who believed that the survival of the Communist system depended on the strict application of Marxist-Leninist policies and Stalinist practices. One of the pillars of Gheorghiu-Dej's plans was industrialization.

Industrialization

Industrialization began in 1949 with two ambitious one-year plans, followed by a five-year plan, a four-year plan, and a six-year plan. In 1958, Romania began to establish contacts with manufacturers in Western Europe and the United States to discuss Romania's intention to develop a heavy steel industry. These contacts resulted in contracts for the purchase of equipment to be used in a planned metallurgical complex at Galaţi.

By 1961, Romania had the fastest rate of industrial growth in eastern Europe. In the Soviet Union, however, the pace of industrialization was decreasing in favor of higher production of consumer goods. This had a negative effect on the economies of highly industrialized satellite states such as Czechoslovakia and East Germany. Consequently, when Romania approached the Soviet Union in 1960 for assistance under favorable conditions for the construction of the Galaţi complex, it was rejected. On August 3–5, 1961, at a meeting of the Comecon in Moscow, a new plan of industrial optimization of member states was announced. Under this plan, Romania was to limit its role to the supply of agricultural products and other raw materials, oil and gas production, and the chemical and petrochemical industry. This would have meant abandoning Romania's industrialization policy, including the Galaţi steel plant. Gheorghiu-Dej realized that to follow Comecon's new plan would result in Romania's continued dependency on the Soviet Union, and probably the end of his own regime. To survive, he had to defy the Soviet Union and Comecon.

Fortunately, a number of international events that took place during that period helped him take this direction.

Hungarian Uprising

The first event was the Hungarian uprising against the Communist regime in October–November 1956. In return for allowing passage of Soviet troops to invade Hungary and put down the uprising, offering a so-called asylum to Hungary's prime minister, Imre Nagy, and arranging for his subsequent return to Budapest to be executed, Gheorghiu-Dej asked Khruschev to withdraw his troops from Romania. Officially, Soviet forces were in Romania to facilitate the transport of men and materials to Austria. Since the treaty with Austria had removed that country from joint Allied control in 1955, the Romanian Communists skillfully used this to their advantage. At a politically opportune moment during the summer of 1958, Soviet troops were pulled out of the country, thereby substantially weakening Soviet military leverage in Romania's affairs. Concurrently, Gheorghiu-Dej's government launched a new wave of purges to eliminate any potential anti-Stalinist movements, and tens of thousands of lives were lost in forced labor camps or executions as a result.

Sino–Soviet Discord

Deterioration in the Sino–Soviet Alliance caused by ideological differences began at the end of the 1950s but reached major proportions by 1957, when China decided to deviate from the Soviet model of economic and industrial development. Soviet technical and financial assistance was withdrawn, causing severe hardship in China. Gheorghiu-Dej offered to take the role of mediation between the two powers, which they accepted. His efforts failed, but it gained him China's support for Romania's own deviation from Soviet policy.

Cuban Missile Crisis

With the Soviet military out of Romania, with support not only from China but also from Yugoslavia's Marshal Tito, Khruschev's loss of face in the Cuban missile crisis of October 1962 convinced Gheorghiu-Dej more than ever to move towards autonomy.

Romania's "Declaration of Independence"

During the November RWP Central Committee plenum it was announced that a contract for the construction of the Galaţi steel complex was awarded to a British–French consortium. The complex was inaugurated in 1968.

During 1963 and 1964, further steps were taken toward an independent policy, such as the signing of a contract with Yugoslavia in 1963 for the joint construction of one of the largest hydroelectric plants in Europe, which was built on the Danube at the Iron Gate. In an article published in the official party newspaper *Scânteia* on April 23, 1964, a statement, which was referred to as the "declaration of independence," affirmed the right of all nations to determine their own national destinies.

Nationalism and Autonomy

Gheorghiu-Dej's ideology was never nationalistic, and he would have been content to continue as a Stalinist Communist, dependent on Moscow, wiping all traces of the traditional Romanian nationalism through industrialization and the creation of a new proletariat. What made this untenable was the loss of Moscow's support for Romania's industrialization. Thus Gheorghiu-Dej faced a dilemma. To stay in power he had to proceed with his plan of industrialization. Without Moscow's support, he was forced to appeal for internal support, which he knew he would not obtain by destroying Romanian nationalism. This dilemma was to be inherited by his successor, Nicolae Ceauşescu.

Nikita Khruschev was removed from office on October 14, 1964, and replaced by Leonid Brezhnev. With the change in administration came also an acceptance of Romania's independent policy. The Soviet Union signed an agreement to provide a substantial amount of technical and economic assistance in the development of Romania's heavy industry, and in December, the KGB advisors were withdrawn from Romania.

In January 1965 Gheorghe Gheorghiu-Dej was taken ill with lung cancer, and he died on March 22, 1965. His funeral on March 24 in Bucharest was attended by thirty-three foreign delegations, including some twenty from non-Communist countries as well as President Mikoyan of the Soviet Union and Chou En-lai, the Chinese prime minister.

CEAUŞESCU REGIME

Nicolae Ceauşescu

At the Ninth Congress of the RWP, on July 19–24, 1965, Nicolae Ceauşescu was confirmed as secretary-general of the Central Committee. At the same congress it was decided that the name of the party be changed back to the Romanian Communist Party (RCP). Chivu Stoica was elected president of the State Council.

Nicolae Ceauşescu
Courtesy of Romanian National Tourist Office

Nicolae Ceauşescu was born on January 26, 1918, in the Wallachian village of Scorniceşti, between Craiova and Bucharest. He was the third of ten children from a relatively poor peasant family. His father, Andruţă, squandered what little income they earned on women and alcohol. At the age of eleven, equipped with only a primary education, Nicolae left the farm, as did most of his siblings, in search of work, which was hard to find during the worldwide depression of 1929. He moved in with his sister Niculina in Bucharest, where he became a shoemaker's apprentice.

As a teenager, he joined the then outlawed Communist Party and was arrested a number of times for participating in political activities and street demonstrations. During World War II, Ceauşescu continued to spend time in and out of prisons, including the Târgu Jiu detention camp, where he met senior members of the RCP. During this period, he became closely associated with Gheorghe Gheorghiu-Dej, who was already considered and treated as the most influential party member in the camp. When, in August 1944, Gheorghiu-Dej escaped from Târgu Jiu, Ceauşescu was freed shortly thereafter.

Ceauşescu had a secretive, suspicious nature and a quick temper, and he was prone to violence, but he also had a great deal of energy and enthusiasm. He was not interested in furthering his formal education but was an avid student of Marxism-Leninism, and he accepted its ideology unquestioningly; it became the core of his thinking. With Gheorghiu-Dej as his mentor, he quickly rose in the ranks of the RCP. In 1946 he married Elena Petrescu, whom he had begun to court as far back as 1938. They came from similar backgrounds and possessed a similar outlook on life and political ideology. The Ceauşescus had three children—Valentin, Zoia, and Nicu, their favorite.

In March 1949, Ceauşescu became a deputy minister in the Ministry of Agriculture and was then transferred to the Ministry of Armed Forces. In May 1952 Gheorghiu-Dej promoted him to membership in the party Central Committee, and he was elected, together with Drăghici, as a full member of the Political Bureau. Appointed as central committee secretary for organization and cadres in 1955, Ceauşescu became responsible for all party appointments and promotions, a position that gave him the best possible chance of becoming party leader, as well as maintaining a strong power base. Upon Gheorghiu-Dej's death, Ion Gheorghe Maurer proposed Ceauşescu as secretary-general. His regime lasted from 1965 to 1989.

Foreign Policy

Ceauşescu continued Gheorghiu-Dej's independent policy in international relations with aggressiveness and at times with real courage in the face of the Soviet Union's unpredictable reactions, as was the case in the invasion of Czechoslovakia by the Warsaw Pact countries on August 20, 1968.

Prague Spring

In the spring of 1968, Ludvik Svoboda, president of Czechoslovakia, and Alexander Dubček, prime minister, began to introduce a program of liberalization and civil rights reforms referred to as the Prague Spring. On the night of August 20, Russian, Polish, and East German troops crossed the border and occupied Prague. Romania was the only Warsaw Pact country to refuse to participate in this intervention. On August 21, Ceauşescu, in a speech to a crowd of 100,000 in Bucharest, denounced Soviet intervention and declared that it was "a grave error, and constituted a serious danger to peace in Europe and for the prospects of world socialism."[3]

He called for the immediate withdrawal of foreign troops. Concurrently, he mobilized the Romanian militia in response to reported Soviet troop movements on Romania's border.

Treaty with West Germany

Earlier, in January 1967, Romania had received a secret West German delegation, leading to the exchange of diplomatic missions. Romania was the first Soviet bloc country to establish diplomatic relations with West Germany.

Further Contacts with the West

On August 2–3, 1969, Richard Nixon became the first U.S. president to visit Romania, as well as the first to visit a Soviet bloc state. At Nixon's invitation, Ceauşescu in turn visited the United States in December 1973. A commercial agreement between the United States and Romania was signed in Bucharest on April 2, 1975, under which

Romania became the first Communist state to receive most favored nation status. U.S. President Gerald Ford finalized the agreement in Bucharest in August.

Stronger ties with the West continued to be made with Ceauşescu's visit to the United States in April 1978 at the invitation of President Jimmy Carter, and his visit, in June of that year, to Great Britain at the invitation of Queen Elizabeth II.

Trade and Industry

Ceauşescu's policy of developing diplomatic relations with the non-Communist world was accompanied by the establishment of commercial and economic ties. The exchange of diplomatic missions between Romania and West Germany in 1967 was followed by the visit of a West German trade mission to Romania. In 1971, Romania became a member of the General Agreement on Tariffs and Trade (GATT); in 1972, it met the conditions of both the International Monetary Fund (IMF) and the World Bank, and in 1973 the Common Market extended preferential treatment to Romania.

To encourage Romania's daring independent policy, U.S. President Richard Nixon, Britain's Prime Minister Harold Wilson, and French President Charles de Gaulle all paid Ceauşescu a visit. Nixon's trip to Romania and that of Ceauşescu to the United States were followed up by further commercial contacts, and in 1974, when the U.S. Congress passed a trade act authorizing the president to extend most favored nation status to Communist countries, Romania became the first Communist country to secure it. In December 1978, a contract was signed for the construction of the first nuclear power plant in Romania using GE Canada technology.

Domestic Policy

Ceauşescu's twenty-four-year rule can be divided into two distinct periods. The first, from 1965 to the mid-1970s, was characterized by

President Nicolae Ceauşescu with President Richard Nixon, August 2, 1969
Private collection of Mircea Carp

success, prosperity, liberalization, and hope; the second, from the mid-1970s to its collapse in 1989, was marked by increasing economic decline, industrial stagnation, loss of international support, increasing internal oppression, discontent, dissent, and despair, finally ending in bloodshed and the collapse of communism in Romania.

Ceauşescu's Rise and Prominence

One of Ceauşescu's first acts after being elected secretary-general of the Communist Party was to replace Alexandru Drăghici as minister of the interior with his deputy and to denounce abuses that took place under him by the Securitate. In 1968 he rehabilitated Lucreţiu Pătrăşcanu, the nationalist Communist leader who had been executed in 1954. In the same year, the National Assembly returned the country to the pre-Communist division into counties, and modified the counties in Transylvania in such a way as to allow a fairer distribution of minorities. Ceauşescu promised increased investment in areas with large Hungarian populations, and an additional number of radio and TV programs in Hungarian and German were introduced.

During this first period, Ceauşescu's policy of industrialization resulted in rapid economic growth and a rise in the standard of living. Large sums of money were invested in the new construction of apartment houses to relieve acute housing shortages. Concurrent with the economic improvements, this period was also characterized by cultural liberalization. Western serials were allowed to be shown on Romanian television, and a Pepsi-Cola bottling plant was inaugurated in 1968.

The positive results of Ceauşescu's policies, as well as the recognition and importance that he was given by non-Communist leaders, began to wane with the change that was occurring in the political and economic landscape of the world around him. The world economy in the 1970s and 1980s was shrinking, while worldwide competition was making it increasingly difficult to find markets for Romania's products and to justify further industrial expansion.

Ceauşescu's Decline and Downfall

Things began to go awry in Romania in 1971 and deteriorated gradually throughout the 1970s and 1980s. Yet the economic prosperity which industrialization and trade with the West brought to the population helped to maintain a sense of hope and stability with the majority of Romanians until 1978, when the grim consequences of Ceauşescu's economic and political policies began to take effect.

In May 1971, the period of positive liberalization and progressive leadership took a turn, and a new, repressive phase began, which gradually returned the country to the worst kind of Stalinist oppression, tyranny, and terror. It is not entirely clear if this change was brought about by Ceauşescu's ambitious wife, Elena, who took advantage of her husband's suspicious nature to make him more and more dependent on her advice, thereby manipulating his decisions in such a way as to assume more control of the government herself; or as a result of his 1971 visit to China and North Korea. Ceauşescu was visibly impressed by the pomp of the two dictatorships, the hero-worship of their leaders, and the "cultural revolution" mentality. Shortly after his return to Bucharest, he introduced his own brand of "cultural revolution" and personality cult. The Securitate was again empowered to clamp down on perceived dissidents, and from the early 1970s onward, it expanded into one of the world's most dreaded state police forces. By 1989 it employed an estimated 2,400 officers, and its agents and informers were to be found everywhere. Any information could be used at any time to have someone dismissed, blackmailed, evicted from his home, or barred from higher education. Government media developed a personality cult around Ceauşescu that presented him as the "hero of the working class," "the defender of Romania against all its enemies," and the leader with answers to all problems facing the nation.

In November 1974 the Eleventh Congress of the RCP approved yet another five-year plan of major increases and diversification of heavy industries. The only way to finance this expansion was to increase borrowing from Western banks and governments, to divert investment earmarked for agriculture, and to drastically lower domestic consumption. By 1982 Romania's foreign debt had climbed to $13.2 billion. In order to maintain confidence in Romania's economy, Ceauşescu announced in December 1982 that all foreign debt would be paid off by 1990. He kept his promise, and by March 1989 Romania stood alone in having no foreign debt, but at the expense of the Romanian population who were forced to endure more and more hardship and suffering. Rationing of food was introduced in 1982, followed by gasoline rationing, industrial and domestic heat and hot water restrictions, and electric power cuts. By the late 1980s, these measures became so severe that there was hardly any food to be found in markets, people were dying from lack of heat, and hospitals were faced with unannounced power cuts that interfered with surgical procedures.

To make matters worse, a number of events beyond the government's control added to Romania's ordeal. A catastrophic earthquake in 1977 and severe floods in 1980 and 1981 disrupted production of export products, and Romania's economy was further affected by the 1979 revolution in Iran. Before the revolution, Iran had been both a major importer and a supplier of crude oil for Romania's over-expanded oil refineries. The revolution and the Iraq-Iran War halted this important trade.

Discontent and opposition to Ceauşescu's rule began to emerge in the late 1970s. A miners' strike in 1977 was the first such demonstration. Ceauşescu himself promised the miners improvements in working conditions, and then he proceeded to have the leaders of the strike arrested. More strikes followed in various plants and were similarly quashed.

Opposition increased during the 1980s. On November 15, 1987, workers at a plant in the city of Braşov marched from the plant to the RCP party headquarters, singing "down with the dictatorship"; workers from other plants joined them, and together they ransacked the building. Several miners were arrested.

By 1988, Romania's importance to the strategy of Western countries ended because of Mikhail Gorbachev's policies of glasnost (openness) and perestroika (restructuring), and by autumn of 1989 it was evident that the Communist regimes were collapsing throughout eastern Europe.

In March 1989 an open letter addressed to Ceaușescu by six former party officials accused him of violating human rights and ignoring the constitution. Opposition to human rights violations in Romania also began to appear in the international press and in Voice of America broadcasts. Great Britain and West Germany recalled their ambassadors in protest at Ceaușescu's crackdown on former party officials who criticized his rule.

Despite mounting internal and international protests, on November 20, the Fourteenth Party Congress reelected Ceaușescu as president for five more years. However, an opposition group calling itself the National Salvation Front (Frontul Salvării Naționale), led by former RCP officials, including Ion Iliescu, who later became Romania's first non-Communist president, circulated two open letters to the congress delegates. They urged the ouster of Ceaușescu and warned that the congress might be the last chance to save the country from a bloody struggle if he remained in power.

Then, on December 16, a demonstration against the government took place in the town of Timișoara, sparked by the eviction of a local dissident Hungarian Reformed Church minister, Lászlo Tökes. The next day, as crowds gathered again on the streets of the town, security forces and troops began to fire on the crowd. An estimated 120 people died. For the next two days, tens of thousands of factory workers staged protests, declaring Timișoara a free city. They chanted "today in Timișoara, tomorrow throughout the country." The army did not interfere again with the peaceful demonstrators. In the foreign press, however, the number of deaths reported were as high as 4,000, and news of this traveled quickly across the nation.

While these events were taking place, Ceauşescu was in Iran in an effort to negotiate new trade agreements. Upon his return, he went on the air and told his listeners that the demonstrations had been instigated by fascists and Hungarian nationalists. He then organized a public meeting of support to be convened in front of the Central Committee building in the center of Bucharest. A 100,000-strong crowd gathered as Ceauşescu stepped out on the balcony and began his speech. Within a few minutes his speech was interrupted by chants of "Ti-mi-şoa-ra" and cries of "down with the murderers." The television cameras and radio broadcasts of the event picked up and transmitted the protests, as well as tear-gas explosions, causing more crowds to gather on the street. Ceauşescu made an effort to continue his speech, now promising the population increased wages and pensions, but his voice was drowned by the noise of the crowd. Securitate sharpshooters began firing into the crowd, and shooting continued all night. It was not clear if the army had joined the protesters and were fighting against the security forces or were shooting into the crowd, since General Vasile Milea, the minister of defense, ordered the army not to shoot. The following morning, December 22, Ceauşescu tried again to speak to the crowd, but stones were thrown at him, and he was quickly escorted inside the building. As the news spread that Ceauşescu had Milea shot, many army units defected and joined the protesters, who by noon had broken into the Central Committee building.

Just before noon, helicopters appeared over the building, and one landed on the roof. The Ceauşescus' personal pilot had been instructed to fly them to safety, as mobs tried to break into the building. Nicolae and Elena, followed by two bodyguards and two close allies, former Prime Minister Manea Mănescu and Emil Bobu, all piled into the overcrowded helicopter, and they took off, barely clearing the roof. After a short, agitated flight during which they unsuccessfully tried to radio for reinforcements, the helicopter landed on the main road, and the Ceauşescus were transferred to a commandeered car, then a second one, and were eventually turned over to a military garrison about 100 miles from the capital, where they were placed under guard.

They were tried there by an improvised military tribunal on Christmas day, December 25. Lawyers, prosecutors, and observers, including a member of the National Salvation Front, were flown in by helicopter, and the trial was staged in a nearby schoolroom, a farcical affair, the object of which was to provide a legal pretext for a speedy execution. As expected, the Ceauşescus were found guilty of genocide and destroying the national economy. They were condemned to death and shot the same day before a firing squad, along the wall on the side of the barracks square. So ended more than forty years of communism in Romania.

JEWS OF ROMANIA UNDER COMMUNISM

In 1945, at the end of a period in Europe when nearly six million Jews perished at the hand of Nazis and fascists, there still remained 428,312 Jews living in Romania proper, whereas during the forty years of communism 98% of those Jews left the country. At first glance this may seem strange, but in fact, despite Marshal Antonescu's policy of allowing Jews to emigrate, very few actually left since travel at that time was extremely difficult and dangerous. Great Britain blocked them from entering Palestine, and German troops prevented them from traveling. When World War II ended and the state of Israel was founded (1948), emigration became much easier.

Under communism, the lives of Jews who were mainly tradesmen, shopkeepers, or industrialists, or who held liberal professions, were dramatically affected by the centralization and de-privatization policies of the government. So the Jewish population began to leave, and by 1992, only 9,107 remained in Romania.

NOTES

1. *The Hutchinson Encyclopedia*, 2001 ed. (Oxford: UK Helicon Publishing, 2000), 1074.
2. Gilbert, *Winston Churchill 1941–1945*, vol 7, 754.
3. *The Times* (London), 22 August 1968, 5g.

CHAPTER 13

Cultural Development in the Twentieth Century

EARLY TWENTIETH CENTURY

It was between 1866 and the start of World War I that cultural life in Romania blossomed and developed to the fullest. This period became known as the Age of Great Classics.

Chapter 9 covers cultural development in the first and second half of the nineteenth century, and chapter 13 continues with the cultural development in the twentieth century. However, the work of many of the literary, artistic, and musical figures overlap this arbitrary time division.

Literature

Several literary movements emerged at the beginning of the twentieth century. Poets Alexandru Vlahuţă (1858–1919) and George Coşbuc (1866–1919) founded the periodical *Sămănătorul* (The sower), which was devoted to a movement promoting Romanian national themes and peasant life in literature. One of its most outspoken supporters was Nicolae Iorga (1871–1940), a most distinguished Romanian intellectual—historian, journalist, and writer, as well as politician. Other writers and poets, such as Mihail Sadoveanu (1880–1961) and

Ştefan O. Iosif (1875–1913) became involved in that movement. *Sămănătorism* influenced Romanian literature even past World War I, but then it faded away. Other literary figures of this period, to mention only a few, were the poets Octavian Goga (1881–1938) and Alexandru Macedonski (1854–1920), as well as novelists Ioan Slavici (1848–1925) and Duiliu Zamfirescu (1880–1961).

Nicolae Iorga
(1871–1940)
Courtesy of Regia Autonomă "Monitorul Oficial," Romanian Parliament

Alexandru Macedonski
(1854–1920)
Courtesy of Regia Autonomă "Monitorul Oficial," Romanian Parliament

Ioan Slavici
(1848–1925)
Courtesy of Regia Autonomă "Monitorul Oficial," Romanian Parliament

Visual Arts

Among the talented Romanian painters from this period were Ştefan Luchian (1868–1916) and Gheorghe Petraşcu (1872–1949). Although they both studied at the Academy of Fine Arts in Bucharest and at the Julian Academy in Paris, the two masters developed their own styles. Luchian was influenced by the art of Nicolae Grigorescu and

Ioan Andreescu. His motifs varied from landscapes to portraits and still lifes. Often in ill health, he died prematurely at the age of forty-eight. Petraşcu resisted any postimpressionist movements, preferring realism. He traveled extensively throughout Europe visiting art galleries and painting landscapes of places he discovered. He exhibited frequently at the Venice Biennale and was awarded the Grand Prix at the 1937 Paris International Exhibition.

Self-portrait by Ştefan Luchian (1868–1916)

Courtesy of Regia Autonomă "Monitorul Oficial," Romanian Parliament

Music

George Enescu (1881–1955), the greatest of Romania's composers, was even better known to the public as a brilliant violinist and a gifted conductor. He was born in Liveni in Moldavia, on August 19, 1881. His father, an estate administrator for a local landowner, sang, conducted a choir, and played the violin, and his mother played the guitar and the piano. Enescu joined the Vienna Conservatory where he studied the violin. At the age of thirteen, he became acquainted with Johannes Brahms, whose symphonic music influenced him. Enescu moved to Paris in 1895 and there, in 1898, his first composition, *Poème Roumain*, was played. A year later, at the age of eighteen, he won first prize for violin at the Paris Conservatory. Enescu was Yehudi Menuhin's violin teacher for many years, and Menuhin wrote that Enescu was a creative genius, whether in speaking, teaching, conducting, playing the violin or piano, or composing.

Enescu's best-known compositions are his early works, the two *Romanian Rhapsodies*. Although they are lively pieces of great beauty, his later compositional style became deeper and more complex in nature. In addition to the rhapsodies, Enescu composed three violin sonatas, three piano sonatas, two string quartets, three symphonies, and an opera, *Oedip*.

George Enescu (1881–1955)
Courtesy of Viorel Cosma, author of *George Enesu: A Tragic Life in Pictures*

Architecture

Architecture continued to be influenced by classical and French eclectic styles. One of the most beautiful examples of this architecture is the Cantacuzino Palace (now the Museum of Romanian Music) in Bucharest. It is French eclectic with elements of Art Nouveau and was designed by the architect I. D. Berindei (1900). This period also saw the development of a Romanian national style (initiated by Ion Mincu). Examples of this style are the Soare House (today the Bucur restaurant; Bucharest, 1914) and the Romanian Bank for Development (Bucharest, 1915–1923), both by Petre Antonescu, as well as the Military Circle (Bucharest, 1912), by the architects Dimitrie Maimarolu and Ernst Doneaud.

It must also be noted that the union of Transylvania with Romania after World War I widened the spectrum of architecture by adding the Austro-Hungarian architectural heritage, complete with all Western styles from Gothic to Secession, Bauhaus, and Modern.

THE INTERWAR YEARS

Literature

The interwar period is considered to be the second great period of literary development. Through the review *Gândirea* (The thought), the traditionalism movement developed. Lucian Blaga (1895–1961) was a representative poet of this movement. Blaga was also an essayist, diplomat, and philosopher, having developed an original philosophical system in an attempt to interpret the Romanian spirit through the Romanian landscape. His work continued past World War II.

Lucian Blaga (1895–1961)
Courtesy of Regia Autonomă "Monitorul Oficial," Romanian Parliament

His autobiographical novel *Luntrea lui Caron* (Caron's boat), published posthumously in 1990, is a chronicle of the tragic destiny of an intellectual, and of the Romanian people in general, after World War II. Blaga became a member of the Romanian Academy in 1936.[1]

Modernism produced one of the greatest twentieth-century poets, Tudor Arghezi (1880–1967). A metaphorical poet, Arghezi synthesized traditionalism and modernism. Another poet of the modernism school was Tristan Tzara (1896–1963). Before the age of twenty, he wrote nearly forty poems, all of which were published in the periodical *Simbolul* (The symbol). Translated into French in *Oeuvres Complètes*, the poems have been identified as part of French symbolist and post-symbolist tradition. Tzara left Romania for Zurich, where, on February 5, 1916—together with another Romanian, Marcel Iancu; the French poet, sculptor, and painter Hans (Jean) Arp; and two Germans—he founded the literary movement known as dadaism, from which surrealism developed.

Among other literary figures of this period are Mihail Sadoveanu, Liviu Rebreanu, and George Topârceanu.

Mihail Sadoveanu

A pillar of the Romanian literary world, Mihail Sadoveanu (1880–1961) began his law studies in Bucharest at his father's insistence, but consumed by the desire to write, he quit and decided to make his living as a writer. Four volumes of his prose were published in 1904, of which his *Povestiri* (Stories) won him a prize by the Romanian Academy. In 1910 he was appointed director of the National Theater in Iaşi. After World War I, Sadoveanu settled in Iaşi, in Mihail Kogălniceanu's former house (now the Mihail Sadoveanu Museum) where he lived until 1936. That was the happiest period in his life, and the prolific writer produced some 100 books. In 1929, he was elected a member of the Romanian Academy. During Octavian Goga's right-wing government, Sadoveanu's books were burned in public squares, but in 1939, he received an honorary degree from the University of Iaşi.

Tudor Arghezi (1880–1967)

Courtesy of Regia Autonomă "Monitorul Oficial," Romanian Parliament

Mihail Sadoveanu (1880–1961)

Courtesy of Regia Autonomă "Monitorul Oficial," Romanian Parliament

The horrors of World War II touched him personally as he lost his youngest son in the fighting to liberate Transylvania and his house was bombed. Disillusioned, Sadoveanu became drawn to the ideals of the new "socialist society." He joined the Communist Party and served as a member of the Presidium, as well as vice president of the Grand National Assembly from 1947 to his death. He continued writing, following Communist guidelines. Among his best-known works from that period are *Păuna Mică* (The little peacock), 1948, *Glonț de Fier* (Iron bullet), 1951, and *Nicoară Potcoavă* (Nicoară the horseshoe), 1952. On May 20, 1961, Sadoveanu was awarded the International Lenin Prize for the Promotion of Peace Among Nations. Ill for several years and almost blind, he died soon after, on October 19, 1961.

Liviu Rebreanu

Liviu Rebreanu (1885–1944) made his literary debut in 1909 in the review *Luceafărul* from Sibiu. In 1911 he became literary secretary at the National Theater in Craiova. During the next ten years, he wrote a number of short stories and books, among which his *Ion* earned him admission to the Romanian Academy. He is also known for his novels *Răscoala* (The uprising) and *Pădurea Spânzuraților* (The forest of the hanged).

Liviu Rebreanu
(1885–1944)
Courtesy of Regia Autonomă "Monitorul Oficial," Romanian Parliament

George Topârceanu

George Topârceanu (1886–1937) was known for his beloved humorous poems for children, such as *Balada Unui Greir Mic* (The ballad of a small cricket), *Rapsodii de Toamnă* (Autumn rhapsodies), *Cioara* (The crow), and *Primăvara*

(Spring). During World War I he was taken prisoner in Bulgaria, where he spent two years in a concentration camp, after which he published his war memoirs. In 1926, Topârceanu was awarded the National Prize for Poetry.

Visual Arts

Romania produced many gifted painters during the first half of the twentieth century, among them Octav Băncilă (1872–1944), Theodor Palladi (1871–1956), Iosif Iser (1881–1958), Nicolae Tonitza (1886–1940), and Lucian Grigorescu (1894–1965).

One of the greatest sculptors of the twentieth century was Constantin Brâncuşi (1876–1957). He was to become one of the founders of modern sculpture. Brâncuşi was born in the village of Hobiţa in the foothills of the Carpathian Mountains. As a child, he ran away from home twice, and then at the age of eleven he left his large family of peasants and small landowners for good. After five years of doing menial work in Târgu Jiu, Brâncuşi moved to Craiova, where he entered the School of Arts and Crafts. He graduated with honors in 1898 and then entered the School of Fine Arts in Bucharest, where he won several prizes.

In 1903, Brâncuşi took to traveling throughout Europe, mostly by foot, until, a year later, he settled in Paris and enrolled in the Ecole des Beaux Arts. For a time he worked in Rodin's studio, but then he broke away from Rodin's influence to create his own style of sculpture.

In 1955 the Guggenheim Museum in New York mounted his largest one-man exhibition, and on the occasion of his eightieth birthday, in 1956, the Museum of Art in Bucharest held an exhibition of his works. A major portion of his sculpture is in permanent exhibit at the Pompidou Center in Paris, while other museums of art such as the Museum of Modern Art in New York also own a number of his sculptures. Among Brâncuşi's best-known masterpieces are the series motifs of *Mlle Pogany*, *Prometheus*, *The Sleeping Muse*, and *The Birds*.

His ultimate desire was to create a gigantic outdoor column that would rise gracefully toward the sky, and he tried to promote his idea in cities such as New York and Chicago. In 1937, he was commissioned by the National League of Romanian Women of Gorj to create a memorial to Romanians who died defending the town of Târgu Jiu against the German army during World War I. The Târgu Jiu memorial includes *The Column of Endless Gratitude*, more commonly known as *The Column of the Infinite* or *The Endless Column*, located at one end of the Avenue of Heros, and the Garden of Meditation, located in a park at the other end of the avenue. The garden includes two other works, *The Table of Silence*, a circular table surrounded by twelve circular hourglass-shaped stools, and *The Gate of the Kiss*, a portal, both carved in local stone.

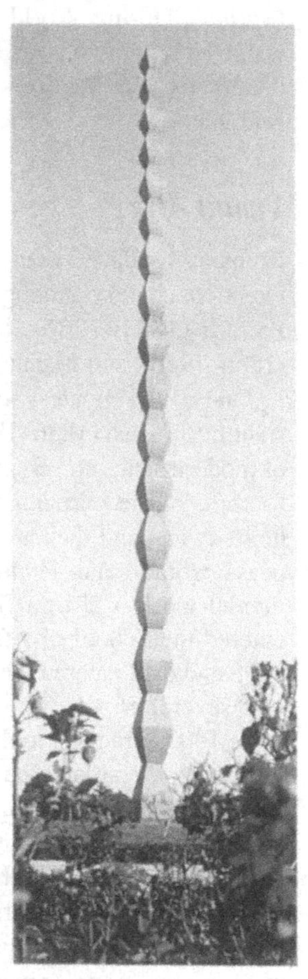

Constantin Brâncuşi's *Column of Endless Gratitude*
Courtesy of Romanian National Tourist Office

The ninety-eight-foot high column, made of a cast iron core and a series of rhomboidal sections reminiscent of the sculpted verandas of old wooden houses of the region, was originally sprayed with a golden yellow metallic alloy, which gleamed in the sun. After many years of neglect, the column lost its coating and began to rust. Then, in the early 1950s, the local mayor attempted to have it demolished as a symbol of capitalism, and only managed to bend it a few degrees off the vertical. In 1966 it was given a coat of bronze paint, and in 2000, the whole column was disassembled, renovated, and reassembled in preparation for the year 2001, which was designated "Brâncuşi Year." Brâncuşi died on March 16, 1957.

Another well-known sculptor of this period was Dimitrie Paciurea (1873–1932).

Music

Music flourished during the relatively peaceful interwar period. The Society of Romanian Composers was founded by a number of composers in 1920. Operas such as *Oedip* by George Enescu, *Năpasta* (The plague) by Sabin Drăgoi, *Capra cu Trei Iezi* (The goat with three kids) by Alexandru Zirra, and the ballet *La Piaţă* (At the market) by Mihail Jora, as well as orchestral music by Mihail Jora, Mihail Andricu, Paul Constantinescu, and others, were performed in Bucharest, Cluj, Timişoara, and Iaşi.

Architecture

The first decade of this period produced an expansion of the neo-Romanian style (adaptations of the Brâncoveanu style) by Petre Antonescu, P. Smărăndescu, C. Pompoiu, and Gheorghe Simotla, reflected in monumental buildings such as Astra Română (Bucharest), Marmorosh-Blank Bank (Bucharest), the Orthodox Cathedral (Cluj), and the Patriarhia Palace (Bucharest).

Concurrently many impressive neoclassical and eclectic buildings continued to be built, such as the Royal Palace (Bucharest, 1930) by architect N. Neciulescu, now the National Art Museum, and the Faculty of Law (Bucharest, 1935) by Petre Antonescu.

The most significant architectural phenomenon of this period was the spreading of modern architecture, such as the ARO building (Bucharest, 1930s) by Horia Creangă, the Military Academy (Bucharest, 1939) by Duiliu Marcu, the International Hotel (Mamaia), and the Belona Hotel (Eforie Nord). Many buildings, both private villas and commercial edifices, were designed in the Bauhaus style.

LATE TWENTIETH CENTURY

Literature and Visual Arts

After World War II, Romania's literary development took a sharp turn. After the transition period to communism (1944–1947), during which new writers and poets such as Ion Caraion, Marin Preda, and Petru Dumitriu emerged, the government began to impose so-called proletarian literature and social realism. Some authors went into exile, while others who would not follow the imposed guidelines were imprisoned. With some exceptions, most literary works of the 1950s are mediocre. It was not until the 1960s, during a period of political détente, that literary movements began again to take shape. A new generation of authors evolved, including Marin Sorescu and Nichita Stănescu. Some of the writers who had been imprisoned in the 1950s were also released, and some of their works were published, such as Vasile Voiculescu's *Povestiri* (Tales).

From the early 1970s on, however, the interference of the authorities in cultural life became intolerable. Many dissident intellectuals began to express their dissatisfaction and suffered the consequences. It became more and more difficult to publish any works, which were subjected to censorship. The same situation affected the visual arts. Nevertheless, in spite of these conditions, artists managed to develop the basic trends from impressionism and postimpressionism to dadaism and surrealism, and they continue to develop after the 1989 revolution in the new free and democratic environment.

Music

Although composers faced many restrictions in freedom of creation during the years of Communist rule, Communist regimes did place much emphasis on music. During that period, about twenty philharmonic and symphonic state orchestras were founded. Ten state lyrical theaters, over forty professional song and dance groups, and dozens of schools of music also sprang up during that time. Among the composers who nevertheless discovered new solutions for the development of music and distinguished themselves are Mihai Moldovan, Tiberiu Olah, Pascal Bentoiu, Aurel Stroe, Theodor Grigoriu, Stefani Niculescu, Cornel Ţăranu, Wilhelm Berger, Dumitru Capoianu, and Myriam Marbe.

Architecture

Communist Period

Architecture during the communist period evolved in several distinct phases:

1940–1960

Russian-inspired Stalinist architecture was introduced, the best example of which is the massive Casa Scânteii (now the House of the Free Press; Bucharest, 1950s) by architects G. Maicu and N. Bădescu. It is a replica of the Lomonosov University of Moscow.

A number of buildings were also built in an eclectic blend of neoclassical and Romanian style, such as the Bucharest Opera House (1953) by Octav Doicescu.

1960–1972

Modern architecture covering all fields—housing, institutional, leisure, and industrial—was being built, such as the Bucharest Băneasa Airport, Bucharest Otopeni Airport, Constanţa Railway Station, and the Bucharest Circus Building.

Other modern buildings that were completed during this period were the Intercontinental Hotel (Bucharest, 1970–1971) by architects Gheorghe Nedrag, I. Moscu, and R. Belea, and the National Theater (Bucharest, 1967–1970) by H. Maicu, R. Belea, and N. Cucu.

1960–1989

Ethnic-driven modern architecture, grafting Romanian folklore themes onto modern structures, made its appearance in the 1960s and continued through to the end of the communist period. Examples include the Craiova Theater, Târgu Mureş Theater, Baia-Mare Cultural Center, and the Polytechnic Institute of Braşov.

This period also produced the infamous House of the People (now the Palace of Parliament; Bucharest, late 1980s), devoid of any style. It was conceived by Nicolae Ceauşescu who was influenced by similar structures in North Korea. The palace dominates the entire Civic Center and is the second largest building in the world, after the Pentagon. It has twelve floors, four underground levels, and includes 1100 rooms.

Post-Revolution

Modern and post-modern architecture reflects the introduction of western technology and the demands of the market-driven economy. Examples are the high-rise structures such as the Bucharest Financial Plaza (1992/1993) and the World Trade Center (Bucharest, 1993/1994) by architects V. Vion and N. Taralunga.

NOTE

1. In 1866 the Romanian Literary Society was established by an act of parliament. Its initial scope, similar to that of the French Academy, was to make up the dictionary and glossary of the Romanian language. In 1867 its name was changed to the Romanian Academic Society, and its aims, as originally defined, were to work for the promotion of the letters and sciences among Romanians. Finally, in 1879, the Romanian Academic Society was converted into a national institute to be called the Romanian Academy, with the aim of maintaining high cultural standards in language, national history, letters, sciences, and the fine arts. Titular, corresponding, and honorary members elected to the Romanian Academy include top literary, artistic, and scientific personalities.

EPILOGUE

Post-Communist Romania

TRANSITION

While the Ceauşescus were held in custody and tried at a military base near Bucharest, fighting continued on the capital's streets between protesters, security forces still loyal to the Ceauşescus, and the army units who were defecting to the side of the protesters. Demonstrations and street fighting were also taking place in other cities around the country. After the execution of the Ceauşescus, when news of it reached the public, all quieted down, and the National Salvation Front (NSF) began to take control of the situation.

When the dust and smoke of the December 1989 revolution settled, it was discovered that the total actual number of deaths had been greatly exaggerated by the international press, which had reported as many as 60,000 casualties, the real figure being around 1,000. There were also indications that a coup had actually been organized even before the Timişoara demonstrations.

The NSF formed a provisional council to take control of the country and to prepare for elections. The main figure to emerge was Ion Iliescu, who served from 1990 to 1996 and again from 2000 to the present.

ION ILIESCU

Born on March 3, 1930, in Olteniţa, Ilfov District, Iliescu studied at the Bucharest Polytechnic Institute and the Energy Institute of Moscow. He joined the Romanian Communist Party (RCP) in 1953 and was elected as alternate member of the Central Committee in 1965 and full member in 1968. In 1971 Iliescu accompanied Ceauşescu on a visit to China and North Korea. During the trip, an ideological difference developed between them, and Iliescu was accused of intellectual "deviationism." He was kept under observation, but in 1979 he was given the post of director of the Political Bureau. When another disagreement developed between Ceauşescu and Iliescu in 1984, this time over the Danube-Black Sea Canal, Iliescu was dropped from both the Central Committee and the Political Bureau. He was appointed as director of the State Technical Publishing House in Bucharest, where he worked until the 1989 revolution.

FIRST POST-COMMUNIST ELECTIONS

As president of the provisional council, Ion Iliescu appointed Petre Roman, a university professor who was head of the hydraulics department in the Faculty of Hydroenergy at Bucharest Polytechnic Institute, as prime minister.

On January 3, 1990, Iliescu signed a decree reestablishing political parties, and they returned to the political scene with a vengeance. By 1993, some 159 political parties had been registered. On December 22, 1989, shortly after Ceauşescu's arrest, Corneliu Coposu, Iuliu Maniu's former political secretary and deputy general-secretary of the National Peasant Party (NPP), had announced the return of his party, subsequently turned into the National Peasant–Christian Democrat Party, to public life. Coposu had been arrested by the Communists in 1947 and, together with Maniu and the entire NPP board, had spent seventeen years in prisons and forced labor and another twenty-five

President Ion Iliescu (1989–1996 and 2000–)

Courtesy of Embassy of Romania, London

Corneliu Coposu, a leader of the National Peasant Party
Private collection of Mircea Carp

Ion Raţiu, a leader of the National Peasant Party in exile
Courtesy of Nicolae Raţiu

years under observation, subjected to repeated house searches and harassment by the Securitate. He was one of the few political leaders to survive the Communist jails. Radu Câmpeanu and Ion Raţiu, the respective leaders in exile of the National Liberal and National Peasant Parties, returned to Romania before the 1990 elections as presidential candidates. On February 1, 1990, a provisional government, the Council of National Unity, was formed by the NSF in preparation for a general election to be held on May 20. It consisted of the NSF, NLP, and NPP. The NSF won the parliamentary elections with 66 percent of the vote, and in the presidential race Ion Iliescu was elected as the first post-Communist president with an overwhelming 85.31 percent, while Câmpeanu received 10.57 percent and Raţiu only 4.12 percent.

It was a daunting task that Iliescu undertook. In Romania, unlike in other ex-Soviet satellite states such as Poland, Hungary, and Czechoslovakia, there was no period of liberalization or gradual return to a market economy. Even in the Soviet Union, the policies of Gorbachev began to take effect as far back as 1985. Communism in Romania had to be forced out by a bloody revolution. Neither politicians nor the general public had any previous knowledge or experience of how a democratic society functions or how a market-driven economy operates. After forty-five years of a brutal and ruthless type of communism, the electorate had no understanding of the significance of political parties, free elections, or business entrepreneurial skills. Iliescu himself was born into a Communist family and joined the Communist Party at the age of twenty-three.

UNREST, DEMONSTRATIONS, AND VIOLENCE

Even before the May elections, demonstrators in Bucharest accused the NSF of neo-communism and demanded the resignation of former Communists. Demonstrations continued into June, mainly by university students but also by supporters of opposition parties. Students occupied Bucharest's University Square, and some of them began a hunger strike against state-controlled television. On June 13, 1990, rioters attacked government buildings, including police headquarters, offices of state-run television, and the Foreign Ministry. Failure of the police to disperse the rioters prompted the government to appeal to miners from the Jiu Valley in support of the police. According to the press, miners armed with wooden clubs and heavy wire bludgeons swarmed into Bucharest at dawn on Thursday, June 14, beating anyone suspected of opposing the government and ransacking the offices of the opposition parties.[1] At a news conference at government headquarters, Prime Minister Roman conceded that some miners had engaged in violence against innocent people: "There were unpleasant moments when some people were molested without any reason at all. I must say it in public that we are deeply sorry for that."[2] The government had tried to stop them from operating on their own, Roman said, "but there were cases in which they took action without us being able to control them."[3] The next day Iliescu sacked Interior Minister Mihai Chitac, blaming him for the failure of the police to maintain order. The miners left behind at least seven dead and many injured. The effect was to tarnish Romania's image abroad. The United States suspended non-humanitarian aid to Romania, and its ambassador condemned the government and the president for inspiring continued violence

Iliescu's Romania was also subjected to other international events that added to its plight. The fragmentation of Yugoslavia in 1990 followed by wars between former Yugoslav republics disrupted trade with the West that was so necessary for its recovery, while Western industries preferred to invest in other ex-Communist states with fewer problems. A travel advisory for Romania issued by the U.S. Department of State in 1990 exacerbated the situation by discouraging business travel and tourism. Thus with Romania essentially isolated from the Western world, special interest groups were able to project a negative image of the country, and the Western media obliged.

Personal freedom restrictions were lifted, and economic reform began slowly. In November, food subsidies began to be reduced, causing a sharp rise in inflation. In September 1991 the Jiu Valley miners went on strike and returned to Bucharest, this time to protest working conditions. Petre Roman resigned and formed a splinter party, the Democratic Party–National Salvation Front (PD–FSN), while Iliescu's party was renamed the Democracy Party of Romania (PDSR). A new government was formed on October 1 under an independent prime minister, Teodor Stolojan, including members of the NLP. The government continued efforts to reform the economy and undertook the task of writing a new constitution, which was adopted by a referendum in December. Under the new constitution, Romania became a parliamentary democracy.

ILIESCU REELECTED

The first national elections after Parliament adopted the new constitution took place on September 27, 1992. Only thirteen of the registered political parties were able to secure 3 percent of the vote, the minimum necessary to entitle them to a seat in Parliament. Iliescu's PDSR party won the elections with 21.71 percent of the vote, defeating the Democratic Convention of Romania (CDR), an opposition coalition initially composed of two factions of the NLP, The National Peasant-Christian Democrat Party (NPP-CD), the Civic Alliance Party (PAC), the Social Democratic Party of Romania (PSDR), and the Ecological Party of Romania under Emil Constantinescu. Iliescu was reelected in the presidential run-off election on October 11, 1992, receiving 61 percent of the vote. A new government under Nicolae Văcăroiu was formed as a coalition with the Greater Romania Party (PRM) and the Socialist Labor Party (PSM).

Some progress began to be felt after 1992. In 1993 Romania became a full member of the Council of Europe, and the Congress of the United States again granted it most favored nation trade status. On

January 26, 1994, Romania became the first East European country to sign NATO's Partnership for Peace program, and in September 1995, it hosted its first NATO joint maneuvers. Another major achievement by this government was the historic treaty between Romania and Hungary signed on September 16, 1996, in Timişoara, in which the two countries agreed to respect each other's borders and to protect the rights of the Hungarian minority in Transylvania. This was seen as a key step to the European Union and NATO membership. Some progress was also made in privatization and private sector development.

OPPOSITION WINS

By the 1996 elections, the fifteen-party Democratic Convention of Romania (CDR) looked hopelessly divided, and Iliescu confidently expected to win. Surprisingly, however, the CDR won the election by a landslide, with 200 of the 341 seats in the House of Deputies and 87 of the 143 senatorial seats. In the first round of the presidential elections, Ion Iliescu obtained 32.25 percent of the votes; Emil Constantinescu received 28.21 percent, and Petre Roman received 20.21 percent. In the second round, however, Roman supported Constantinescu, who won with 54.42 percent against Iliescu's 45.59 percent. Victor Ciorbea, the mayor of Bucharest, was appointed prime minister.

President Emil Constantinescu (1996–2000)

Courtesy of Embassy of Romania, London

Emil Constantinescu was born on November 19, 1939, in Tighina (now in the Republic of Moldova). He was a practicing lawyer, a geology lecturer at the University of Bucharest, becoming president of the university in 1992. He was also a visiting professor at Duke University in the United States.

The CDR coalition included the two historic parties, the NPP–Christian-Democrat, and the NLP, as well as the reform-oriented Democratic Party and other democratic parties. The victory was hailed both in Romania and in the West as a historic turning point, a new beginning for Romania. Constantinescu promised radical reforms and accelerated return to a market economy, privatization, and a major drive against corruption.

President Constantinescu with President Bill Clinton and Mihai P. Carp, member of the U.S. Embassy in Bucharest, during Clinton's visit to Bucharest, July 13, 1997.
Private collection of Mircea Carp

Unfortunately, the peoples' expectations soon evaporated. The large number of political parties in the CDR made it difficult for Parliament to function efficiently. Disagreement within the coalition led to two changes of prime ministers. In March 1998 Victor Ciorbea resigned and was replaced by Radu Vasile, who made an effort to improve conditions but without success. He was dismissed in December 1999 for being too lenient with the trade unions, and was replaced by Mugur Isărescu, head of the Romanian National Bank. Isărescu had rebuilt the credibility of the central bank, kept out of partisan politics, and used the bank's resources to create the building blocks of a market economy, while supporting Romanian culture and arts. However, intrinsic corruption still flourished, the economy declined steadily, and by 1999 inflation had reached staggering proportions with the cost of electricity rising 500 percent as subsidies ended. Violent protests over economic conditions took place toward the end of 1999. Isărescu did manage to make some reforms when he became prime minister, but not enough to return to 1996 levels. The CDR coalition began to split up, and on July 17, 2000, President Emil Constantinescu made an announcement on national television that he would not seek reelection. In foreign policy, the government continued its efforts toward integration into NATO and the European Community.

2000 ELECTIONS: THE RETURN OF ILIESCU TO POWER

There has been much speculation as to the reason for Constantinescu's decision not to seek reelection, the most plausible being his slim chance of winning, according to opinion polls. Angered by the lack of expected progress, the electorate gave the PDSR 37.09 percent of the votes, with the PRM gaining 21.01 percent; the CDR came in last with only 5.04 percent of the votes. Ion Iliescu was elected president with 36.50 percent of the votes. He appointed Adrian Năstase, former foreign minister, as prime minister.

As of this writing, one-and-one-half years after the November elections, Romania's economy is improving slowly, although unemployment remains relatively high, while wages are still extremely low, and Romania is still lagging behind most former communist states. So, what does the future hold? It depends on many conditions, some of which are created by the government or subject to its control, while others are affected by international events or policies over which Romania has very little control.

Indeed, the present government is actively pursuing policies designed to bring about Romania's recovery. A basic objective has been its integration into the European and Euro-Atlantic political, economic, and strategic organizations. Accession to the European Union (EU) and North Atlantic Treaty Organization (NATO) is perceived as crucial to achieving security, stability, and the rule of law. To succeed in these goals, Romania has to maintain an active dialogue with the West and improve its image internationally. It will have to continue giving support and encouragement to interested foreign investors and international financial institutions, and facilitate access of international capital and markets to private and public sectors. Romania is also continuing its efforts to join the Organization for Economic Cooperation and Development (OECD) and to back the interests of its citizens, both at home and abroad.

One way of encouraging foreign investment is through tourism. What better way is there of familiarizing potential investors than to have them bring their families to Romania on vacation, getting to know the country and its people, its advantages and potential? Romania is easily accessible by air, rail, road, and waterways. It has the potential of becoming one of Europe's favorite vacation choices, with a seacoast and mountains unsurpassed in beauty, a great variety of resorts, and natural mineral spring spas, monuments of historical and artistic interest, as well as over 400 museums, and many cultural and spiritual events. To achieve this goal, Romania must follow through with plans to improve its tourist infrastructure, since visitors have many other attractive options at reasonable prices throughout Europe.

Romania has a vast network of railways with international connections to all parts of Europe, but there is a need for updated new railcars and improved facilities. There is also a system of roads crisscrossing the country and connecting with inter-European road systems, but many are still in dire need of maintenance. Work is underway to modernize over 1500 miles of national roads connected to international traffic. Romania must also continue to fight all threats to its security, such as organized crime, corruption, and drug and people trafficking.

Then there are the kind of conditions that create obstacles to recovery that are not under Romania's direct control. Events such as the disintegration of Yugoslavia and the NATO military strikes crippled important Romanian import and export shipments. There has to be a turnaround in the persistent, negative western media attention given to Romania. Romania's strategic location and its resources have made it vulnerable throughout history. From the Romans to Austro-Hungary, Czarist Russia, and the Ottomans, as well as the "Tolstoy" agreement of the twentieth century, great powers have schemed to annex, control, or keep its lands under their zones of influence. Just as in the past Romanians have been able by force or shrewd negotiations to remain autonomous and independent, so Romania must continue to remain vigilant in the twenty-first century.

NOTES

1. *Washington Post*, June 16, 1990, A1.
2. Ibid.
3. Ibid.

Historical Chronology

To 650 B.C. Prehistoric ages (see chapter 1)

c. 650 B.C. Greeks set up trading posts on the western shores of the Black Sea and the Danube

512 B.C. Persian King Darius launches campaign against Scythians; takes Thrace and Macedonia, and builds bridge across Danube; later accounts of this campaign by Herodotus constitute first historical mention of Getae

509 B.C. Establishment of the Roman Republic

335 B.C. Alexander the Great of Macedon crosses the Danube in campaign against the Thracians; Getae are mentioned in accounts of this campaign

292 B.C. Dromichaites is first Geto-Dacian king mentioned by Greek historians

279 B.C. Invasion of Dacian region by Celts

100–44 B.C. Life of Julius Caesar

82 (or 70) B.C. Geto-Dacian King Burebista unites all tribes

36 B.C. Beginning of the Roman Empire

c. 4 A.D. Birth of Jesus

30 A.D. Jesus crucified in Jerusalem

46 A.D. Romans annex Dobrudja to province of Moesia

87–106 Reign of Geto-Dacian King Decebal (Decebalus); two Dacian wars during Roman Emperor Domitian's reign
- **101** Romans, under emperor Trajan, attack Dacia
- **106** Romans attack Dacia again and conquer the kingdom, which is destroyed; Romans turn Dacia into a province and colonize it

106–271 Dacia is a Roman province; colonization creates a Daco-Roman population, speaking a Latin language, which will lead to the formation, over a long period of time, of the Romanian people
- **212** Under Emperor Caracalla, all free inhabitants of the empire are granted Roman citizenship
- **230–249** Invasions of Carps, Sarmanians, and free Dacians
- **249–251** Anti-Christian persecutions in Dacia under emperor Decius

271–275 Roman emperor Aurelian withdraws Roman legions and administration from Dacia and creates an Aurelian Dacia south of the Danube

271–11th C. Epoch of great migrations

286 Roman emperor Diocletian reorganizes the Roman Empire, dividing it into East Roman and West Roman Empires; persecution of Christians; Christianization of Daco-Romans begins

313 Milan Edict by which Christianity is officially adopted throughout the Roman Empire

330 Emperor Constantine I (the Great) establishes the new Roman imperial capital at Byzantium and changes its name to Constantinople; builds second bridge across the Danube, at Sucidava

395–1453 Byzantine Empire (East Roman Empire): in 395 East Roman Empire and West Roman Empire split permanently, each with an emperor; the Byzantine Empire lasts until 1453, when the Ottoman Empire's sultan Mehmed II takes Constantinople in 1453

395 Dobrudja becomes part of the East Roman Empire; Christianity becomes the sole religion of the empire

476 Last Roman emperor in the West—Romulus Augustus

c. 570–632 Life of the Prophet Mohammed and foundation of Islam

9th–11th C. Small state formations appear in the Carpatho-Danubian region (cnezats and voievodats)

800 West Roman Empire is revived with the coronation of Charlemagne by Pope Leo III

843 Roman Empire of the West is split into two by the Treaty of Verdun; it eventually becomes France and Germany

896 Magyars (Hungarians) arrive on the Pannonian Plain and settle there

10th–13th C. Gradual expansion eastward by the Hungarians, resulting in complete occupation of Transylvania by the early thirteenth century

962–1806 Holy Roman Empire: the coronation of Otto I by Pope John XII on February 2, 962, is considered as the restoration of the empire of Charlemagne; it endures until the renunciation of the imperial title by Francis II in 1806

972 Formation of the Hungarian State

976 First mention of the Vlachs (Romanians south of the Danube)

1000 Byzantine Empire captures Macedonia, bringing the imperial frontier back to the Danube and reestablishing contact with the south Danubian Vlachs

1054 Schism between Greek and Latin Christian churches begins

1095–1272 Crusades (nine)

1241–1242 Tatar hordes invade Romanian territory, wipe out the Cumans, and devastate lands south and east of the Carpathians

1290–1922 Ottoman Empire: In 1290, Osman I (Othman I) proclaims his independence from the Seljuk Turks and begins the expansion of the empire that is named after him; it ends with the establishment of Turkey as a republic in 1922

c. 1310 Wallachia becomes the first Romanian principality, under Prince (Voievode) Basarab I the Great (cel Mare)

1330 Battle of Posada; army of Basarab I defeats an attempt by Hungarian King Charles I (Charles Robert of Anjou) to reimpose his suzerainty over Wallachia

1334 Plague begins in Constantinople; spread by Crusaders throughout Europe, it is estimated to have wiped out in fewer than twenty years as much as three-fourths of the population of Europe

1359 Moldavia becomes the second Romanian Principality, under Prince Bogdan I

1386–1418 Reign of Mircea the Old (cel Bătrân) in Wallachia

1389 Turks defeat Serbs at Kosovo

1393 Turks occupy Trnovo, Bulgarian capital

1417 Peace treaty signed between Mircea the Old and Mehmed I; Wallachia recognizes Ottoman suzerainty, and Dobrudja is annexed by Turks

1441 John Hunyadi, Hungarian national hero, is chosen prince (voievod) of Transylvania under King Ladislaus (1441–1456)

1448, 1456–1462, and 1476 Reign of Vlad III Dracula (Ţepeş) in Wallachia

1453 Ottomans, led by Sultan Mehmed II, take Constantinople; by end of the fifteenth century, Ottomans are in possession of most of the Byzantine Empire

1456: July 4–22 Battle of Belgrade

1457–1504 Reign of Stephen the Great (cel Mare) in Moldavia

- **1467: December 15** Battle of Baia; Stephen the Great defeats an attempt by Matthias Corvinus, king of Hungary, to impose his suzerainty over Moldavia
- **1475: January 10** Battle of Vaslui; Stephen the Great defeats a large Ottoman invading force
- **1497: October 26** Battle of Codrul Sosminului; Stephen the Great defeats a Polish invasion of Moldavia, led by King John Albert, who attempts to impose his suzerainty over Moldavia

1526: August 29 Battle of Mohács; Ottomans defeat forces of the kingdom of Hungary

1541 Buda is taken by the Ottomans, and Hungary is divided into three, with the southern and central regions annexed and reduced to an unpopulated desert, the western and northern regions under Hapsburg rule, and Transylvania, including Banat and Crişana, allowed to become an autonomous principality tributary to the Porte; Austrian and Turkish influences fight for supremacy in Transylvania for nearly two centuries

1552 Banat and part of Crişana are annexed by the Ottomans and become a Turkish district with center at Timişoara

1593–1601 Reign of Michael the Brave (Mihai Viteazul) in Wallachia

- **1595** Michael the Brave defeats Ottoman invading armies
- **1599** Michael the Brave leads his troops into Transylvania; in Alba, Iulia, Michael is declared prince of Wallachia
- **1600: May** Michael the Brave takes Moldavia and is declared Prince of Wallachia, Transylvania, and Moldavia, thus achieving the first unification of the three principalities into one Romanian state
- **1601** External and internal opposition to the union of the three principalities: Austria and Poland send troops into Wallachia and Moldavia and force the abdication of Michael the Brave, ending the short-lived union; Michael the Brave is assassinated on August 19, 1601

1613–1629 Reign of Gabriel (Gábor) Bethlen in Transylvania

1618–1648 Thirty Years War in Europe

1686–1688 Holy Roman Empire armies capture Buda
- **1686: July 6** Treaty of Vienna
- **1687** Ottomans defeated at Mohács; Hapsburgs are recognized as kings of Hungary
- **1688** Diet of Transylvania accepts the protection of the Hapsburg Empire

1688–1714 Reign of Constantin Brâncoveanu in Wallachia

1697: March 27 Union of the Romanian Orthodox churches in Transylvania with the Roman Catholic Church, creating the Greek Catholic or Uniate Church

1699: February 5 Treaty of Carlowitz; the Ottomans recognize Hapsburg domination in Transylvania

1711: October 17 Nicolae Mavrocordat is appointed governor of Moldavia by the Ottoman Porte, the first of the Phanariot rulers; the Phanariot regime continues until 1821

1716: January 5 Phanariot regime is extended to Wallachia by the appointment of Nicolae Mavrocordat, former ruler of Moldavia, as governor of Wallachia

1718: July 21 Treaty of Passarovitz; Oltenia and the Banat are annexed by Austria

1739: September 18 Treaty of Belgrade; Oltenia is returned to Wallachia

1760 European Enlightenment: Voltaire, Diderot, Hume

1769 James Watt patents his steam engine, considered to have triggered the Industrial Revolution in Europe

1772–1775 Poland is dismembered and partitioned between Austria, Prussia, and Russia

1775: May 18 Bucovina annexed by Austria

1784–1785 Peasant revolt in Transylvania, led by Horea, Cloşca, and Crişan

1789: July 14 French Revolution begins

1792–1802 Revolutionary Wars

1806: August 6 Dissolution of the Holy Roman Empire

1812: May 28 Treaty of Bucharest; Bessarabia, formerly a part of Moldavia, annexed by Russia

1821 Greek War of Independence and anti-Ottoman revolt in Wallachia

1825 Steam-powered freight and passenger railway transportation starts in Britain

1828 (November)–1834 (March) Wallachia and Moldavia under Russian occupation

1829: September 14 Treaty of Adrianople

1831: July Organic Regulations introduced in Moldavia

1832: January Organic Regulations introduced in Wallachia

1848 French Revolution, which ends in the creation of the Second Republic, followed by revolutions and revolutionary movements all over Europe, including Moldavia, Wallachia, and Transylvania

1854–1856 Crimean War

1856: February–March Congress of Paris

1859

- **January–February** Alexandru Ioan Cuza elected as ruler of both Moldavia and Wallachia
- **September** Prince Alexandru Ioan Cuza is recognized as ruler of both principalities by the major powers

1861: December 4 Conference of Constantinople; the union of the two principalities is recognized for the duration of Cuza's reign

1862: February 5 The national assemblies of Moldavia and Wallachia are merged into one parliament; Cuza proclaims the union; Bucharest becomes the capital

1866

- **February 22** Abdication of Alexandru Ioan Cuza
- **May 22** Carol of Hohenzollern-Sigmaringen takes the oath as Prince Carol of Romania
- **July 11** A new constitution is adopted and ratified; it gives the country the official name of Romania and specifies that its national flag is the tricolor blue, yellow, and red

1877

- **April 24** Russia declares war on the Ottoman Empire
- **May 9** Parliament proclaims the independence of Romania
- **May 21** Romanian troops go into action in support of Russian forces

1878

- **February 19** Treaty of San Stefano
- **July 13** Treaty of Berlin
- **October 20** Dobrogea and the Danube Delta become part of Romania

1880: February 20 Romania's independence officially recognized by all European powers

1881: March 26 Parliament proclaims the Romanian Kingdom; Prince Carol becomes King Carol

1883: October 30 Romania signs the secret Treaty of Vienna with Austria-Hungary, thus becoming a member of the Triple Alliance

1907: February–April A violent peasant uprising spreads across the country and is brutally squashed, resulting in a high death toll and much destruction

1913: August 10 Treaty of Bucharest, at the end of the Second Balkan War; Bulgaria forced to cede southern Dobrogea to Romania

1914

- **June 28** Archduke Franz Ferdinand assassinated by Serb nationalists in Sarajevo
- **July 28** Austria-Hungary declares war on Serbia, signaling the onset of World War I
- **October 10** King Carol I dies; Prince Ferdinand of Hohenzollern crowned as King Ferdinand I the next day, October 11, 1914

1916

- **August 17** Treaty signed between Romania and the Allied powers (France, Great Britain, Russia, and Italy)
- **August 27** Romania declares war on the Central Powers and invades Trnasylavania
- **December 6** German forces enter Bucharest, splitting Romania into two parts; King Ferdinand and the Romanian government set up headquarters in Iaşi

1917

- **February** Russian Revolution ends in the abdication of Czar Nicholas on March 14, 1917
- **November** Bolshevik Revolution; Russia unilaterally ceases hostilities on November 26, 1917

1918

- **March 27** Bessarabia votes for unification with the Kingdom of Romania
- **May 17** Treaty of Bucharest signed between Romania and the Central Powers
- **November 10** Allied troops cross the Danube into Romania, and Romania declares war on the Central Powers
- **November 11** Armistice signed between the Allies and the Central Powers at Compiègne, ending World War I
- **November 28** Bucovina votes for unification with the kingdom of Romania

1919

- **June 28** Treaty of Versailles signed
- **December 29** Bessarabia, Bucovina, Transylvania, Crişana, Maramureş, and the Banat are formally united with Romania

1927–1930 King Ferdinand dies on July 20, 1927; Romania is ruled by a three-member regency in the name of King Michael I, son of Crown Prince Carol, who is only six years old

1929: October 29 Wall Street stock market crash

1930: June 8 Crown Prince Carol returns to Romania and is crowned as King Carol II

1933: January 30 Hitler becomes chancellor of Germany

1936: October 26 Axis Rome-Berlin formed

1938: February 24 King Carol II submits a new constitution based on a Royal Dictatorship

1939: September 3 Britain and France declare war on Germany

1940

- **May 10** Churchill becomes prime minister of Great Britain
- **June 27** Romania forced to cede Bessarabia and northern Bucovina to the Soviet Union
- **August 30** Romania forced to cede northern Transylvania to Hungary
- **September** Romania forced to return southern Dobrogea to Bulgaria
- **September 4** King Carol II appoints Ion Antonescu as prime minister with full dictatorial powers
- **September 6** King Carol II turns the throne over to his son Michael, who once again becomes King Michael I; Romania is declared a "National Legionary State"

1941

- **February 14** National Legionary State officially abolished
- **June 22** Germany invades the Soviet Union; Romania declares war on the Soviet Union
- **August 11** Roosevelt and Churchill agree on the Atlantic Charter
- **December 7** Japanese bomb Pearl Harbor; Britain declares war on Romania
- **December 11** Hitler declares war on the United States

1943: September 3 Italy surrenders

1944

- **June 6** D-Day: Allied landings begin in Normandy
- **September 12** Armistice signed between Romania and the Soviet Union (representing the Allies)

1945

- **May 8** End of war in Europe
- **August 6–9** Atomic bombs dropped on Hiroshima and Nagasaki
- **August 14** Japan surrenders

1947: December 30 King Michael abdicates and leaves country; Romania proclaimed the Romanian People's Republic

1948

- **February 21** Gheorghe Gheorghiu-Dej elected secretary-general of the Romanian Communist Party, which changes its name to Romanian Workers' Party
- **May** State of Israel created
- **August 23** NATO created
- **September** Federal Republic of Germany established

1949: October German Democratic Republic established

1952: June 2 Gheorghe Gheorghiu-Dej appointed president of the State Council

1953: September Khrushchev becomes first secretary of the Communist Party of the Soviet Union

1961: August Construction of the Berlin Wall

1962: October Cuban missile crisis

1965: March 22 Gheorghe Gheorghiu-Dej dies; Nicolae Ceauşescu becomes secretary-general of the Romanian Communist Party; Chivu Stoica becomes president of the Council

1967: December 9 Nicolae Ceauşescu becomes president of the Council

1969: August 2–3 Richard Nixon becomes the first U.S. president to visit Romania

1974: March 27 Grand National Assembly elects Nicolae Ceauşescu as the first president of the Socialist Republic of Romania

1975: April 2 Romania becomes the first Communist state to be given most favored nation status by the United States

1977: June Leonid Brezhnev becomes president of the Soviet Union

1985: June Mikhail Gorbachev becomes first secretary of the Communist Party in the Soviet Union; Glasnost and Perestroika programs launched

1989

- **January** Political pluralism returns to Hungary
- **March** Political pluralism returns to Poland; Solidarity is made legal
- **November** Political pluralism returns to East Germany; Berlin Wall opened
- **December 16–17** Antigovernment demonstrations in Timişoara instigated by eviction of dissident Protestant minister; security forces and troops fire on demonstrators; media reports of large number of casualties create unrest in other parts of the country
- **December 21–25** Revolution starts in front of Central Committee Building in Bucharest during a speech by Ceauşescu; his speech is interrupted by demonstrators, security forces fire into crowds, and the Ceauşescus fly in an escape helicopter, but they are intercepted and are placed under guard at a military garrison some 100 miles from the capital
- **December 25** After a summary trial that convicts them of genocide and destroying the economy, Nicolae and Elena Ceauşescu are executed

1990

- **January 3** Political parties are reestablished in Romania
- **February/March** Soviet Union votes to return to pluralism
- **May 29** Boris Yeltsin elected chairman of the Russian Supreme Soviet and president of the Russian SFSR
- **October 3** Reunification of Germany

1991: December Soviet Union dissolves; Commonwealth of Independent States set up. A new constitution is adopted in Romania by a referendum, under which Romania becomes a parliamentary democracy

1992: September 27 Ion Iliescu reelected president of Romania in national elections

1993: January 1 Czechoslovakia divides into separate Czech and Slovakian republics

1996: November Opposition CDR coalition wins the elections, and Emil Constantinescu becomes president of Romania

1997 Slobodan Milošević elected president of Yugoslavia (now only comprised of Serbia and Montenegro)

1998 Serb offensive launched against Albanian separatists in Kosovo, causing a refugee crisis

1999 NATO launches a bombing campaign against the Serbs after peace talks fail; President Milošević indicted for crimes against humanity by the International War Crime Tribunal; Serbs surrender and withdraw their forces from Kosovo

2000 Under international pressure, President Milošević steps down
- **November** Ion Iliescu's party, the PDSR, wins the elections in Romania; Iliescu reelected as president of Romania

2001 Ex-president Milošević arrested and taken to be tried by the International War Crimes Tribunal

Bibliography

Arendt, Hannah. *Eichmann in Jerusalem.* The Viking Press, 1963. rev. and enl. New York: Penguin Books, 1979.

Arrian (Flavius Arrianus). *Anabasis of Alexander.* Translated by E. Iliff Robson. London: William Heinemann, 1929.

Baleanu, V. G. *Romania's November 2000 Elections: A Future Return to the Past?* Camberley, Surrey, England: Conflict Studies Research Centre (Occasional Brief No. 80), Nov. 17, 2000.

Braham, Randolph L. *Genocide and Retribution: The Holocaust in Hungarian Ruled Northern Transylvania.* Boston: Kluwer-Nijhoff Publishing, 1983.

———, ed. *The Destruction of Romanian and Ukrainian Jews During the Antonescu Era.* Boulder, Co.: Social Science Monographs, 1997.

Brătianu, G. I. *Origines et Formation de l'Unité Roumaine.* Bucharest: Institut d'Histoire Universelle "N. Iorga," 1943.

Browning, Gordon Frederick. *Tristan Tzara: The Genesis of the Dada Poem, or from Dada to Aa.* Stuttgart: Akademischer Verlag Hans-Dieter Heinz (no. 56), 1979.

Butnaru, I. C. *The Silent Holocaust—Romania and its Jews.* New York: Greenwood Press, 1992.

Carol I. Translated by Dan Berindei. *Cuvântiri şi scrisori* volume 2 (Bucharest, 1909): 427.

Carp, Matatias. *Cartea Neagră*, volume 2 (Bucharest: Diogene, 1996).

Castellan, Georges. *History of the Balkans from Mohammed the Conqueror to Stalin.* Translated by N. Bradley. Boulder, Co.: East European Monographs, 1992.

———. *A History of the Romanians.* Translated by Nicholas Bradley. New York: Columbia University Press, 1989.

Ceauşescu, Ilie, Florin Constantiniu, and E. Mihail. *A Turning Point in World War II—23 August 1944 in Romania.* New York: Columbia University Press, 1985.

Cioranescu, Alexandre. *Vasile Alecsandri.* New York: Twaine Publishers, 1976.

Codreanu, Corneliu Zelea. *La Garde de Fer.* Paris: Editions Prométhée, 1938.

Constantiniu, Florin. *O Istorie Sinceră a Poporului Român.* Bucharest: Univers Enciclopedic, 1999.

Cottrell, Arthur, ed. *The Encyclopedia of Ancient Civilizations.* London: The Rainbird Publishing Group, 1980.

Dear, I. C. B., gen. ed. *The Oxford Companion to the Second World War.* Oxford: Oxford University Press, 1995.

Deletant, Dennis. *Romania under Communist Rule.* Iaşi, Romania: The Center for Romanian Studies, 1999.

Dogan, Matei. *Analiza statistică a democraţiei parlamentare din Romănia.* Bucharest: Ferderaţia Comunităţilor Evreieşti; Monographie., 1946. XXI.

Dragan, J. C. *We, the Thracians and our Multimillenary History.* Milan: Editrice Nagard, 1976.

DuNay, André. *The Origin of the Romanians, the Early History of the Romanian Language.* Toronto-Buffalo: Matthias Corvinus Publishing, 1996.

Eliade, Mircea. *The Romanians, A Concise History.* Translated by Rodica Mihaela Scafeş. Bucharest: "Roza Vînturilor" Publishing, 1992.

Eminescu, Mihai. *Poems and Prose of Mihai Eminescu.* Edited by Kurt W. Treptow. Iaşi, Romania: The Center for Romanian Studies, 2000.

Fischer-Galaţi, Stephen. *Twentieth Century Romania.* New York: Columbia University Press, 1970.

Fisher, H. A. L. *A History of Europe.* Vol. 1, *From the Origins to the End of the 17th Century.* London, England: Eyre & Spottiswoode, 1938.

Florus, Lucius Annaens. *Epitome of Roman History.* Edited by G. P. Goold; translated by Edward Seymour Forster. London: William Heinemann, 1984.

Gallagher, Tom. *Romania after Ceauşescu.* Edinburgh: Edinburgh University Press, 1995.

Geist, Sidney. *Brancusi, A Study of the Sculpture.* London: Studio Vista Ltd., 1968.

Georgescu, Vlad. *The Romanians—A History.* Edited by Matei Calinescu; translated by Alexandra Bley-Vroman. London: I. B. Tauris & Co., 1991.

Ghyka, Matilda. *A Documented Chronology of Roumanian History from Pre-historic Time to the Present Day.* Translated by Fernand G. Reiner and Anne Cliff. Oxford: B. H. Blackwell, 1941.

Gilbert, Martin. *Dent Atlas of the Holocaust.* 2nd ed. London: J. M. Dent, 1993.

———. *Winston S. Churchill, 1941–1945.* Vol. 7, *Road to Victory.* London, England: Heinemann, 1986.

Giurescu, Dinu C. *A Historic Perspective.* Edited by Stephen Fischer-Galaţi. New York: Columbia University, 1998.

———. *Illustrated History of the Romanian People.* Translated by Sonia Schlauger. Bucharest: Editura Sport-Turism, 1981.

Glenny, Misha. *The Balkans 1804–1999.* London: Granta Books, 1999.

Golea, Traian. *Romania Beyond the Limits of Endurance – A Desperate Appeal to the Free World.* Miami Beach, Fl.: Romanian Historical Studies, 1988.

Hazard, Elizabeth W. *Cold War Crucible: United States Foreign Policy and the Conflict in Romania, 1943–1953.* Boulder, Co.: East European Monographs, 1996.

Herodotus. *Histories.* Vol. 1, 2. Translated by George Rawlinson. 1910. Reprint. London: Everyman's Library, 1964.

Hilberg, Raul. *The Destruction of the European Jews.* New York: Holmes & Meier, 1985.

Hillgruber, Andreas. *Hitler, König Carol und Marschall Antonescu, Die deutsch-rumänishen Beziehungen 1938–1944.* Wiesbaden, Germany: F. Steiner, 1954.

Hitchins, Keith. *The Romanians 1774–1866.* Oxford: Clarendon Press, 1996.

———. *Rumania 1866–1947.* Oxford: Clarendon Press, 1994.

Hoddinott, R. F. *The Thracians.* Over Wallop, England: Thames & Hudson, 1981.

Howard, Peter. *Camboglanna/Birdoswald Fort on Hadrian's Wall, a History and Short Guide.* Huddersfield, England: Cameo Books, 1972.

Illyés, Elemér. *Ethnic Continuity in the Carpatho-Danubian Area.* New York: Columbia University Press, 1988.

Ioanid, Radu. *The Holocaust in Romania.* Chicago: Ivan R. Dee, 2000.

Ionescu, Ghiţă. *Communism in Rumania, 1944–1962.* London: Oxford University Press, 1964.

Iorga, N. *A History of Roumania, Land, People, Civilisation.* Translated by Joseph McCabe. London: T. Fisher Unwin, 1971.

Jelavich, Barbara. *Russia and the formation of the Romanian National State 1821–1878.* Cambridge, England: Cambridge University Press, 1984.

Light, Duncan and David Phinnemore. *Post-Communist Romania—Coming to Terms with Transition.* Houndmills, Basingstoke, England: Palgrave, 2001.

Malcom, Noel. *George Enescu, His Life and Music.* Stroud, England: Alan Sutton Publishing Ltd., 1990.

McKendrick, Paul. *The Dacian Stones Speak.* Chapel Hill: University of North Carolina Press, 1975.

Miller, William. *The Story of the Nations; The Balkans.* London: T. Fisher Unwin, 1896.

Mommsen, Theodor. *The Provinces of the Roman Empire—The European Provinces.* Selections from *The History of Rome*, Vol. 5,

Book 8. Edited by T. Robert S Broughton. Chicago: University of Chicago Press, 1968.

Montias, John Michael. *Economic Development in Communist Rumania.* Cambridge, Ma: MIT Press, 1967.

Muller, James W. *Churchill as Peacemaker.* Cambridge, England: Cambridge University Press, 1997.

Nelson Daniel. "Ten Years On, Romania Has Earned Our Help." *The Washington Post,* December 26, 1999. B2

Oţetea, Andrei, ed. *A Concise History of Romania.* English edition edited by Andrew MacKenzie. London: Robert Hale, 1985.

Pârvan, Vasile. *Dacia.* Cambridge, England: Cambridge University Press, 1929.

Pascu, Ştefan, ed. *The Independence of Romania.* Bucharest: Editura Academiei Republicii Socialiste România, 1977.

Rady, Martyn. *Romania in Turmoil.* London: I. B. Tauris & Co., 1992.

Ratesh, Nestor. *Romania: The Entangled Revolution.* Washington, DC: The Center for Strategic and International Studies, 1991.

Raţiu, Ion. *Contemporary Romania.* Richmond, England: Foreign Affairs Publishing Co. Ltd., 1975.

Rogger, Hans and Eugen Weber, eds. *The European Right, A Historical Profile.* London: Weidenfeld & Nicholson, 1965.

Seişanu, Romulus. *Rumania.* Miami Beach, Fl.: Romanian Historical Studies, 1987.

Seton-Watson, R. W. *A History of the Romanians: from Roman times to the completion of unity.* Cambridge: University Press, 1934.

Shaw, Stanford J., and Ezel Karal Shaw. *History of the Ottoman Empire and Modern Turkey.* Vol I & II. Cambridge, England: Cambridge University Press, 1977.

Strabo. *The Geography of Strabo.* Vol. 3. Translated by Horace Leonard Jones. London: William Heinemann, 1924.

Tappe, E. D. *Documents concerning Rumanian History (1427–1601).* The Hague: Moreton & Co., 1964.

The Times (London), August 22, 1968. 5G.

Treptow, Kurt W. *Vlad III Dracula, The Life and Times of the Historical Dracula*. Iaşi, Romania: The Center for Romanian Studies, 2000.

———, ed. *Classics of Romanian Literature*. Vol. 1, *Selected Works of Ion Creangă and Mihai Eminescu*. New York: Columbia University Press, 1991.

———, ed. *A History of Romania*. 3d ed. Iaşi, Romania: Foundation for Romanian Culture and Studies, 1997.

Troncotă Cristian. *Eugen Critescu, asul seviciilor secrete româneşti*. (Bucharest, 1996): 118–119.

Wags, Robert J. *Europe since 1945–A concise history*. 3d. ed. New York: St. Martin's Press, 1991.

Washington Post, June 16, 1990. A1.

Watson, Ian. *Hadrian's Wall*. London: English Heritage Educational Service, 1997.

Index

About the Author

NICOLAE (NICK) KLEPPER was born in Bucharest, Romania. In 1939, he was completing his first year of high school and looking forward to a trip with his parents, which was to take them to San Salvador. His father, a prominent architect, had been assigned to write a series of articles on Inca and Aztec cultures in Central America. By the time they arrived in America, World War II had broken out and the Kleppers decided to remain there for the duration of the war. They never went back to Romania, settling in New York instead.

Later, returning from a tour of duty with the U.S. Army in Europe, Klepper decided to devote his career to international business. After obtaining Engineering and Business degrees from the University of Denver, he worked and lived in Europe, Africa and the Middle East for the next twenty-five years.

For fifty years Klepper had no contact with his country of birth, and had even forgotten his native language. All that changed in 1989, when he watched TV film footage of the revolution and collapse of Communism in Romania. Klepper's first book, *Taste of Romania, Its Cookery and Glimpses of Its History, Folklore, Art, Literature, and*

Poetry (Hippocrene Books, 1997), was the result of his renewed interest in Romania, and his desire to make his native country better known to the world. It was followed by an expanded second edition and a third edition. *Romania: An Illustrated History* is his second book.

Now a retired business executive, Klepper has three sons and a daughter, all scattered around the world, and lives with his Scottish wife Ann in Edinburgh, Scotland.